MORAL EPISTEMOLOGY

How do we know right from wrong? Do we even have moral knowledge? *Moral Epistemology* studies these and related questions concerning our understanding of virtue and vice. It is one of philosophy's perennial problems, reaching back to Plato, Aristotle, Aquinas, Locke, Hume, and Kant, and has recently been the subject of intense debate as a result of findings in developmental and social psychology.

In this outstanding introduction to the subject, Aaron Zimmerman covers the following key topics:

- what is moral epistemology? What are its methods? Includes a discussion of Socrates, Gettier, and contemporary theories of knowledge
- skepticism about moral knowledge based on the anthropological record of deep and persistent moral disagreement, including contextualism
- moral nihilism, including debates concerning God and morality and the relation between moral knowledge and our motives and reasons to act morally
- epistemic moral skepticism, intuitionism, and the possibility of inferring "ought" from "is," discussing the views of Locke, Hume, Kant, Ross, Audi, Thomson, Harman, Sturgeon, and many others
- how children acquire moral concepts and become more reliable judges
- criticisms of those who would reduce moral knowledge to value-neutral knowledge or attempt to replace moral belief with emotion.

Throughout the book Zimmerman argues that our belief in moral knowledge can survive skeptical challenges. He also draws on a rich range of examples from Plato's *Meno* and Dickens' *David Copperfield* to Bernard Madoff and Saddam Hussein.

Including chapter summaries and annotated further reading at the end of each chapter, *Moral Epistemology* is essential reading for all students of ethics, epistemology, and moral psychology.

Aaron Zimmerman is an Associate Professor of Philosophy at the University of California, Santa Barbara. His research is focused on the intersection of thought, language, and reason, and he also writes and teaches on David Hume's philosophical work.

New Problems of Philosophy
Series Editor: *José Luis Bermúdez*

The *New Problems of Philosophy* series provides accessible and engaging surveys of the most important problems in contemporary philosophy. Each book examines either a topic or a theme that has emerged on the philosophical landscape in recent years, or a longstanding problem refreshed in light of recent work in philosophy and related disciplines. Clearly explaining the nature of the problem at hand and assessing attempts to answer it, books in the series are excellent starting-points for undergraduate and graduate students wishing to study a single topic in depth. They will also be essential reading for professional philosophers. Additional features include chapter summaries, further reading, and a glossary of technical terms.

Also available:

Fiction and Fictionalism
R. M. Sainsbury

Noncognitivism in Ethics
Mark Schroeder

Analyticity
Cory Juhl and Eric Loomis

Embodied Cognition
Lawrence Shapiro

Physicalism
Daniel Stoljar

Forthcoming:

Self Knowledge
Brie Gertler

Folk Psychology
Ian Ravenscroft

Perceptual Consciousness
Adam Pautz

Semantic Externalism
Jesper Kallestrup

Consequentialism
Julia Driver

Philosophy of Images
John Kulvicki

MORAL EPISTEMOLOGY

Aaron Zimmerman

Routledge
Taylor & Francis Group

LONDON AND NEW YORK

This edition published 2010
by Routledge
2 Park Square, Milton Park, Abingdon, Oxon OX14 4RN

Simultaneously published in the USA and Canada
by Routledge
270 Madison Ave, New York, NY 10016

Routledge is an imprint of the Taylor & Francis Group, an informa business

© 2010 Aaron Zimmerman

Typeset in Joanna and Scale Sans by Bookcraft Ltd, Stroud, Gloucestershire

Printed and bound in Great Britain by TJ International Ltd, Padstow, Cornwall

All rights reserved. No part of this book may be reprinted or reproduced or utilised in any form or by any electronic, mechanical, or other means, now known or hereafter invented, including photocopying and recording, or in any information storage or retrieval system, without permission in writing from the publishers.

British Library Cataloguing in Publication Data
A catalogue record for this book is available from the British Library

Library of Congress Cataloging in Publication Data
Zimmerman, Aaron (Aaron Zachary)
Moral epistemology / by Aaron Zimmerman.
p. cm. — (New problems of philosophy)
Includes bibliographical references and index.
1. Ethics. 2. Knowledge, Theory of. I. Title.
BD176.Z56 2010
170'.42—dc22
2009048670

ISBN 10: 0-415-48553-1 (hbk)
ISBN 10: 0-415-48554-1 (pbk)
ISBN 10: 0-203-85086-6 (ebk)

ISBN 13: 978-0-415-48553-1 (hbk)
ISBN 13: 978-0-415-48554-8 (pbk)
ISBN 13: 978-0-203-85086-2 (ebk)

For Max

CONTENTS

ACKNOWLEDGMENTS

I would like to thank Tony Bruce for asking me to write this book, and Joshua May, Walter Sinnott-Armstrong, Pekka Väyrynen, Jonathan Way, and an anonymous Routledge referee for written comments. Discussions with Tony Anderson have also proved helpful.

Puzzlement over the source and nature of moral knowledge is what brought me to philosophy more than fifteen years ago. And I have tried to write a book for the person I was at that time – a philosophically-minded sophomore just trying to figure things out. I hope this book finds its way into that student's hands, and that it is sufficiently clear and cogent to inform his or her intellectual struggle. If it does this, and does not bore his or her teacher to tears, the book will have achieved its intended end.

I have always wanted to share my passion for philosophy with my mish-pocha – the audience of people for whom I care most: my wife, Kira Goldberg, my parents, Hope and Daniel Zimmerman, and the rest of the Zimmermans, the Nathans, the Mansells, the Cherlins, the Goldbergs, the Mandelbaums, the Thatchers, the Finkels, the Moores, the Magnuses, the Fiorentinos, the Kays, the Kyriokous, the Tzahs, the Kay-Grosses, the Lebows, the Palogers, the McElroys, the Weisses, the Stanleys, the Fitelsons, the Wolfs, the Browns, the Stormers, the Friedmans, the Lendermans, the Schers, the Kriegers, the Filuses, and the many other families who have shown me so much love. Perhaps this book is not yet the book for this crew. If not, I will keep trying.

If you find certain passages in what follows overly dense or hard to follow, please feel free to question me via electronic mail. I will do my best to clarify what can be clarified and to own up to the irredeemable obscurity of what cannot. If you like, you can think of my inbox as the "meaningless distinction" hotline. (Thanks Tina.)

Aaron Zimmerman
Los Angeles, California
azimmerman@philosophy.ucsb.edu

1

MORAL EPISTEMOLOGY: CONTENT AND METHOD

1.1 What is moral epistemology?

Roughly speaking, moral epistemology is the study of whether and how we know right from wrong. This colloquial characterization is only "roughly" correct because as epistemologists we are concerned with more than just knowledge, and as moral theorists our interests extend beyond mere right and wrong. So, for instance, once we know that a proposition is false, we know that those who believe it do not know it. But this need not end our critical evaluation of the believer or believers in question. We may still ask whether they were misled by what was otherwise excellent evidence, or whether, instead, they lacked on balance good reasons for believing what they did. We can ask whether they were led astray by "internal" problems like poor vision, bad memory, or defective methods of reasoning, or whether the cause of error was instead "external." Were the lighting conditions poor? Were they, perhaps, deliberately tricked by a crafty adversary? And we can ask whether those who do not know those propositions they believe are generally reliable on the matters at hand or whether they quite often go astray. Should we trust them in the future, or have they earned our suspicion?

Similarly, once we know that an action is immoral we know that those who perform it thereby do something wrong. But we may still want to know what makes the action bad and how the nature of these particular instances of immorality ought to shape our critical reactions. Is the act uncaring or cruel? Is it unjust or unfair? Do the perpetrators deserve blame for what they've done, or did they have a good excuse? Are they just rotten people, or is this act of immorality an exception to an otherwise acceptable pattern of behavior?

In sum, epistemology is concerned with knowledge and the truth required for it, but it is also concerned with belief, justification, reasons, evidence, cognitive malfunction, proper functioning, reliability, and a host of cognate notions. Moral philosophy is concerned with morally right and wrong actions and the moral goodness and badness endemic to them, but it is also concerned with virtues and vices such as kindness and cruelty, fairness and greed; it explores the nature of moral obligations and rights, and the more or less general rules that we must observe to fulfill the former and avoid violating the latter; and it has a great deal to say about moral excellence and culpability and the attitudes, rewards, and punishments that we ought to level at those who act in morally laudable or blameworthy ways.

Moral epistemology thus explores the application of an enormous and somewhat varied set of concepts to a range of behaviors and institutions that are, if anything, even more numerous and varied. In consequence, the field is an exceedingly difficult one to circumscribe. So, for example, as moral epistemologists we are concerned with knowledge and ignorance regarding the morally right thing to do; the way to arrive at justified or well-grounded beliefs as to which actions and institutions are just; an enumeration of the sort of psychological maladies and sociological conditions that result in an improper appreciation of the viciousness of cruelty; and so on for each such combination of the many things separately investigated by mainstream epistemologists and moral philosophers. Knowing right from wrong is no more than a chunk of the iceberg's visible portion.

The looming multiplication of topics means that work in moral epistemology must of necessity be either wholly superficial or rather drastically limited in scope, and I aim to partially avoid the first of these vices by embracing the second to a greater degree than I would otherwise like. For this reason, among others, I will focus the discussion to follow on different views of basic moral knowledge and justification: our knowledge of the premises of those moral arguments we offer to one another in contrast with their conclusions; the justification with which we hold our most common moral beliefs; the assumptions almost all of us make when we consider these matters. As a result, I will only touch on the difficulties endemic when we try to "weigh" conflicting considerations so as to arrive at an all-things-considered verdict about a particular scenario of moral interest. That is, I will have relatively little to say about which if any of the numerous mutually exclusive courses of action available to a person at any given time are the morally right or permissible options for her to pursue. And I will address only in passing our judgments about whether and how a person who is forced to weigh competing moral considerations can come to know her all-things-considered moral duty or what is all-things-considered the morally best course of action for her to undertake.[1] I won't ignore these topics entirely, but because there is little current consensus on them, a survey of the difficulties involved is the only way to avoid an overly dogmatic presentation.

And there are two other advantages to this approach. First, it allows us to begin at the beginning with those moral beliefs and judgments that are conceptually and developmentally most fundamental. And second, it establishes a forum for the discussion of moral skepticism: the view that we cannot know right from wrong, either because evidence sufficient to support knowledge is not forthcoming, or because there are no moral facts to be known. Of course, by focusing on our most basic moral beliefs we are prevented from providing much if anything in the way of a guide to those already competent moral judges who are trying to figure out how to resolve the moral dilemmas (real or imagined) that they have encountered in trying to lead good lives. At best, we can hope to provide moral people with a better understanding of their knowledge, while supplying the ignorant and incompetent – who nevertheless possess the intelligence needed to follow our discussion – with an account of their deficiencies (cf. Aristotle, *Nicomachean Ethics*, 1095b [Aristotle, 1984, 1729–1867]).

1.2 Socrates, Gettier, and the definition of "knowledge"

One of the most intriguing questions in our field is whether virtue can be taught. Religious leaders and ethics professors, the writers of self-help books, and the principals of reform schools all claim to possess the kind of knowledge of virtue they must have if they are to teach it to their students or disciples. Can we learn how to be virtuous from a book? Does the acquisition of moral knowledge require training? Or is it, perhaps, largely innate? A number of different hypotheses come readily to mind. Perhaps some exceptional people can teach themselves virtue from the Torah, the Bible, the Koran, the Hindu Vedas, the writings of the Buddha, or the works of the great moral philosophers. After all, the physicist and climate apostate Freeman Dyson is supposed to have taught himself calculus from an encyclopedia entry. Why can't the privileged few learn virtue in the same way? (When a sweet and loving child emerges from a horribly debauched environment, the attribution of "moral genius" is almost irresistible.) Perhaps, though, other people, indeed most children, really do need the flesh-and-blood instruction, training, and encouragement that good parents and teachers try to provide. Those of us who learned calculus in high school or college only managed to do so by asking a number of questions and solving a whole range of exercises and problems. Why should learning virtue be any easier? Indeed, it might turn out that some people lack the innate equipment to ever acquire virtue, no matter how much help they are given, and no matter how forcefully they are coerced into the pursuit. Surely, there are some kids – if only those with severe learning disabilities – who couldn't learn calculus if their lives depended on it. Mightn't virtue also be unattainable for some? Might some children – if only those with psychological problems of a rather drastic sort – be innately incapable of acquiring moral knowledge from even the most caring, perceptive, gifted communicator? When, as Shakespeare says, "good wombs have borne bad sons," must anguished parents find recourse in either the hospitalization or imprisonment of their children?

These issues have a long and storied history. Indeed, they were hotly debated in Athens over 400 years before the birth of Christ, during the time of Socrates, Plato, and Aristotle, the greatest philosophers of antiquity. The sophists were intellectuals who claimed to be able to teach virtue. But you cannot teach what you do not know. So do the sophists then know how we ought to behave? If they do, they would seem eminently qualified to lead. In the final analysis we *are* the state. So someone who knows what we should do must know what the state should do. Shouldn't the leader of the nation be someone who can articulate its proper mission and instruct us on the best means to its attainment? Shouldn't the true teachers of virtue then lead us all?

In Plato's dialogue *Meno*, Socrates discusses these issues with Meno, a Thessalian aristocrat. The best men – Pericles and Thucydides among them – sometimes produce bad sons. No doubt, they would have produced good children were it in their power to do so, and this suggests that virtue cannot be taught. But the sophist Protagoras was paid to teach virtue for more than forty years. Surely, his ability to maintain a paying clientele over so long a period speaks in favor of his expertise. The question is therefore extraordinarily difficult to resolve. After pursuing several lines of attack, Socrates introduces a novel hypothesis. When a virtuous person does the right thing, this is not an accidental matter. In fact, we will only judge that someone is virtuous if we are confident that he will act justly in the absence of some unforeseeable accident or unlucky circumstance. But, for all that, we must admit that a good person will not be able to share his virtue with his children unless they are blessed by nature (or the gods) in some way or other. Perhaps then the righteous man has the *right opinion* as to how we should act, but he lacks genuine *moral knowledge*. Perhaps the true opinion explains his reliably virtuous actions and the lack of knowledge explains his inability to communicate virtue to his offspring. "If it is not through knowledge, the only alternative is that it is through right opinion that statesmen follow the right course for their cities" (99b–99c).

But what is the difference between knowledge and true belief? Though Socrates claims to know very little, he tells us that he is absolutely certain that there is a difference between these two states of mind (98b). The preceding discussion gropes toward an account.

> True opinions, as long as they remain, are a fine thing and all they do is good, but they are not willing to remain long, and they escape from a man's mind, so that they are not worth much until one ties them down by giving an account of the reasons why. After they are tied down, in the first place they become knowledge, and then they remain in place. This is why knowledge is prized higher than correct opinion, and knowledge differs from correct opinion in being tied down. (97a–98)

Socrates' tentative claim here is that one's correct opinion on some matter can "become" knowledge once one has acquired some grasp of the reasons why it is true. Having an explanation of some fact solidifies or deepens one's conviction in its truth, helps one remember it, and enables one to communicate it to others. Knowledge, according to Socrates, differs from true belief in all these respects; and if we keep these differences in mind, we will credit virtuous people with certain true opinions as to what is just and good, but we will persist in denying them any moral knowledge.

There are, I think, few contemporary thinkers who would endorse the hypothesis left on the table at the *Meno*'s end.[2] First, for a person to actually *be* virtuous, she would seem to need more than a set of correct opinions on moral matters. A virtuous person must be compassionate, loving, brave, and kind; and it is unlikely that these largely emotional capacities can be correctly identified with the possession of moral views that just happen to be true. Perhaps, as we will discuss, there is a kind of wisdom that really is sufficient for virtue, but wise people have more going for them than true opinions. Second, it is far from obvious that those who know something must be able to teach it to all those they wish to instruct; so why deny the virtuous moral knowledge simply because they do not invariably teach their children to be good?

Third, it is not at all clear that the children of the virtuous are ignorant of virtue. Mightn't they know how they ought to behave, and yet fail to act as they know they ought? Perhaps the virtuous do succeed in providing their children with moral knowledge of a kind, and yet moral knowledge is insufficient for moral action. This last question would hound Socrates throughout his days and trouble Plato and Aristotle a great deal. Indeed, as we will see, it remains a central topic for moral epistemologists working today.

Still, even if we reject Socrates' tentative explanation as to why virtue is not so easily inherited from the virtuous, the distinction behind his hypothesis holds considerable interest. Can someone have the right opinion on moral matters and yet fail to possess moral knowledge? To evaluate Socrates' positive answer to this question, we need to assess his description of knowledge. And it turns out that this is no idle enterprise, as for thousands of years philosophers looked to his remarks for guidance. Mightn't Socrates have provided us with the materials we need to *define* "knowledge" in terms of its difference from opinions that just happen to be true? Can we use his comments to formulate a relatively short, informative account of the kind of thing "knowledge" denotes, an account that might supply someone ignorant of this expression with an adequate grasp of its meaning?

Well, though Socrates doesn't offer us anything like a definition of "knowledge" in the *Meno*, theorists inspired by him did.[3] For instance, Roderick Chisholm would go on to define "knowledge" as a true belief held with adequate evidence (Chisholm, 1957), and A. J. Ayer would define it as conviction in some truth of which one has the right to be certain (Ayer, 1956/1990). Though interesting in their own right, the details of these accounts needn't detain us here. For, in a landmark work, Edmund Gettier (1963) was widely credited with refuting them — and all similar analyses — by supplying compelling examples of people who seemingly fail to know facts that they nevertheless justifiably believe. In the wake of Gettier's essay, the quest to provide Socratic definitions of "knowledge" has gradually ground to a halt.

Suppose, to gloss one of Gettier's examples, that the boss tells me that I am getting a promotion. And suppose, that as I know I only have $20 left to my name, I quite reasonably infer that the man getting the promotion only has $20 left to his name. Indeed, though it is exceedingly coy, we might suppose that in response to an inquiring colleague I go on to assert what I have here inferred. "Who is getting the job?" he asks. "Well, I'm not at liberty to disclose his name," I answer, "Though I will say that he's someone who's been reduced to his last $20." Now imagine that for some reason or other the boss has lied to me, and it is really Jones who is getting the bump-up. But yet imagine too that, as chance may have it, Jones is in the exact same financial position as I am. He also has just $20 left to his name. Then I will be justified in believing that the man being promoted has only $20 left to his name, and this belief will be true, but the accidental nature of its truth will dissuade most of us from thinking of it as knowledge. I'm right in believing that the guy getting the promotion only has $20, but I do not know that this is so.

Now if testimony can provide us with good evidence, I have good evidence for what I believe in the case at hand; and, again, what I believe is in fact true. But my belief still fails to constitute knowledge; so Chisholm's account must be rejected. And I surely have the right to trust those – like my boss – whose testimony I have no reason to doubt. So Ayer's account cannot be quite right either. If our ordinary thinking about the matter is to be respected, knowledge cannot be equated with justified, true belief.

Philosophers responded to Gettier's examples by requiring, in one way or another, that it be *no accident* that one's belief is true if it is to be properly characterized as knowledge, with Alvin Goldman (1967, 1976, 1986) and Robert Nozick (1981, ch. 3) providing what were perhaps the most widely discussed analyses of this kind. But these and all subsequent attempts to reflect on our ordinary thinking about knowledge so as to arrive at a relatively simple, interesting, explanatory account of the phenomenon failed to secure widespread acceptance (Shope, 1983). For this reason, among others, many contemporary theorists now find themselves agreeing with Timothy Williamson's (2000) claim that "knowledge" expresses a relatively simple concept that resists reductive definition or analysis.[4] This isn't to say that epistemology is now a dead discipline. We can still investigate knowledge in general, and moral knowledge in particular. But it now seems as though we are going to have to accomplish this task without the aid of a widely accepted definition of "knowledge."

Indeed, many epistemologists now draw similar conclusions when they turn to cases in which someone forms a false opinion through no fault of her own – cases in which even the most careful investigator would be led into error. Suppose, again, that the boss has lied to me, and I am wrong in thinking that I will be promoted. Still, so long as I have no reason to suspect that the man is lying, my confidence in the promotion is entirely *reasonable*. I am, we would say, entirely *justified* in drawing a false conclusion in this context. But in what does having a justified belief consist? Can we adequately define "justification" as it is used in cases such as these? Can we supply a brief, insightful account of the phenomenon that "justification" is used to denote, an account that might supply someone ignorant of this term with an adequate grasp of its meaning?

Again, recent history is littered with proposals that have yet to secure agreement. We have accounts drawn from the definitions of Chisholm and Ayer cited above: someone is justified in believing something just in case she has adequate evidence of its truth; someone is justified in believing something if she has a right to be convinced that it is the case (cf. Feldman and Conee, 1985; Pollock, 1986). But philosophers often classified as "naturalists" or "externalists" have argued for the inadequacy of these equations. Instead, they suggest, one is justified in believing something when one's belief is generated by a reliable mechanism or procedure (Goldman, 1986). Or perhaps one is justified in believing something just in case one's belief results from the exercise of an epistemic skill or ability, the proper functioning of a psychological module or set of modules, or the expression of some epistemic virtue (Sosa, 1980, 2007; Greco, 1993; Zagzebski, 1996).

The details of these debates needn't concern us here. We need only register the suspicion, most expressly voiced by William Alston (2005), that there is no single concept associated with "justification" even when it is limited in its application to opinion, credence, or conviction. Perhaps, that is, our differing evaluations of the ways in which we sometimes go right and sometimes go wrong when forming, maintaining, and revising of our beliefs track distinct properties that are nevertheless all important in one way or another. Again, it seems we must set about examining the various ways in which our moral beliefs might be said to be justified or unjustified without first having anything like a definition of "justification" in place.

1.3 The standard method: levels of inquiry

The search for definitions has proved inconclusive at best. So let us turn away from the analytic project and note the sense in which theorizing about knowledge in general – and moral knowledge in particular – must begin with observation of human behavior and human psychology.

We can start with an examination of moral theories. Surely, if we are to develop a view as to how people and institutions ought morally to act we must have on hand some description of the ways in which they actually do act. How do we behave? What causes or explains our acting in these ways? Which behaviors are constant across space and time, and which behaviors vary?

Even "theorists of the ideal" bent on describing how a moral utopia would function must concern themselves with the best that common observation, psychology, and sociology have to offer. After all, the imagined utopia is supposed to be a community of people, not angels. If an imagined ideal state is to represent a genuinely human possibility, its conjurer must take into account our distinctively human abilities and frailties (Flanagan, 1993).

> *Zero-level moral inquiry*: a description of the motives and behaviors of people and institutions.

The next step on the way to a moral theory consists in a description of our *critical practices* with regard to the actions and motives we've identified at the zero level. Which actions do we think of as morally right and which do we think of as morally wrong? Which institutions and practices fill us with moral condemnation, and which agents inspire our awe and admiration? Which of these evaluations, criticisms, and emotional reactions vary across time and differ between geographically isolated communities – which even vary between different people in a given community – and which exhibit greater constancy?

When a philosopher writes of her "intuition" that the behavior of some agent in a hypothetical scenario is wrong, unjust, or blameworthy – if she says that someone would be wrong to push a fat man in front of a trolley to save the lives of those it would otherwise trample (Thomson, 1976, 2008), or that a person is morally blameworthy if, because he doesn't want to ruin his clothes, he blithely walks past a child drowning in shallow water (Singer, 1972) – she is perhaps best understood as engaging in this kind of first-level moral theory. If everyone shares her intuitions, she will have described critical practices and judgments that are universally engaged in and assented to. But even if her intuitions do not extend beyond herself and her readership, her effort will be of some utility, as she will have helped articulate the evaluations of that particular community.

> *First-level moral inquiry*: a description of the distinctively moral evaluations (e.g. criticism and praise) that people level at the motives and behavior of people and institutions.[5]

Still, moral theory *proper* begins where first-level moral inquiry ends. Once we have identified the critical practices of a community we can then try to critically evaluate those critical practices themselves. Evaluative practices change, so we don't have to continue resenting, condemning, and calling "wrong" all and only those things that we have called "wrong" up to this point in time. Thus, we can ask, is there any sense to be made of our often pre-reflective (Haidt, Koller, and Dias, 1993; Haidt, 2001) use of "right" and "wrong"? Do we apportion moral praise and blame in conformity with a set of tacit rules, or will our intuitive moral classifications elude even the most careful attempts at codification? If there are rules that can be extracted from the pattern of reactions we've identified at the first level, what if anything can be said in favor of retaining them?

> *Second-level moral inquiry*: an evaluation (critical review) of the distinctively moral evaluations uncovered by first-level moral inquiry.

I've said that proper academic moral theorizing takes place at the second level. But there are philosophers who mingle the first and second levels in the style of an Emily Post by recommending or endorsing every moral evaluation attributable to common thought. Still, where this approach does not result in immediate incoherence – an incoherence mirroring the practices being described – it ensures for itself a conservative outcome. It leaves the theorist thinking that a radical moral theory (such as Singer's strain of utilitarianism) is obviously untenable simply because it fails to describe "our" moral verdicts.

The need for second-level inquiry presses itself upon us with particular force when we have identified a set of evaluative practices that differ significantly from those we find ourselves embracing. Thus, when she is exposed to a liberal society, a member of an orthodox Jewish or Muslim community who is capable of the relevant form of reflection may wonder whether chastity of the sort she is practicing really is a virtue – as her parents, teachers, and friends maintain – or whether, instead, her community is wrong to condemn, look down upon, and call "wrong" all physical contact between unmarried, unrelated people of differing sexes.

Of course, to evaluate a set of evaluative practices a person must *use* some means of evaluation, and our subject's critique will have its greatest impact if she assesses her community's moral view using that community's own concepts and methods of criticism. Consistency or coherence is therefore one of the most powerful tools employed in moral inquiry conducted at the second level (Aristotle, *Eudemian Ethics*, 1214b1–1215b1.15 [Aristotle (384–322 BC/1984)]). So, for instance, almost all of us agree with Singer (1972) and Peter Unger (1996) that it is morally wrong for someone to walk past a child drowning in shallow water if the passerby's only motive for not wading in is a desire to preserve her expensive footwear. But most of us also think that it is morally acceptable for those so inclined to buy expensive shoes for the pleasure that it brings. So suppose someone surfing online happens to have the Oxfam and Christian Louboutin websites open before her: clicking on link A will help save human lives, whereas clicking on B will garner nothing more significant than a fancy pair of high heels. Those I have surveyed tend to think that though clicking on B is somewhat selfish, it is not immoral or morally wrong. But is there a *relevant* difference between clicking on B and walking past a drowning child when the harm that could be prevented is equivalent, and the goal of action in both cases is the possession or preservation of the same pair of shoes? Is there a difference significant enough to warrant our thinking that the passerby acts immorally, but the somewhat self-centered shopper does not? Perhaps there is. But if we cannot articulate such a difference, the critical scheme we've identified at the first level will seem impugned by a second-level review, and rational inquirers will feel forced to change their ways of thinking (Berlin, 1955–56; Nozick, 1974, 277–79). We might conclude, with Singer and Unger, that the requirements of benevolence are more stringent than we typically assume, or we might instead decide that indifference to human suffering is in fact morally permissible (Thomson, 1971).

But though it is a powerful tool, coherence needn't be thought of as the only consideration employed in second-level moral inquiry. Perhaps a minority community of mavericks can reflect on the moral system operative in their society – and the moral "intuitions" common among its populace – and recognize that though these practices are in some sense coherent, they are leading to more misery and suffering than is necessary, and are morally objectionable on these grounds alone. Perhaps people are being uniformly criticized for harmless pleasures, or condemned as "unnatural" for exhibiting behaviors to which no one should object. I have in mind here the intellectual currents that gave rise to Socrates' criticisms of uncritical religious piety and the British Sentimentalists' rejection of the monkish "virtues" of self-abnegation. But left-leaning moral theorists might also include the birth of the young Hegelians and Marx's critique of the now prevalent bourgeois attitude toward the distribution of property.

John Rawls' (1971) less ambitious criticisms of this same socioeconomic structure might provide another example. For though Rawls does use the coherence of his principles with our considered judgments about particular cases as a tool in arguing against the kinds of severe inequality now prevalent in nations the world over, he also invokes seemingly independently grounded psychological and sociological hypotheses. These include propositions about the nature of envy, the conditions necessary for social stability, and metaphysical claims about the separateness of people.[6]

Of course, attempts to undermine or radically revise common morality are often horribly mistaken. (As, I would argue, were Friedrich Nietzsche's [1886/1966] reactionary attacks on democratic ideals.) But if a thinker not wholly of his time can mount a successful second-level critique, moral theorists can use better or more accurate schemes of evaluation to effectively evaluate worse or less accurate schemes of evaluation, where "better" and "worse," "accurate" and "inaccurate" are not measured in terms of coherence alone.

Epistemological inquiry exhibits the same three-level structure present in the moral case. It properly begins at the zero level with a description of the beliefs we actually hold: What do we believe? What causes or explains our holding these beliefs? On which issues do we agree and on which do we part ways? How have our beliefs changed across time, and how do they differ among geographically and culturally distant peoples?

It then proceeds to a first-level description of our evaluation of these beliefs and believers. Under what conditions will we say that agents "know" what they believe? When do we say that though they fail to know they are nevertheless "justified" in believing what they do or that they fail to know through no fault of their own? And when do we say that people or their opinions are "irrational," "unjustified," "gullible," "hasty," "dogmatic," "unreliable," or "overly skeptical"? Which of these evaluations are constant across the speakers in our community and on which do they differ? Which vary across communities or within communities across times (Weinberg, Nichols, and Stich, 2001)?

Finally, second-level epistemology consists in a critical evaluation of our first-level critical evaluations. Is there, as skeptics often allege, some deep-seated incoherence in our attributions of knowledge? Do people fail to know much of what we credit them with knowing? Or are we perhaps overly stingy with application of "knows" and similar terms? In the end, we might conclude that "common sense" should be left alone. Or we might decide that the skeptics are right. But we might discover that the critics have gone entirely the wrong way in rejecting our ordinary attributions of knowledge, when in fact harsh Cartesian strictures have so infiltrated the population at large that genuine possessors of knowledge are commonly being denied the status that is their due (James, 1897/1956, 18).

Properly conceived, distinctively *moral* epistemology results when links are established between epistemological and moral inquiries conducted at one or more of the levels that we have identified. Suppose, for instance, that some of the beliefs that epistemologists enumerate in their zero-level inquiries have distinctively moral content. Suppose, that is, that alongside our scientific belief that $E = mc^2$ and our belief that the Earth is over four billion years old, we must account for our moral belief that greed is a vice that ought to be discouraged, and our conviction that infidelity is immoral. And suppose that the very evaluations we level at those of our beliefs that have non-moral content are also appropriately leveled at beliefs with moral content. Suppose, that is, that as we actually think of properly instructed children learning and therein coming to *know* that the Earth is over four billion years old, we can similarly speak of children learning and therein coming to *know* that it is immoral to be selfish, mean and unjust. If these suppositions are made, then first-level epistemology will contain first-level moral epistemology as a part, and a second-level epistemological project can aim its sights at those moral beliefs that we've uncovered at the first level. Perhaps though we claim that properly raised children come to know that it is immoral to be cruel and selfish, they can't really come to know any such thing, as our assignments of knowledge in these cases are incoherent or just plain false. Or perhaps (to go the other way) though many people in our society think that we are not yet justified in drawing definitive conclusions regarding the exact circumstances in which the abortion of a pregnancy is morally impermissible, we are already in a position to figure this out. In sum, if we have *moral beliefs* that are relevantly like our non-moral beliefs, moral epistemology is a legitimate line of inquiry.

Working from the moral to the epistemological, we can establish the same claim by showing that moral judgments and beliefs relevantly similar to our non-moral judgments and beliefs figure among the evaluations we uncover when pursuing our first-level moral inquiries. There is, of course, no doubt that some of what P. F. Strawson (1962) calls our "reactive attitudes" either stop short of belief or go beyond it. We often respond to perceived immorality with anger, indignation, loathing, resentment, guilt, and disapprobation, and react to what we take to be moral kindness and sacrifice with admiration, approval, love, and pride. But we also *say* that certain actions are morally wrong and others morally right, some morally obligatory and some impermissible, some vicious and other virtuous. If when we say these things we are at least sometimes expressing moral beliefs rather than (or in addition to) morally fraught emotions and sentiments, and we can meaningfully apply epistemological concepts to the states of mind in question, we can then inaugurate the kind of inquiry distinctive to moral epistemology by asking whether we know that certain acts are wrong, whether we're justified in believing that others are virtuous, and so on.

Moral epistemology is, thus, a fairly natural line of inquiry to pursue. We should note, though, that there are theorists who deny the very existence of beliefs with distinctively moral content. For instance, some philosophers equate moral knowledge with certain kinds of value-neutral knowledge; and some philosophers argue that there are no moral beliefs, or insist that if there are moral beliefs, these states of mind are so unlike our non-evaluative beliefs that they cannot be coherently assessed in epistemic terms. Those interested in these challenges to the very coherence of moral epistemology will find them discussed, at some length, in the final chapter.

1.4 Theories of moral knowledge: an overview

Epistemology is often divided into two questions: the "what" and the "how" (e.g. Sosa, 1980):

- the *"what"* question: what do we know?
- the *"how"* question: how do we know it?

Distinctively moral epistemology might then be divided into:

- the *"m-what"* question: what moral facts do we know?
- the *"m-how"* question: how do we know them?

The moral skeptic issues rather stark responses to these traditional questions. The "m-what" question asks what we know of morality. "Nothing," the skeptic answers. The "m-how" question asks how we know those moral facts we know. "We don't," is the skeptic's reply. According to the skeptic, we have no moral knowledge, and since we have no moral knowledge, there is no such knowledge to explain.

Let's call attempts to respond to skepticism *defensive epistemology*. In partial contrast, we have *constructive epistemology*, which first assumes the existence of some kind of knowledge and then tries to explain the knowledge that has been assumed. Again, if we apply this distinction to distinctively moral epistemology, we arrive at:

- *defensive moral epistemology*: an attempt to show that we have moral knowledge;
- *constructive moral epistemology*: attempted explanations of the moral knowledge we have.

Which project should we pursue here? Should we try to answer the moral skeptic first, and assure ourselves that we have some moral knowledge? If we do this, we can address our "m-how" question directly. We can say, "We have shown that we know that this kind of thing is immoral and this other kind of thing is not," and then ask, "Now how do we know these facts?"

But we needn't follow this approach, as we might skip over defensive epistemology either for once or for good. After all, most of us are not moral skeptics. And those of us who believe in moral knowledge are genuinely curious as to how we – and those around us – came to know that, say, theft is wrong and dishonesty a vice. If we put this curiosity on the back burner, and begin by trying to prove that, at some point or other, we really did come to know these moral facts, we may never get around to positive explanations of the moral knowledge most of us think we have. In this event, moral skepticism will have proved itself a nuisance, a source of philosophically debilitating distractions.

Nevertheless, despite this very real danger, I adopt a "skepticism first" approach in the pages to come. I do so for three – somewhat interrelated – reasons. First, moral skepticism differs from other common forms of skepticism in its depth, popularity, and consequences for ordinary thought and practice. Admittedly, philosophers still discuss skepticism about other minds and skepticism about non-observational knowledge more generally. Even full-blown skepticism about the external world has yet to disappear from view. But most epistemologists working in these areas are fairly certain that we do in fact know that there are other people who think and feel roughly as we do; that we do in fact know that objects will fall when dropped near the Earth's surface; and that those of us with hands do in fact know that we have these appendages. The bulk of the literature in these other areas of epistemology is therefore justly dedicated to the constructive task of explaining just how we know these things. In contrast, there still exist many philosophers today who doubt that there are moral facts or doubt that we have any knowledge of morality. Moral skepticism therefore remains a live option – a "relevant alternative" to non-skeptical accounts of moral judgment.

And there is a second reason for beginning with a discussion of moral skepticism, a reason having to do with the interrelation of the defensive and constructive projects we have described. It is my sincere hope that when you finish this book you will have killed two birds with one stone, as responding to skeptical arguments against the very existence of moral knowledge will have provided you with an excellent understanding of the kind of moral knowledge we do in fact have. By seeing what must be done to answer our "m-what" question in a non-skeptical manner, we will have arrived at a better sense of the various non-skeptical answers to our "m-how" question that might be defended.

I will admit, though, that my attitude toward these matters would differ if I thought the moral skeptic's challenges could not be answered. But, in fact, I think exposure to the best arguments for moral skepticism, and the best responses that can be given to those arguments, will leave you convinced that we do in fact have a substantial body of moral knowledge. Indeed, this is the one prejudice I have indulged in the pages to come. While I have done my best to present debates over whether and how we know right from wrong in a neutral, even-handed way, I have done nothing to hide my sense that even the strongest arguments for moral skepticism still come up short. If I am right about this, we needn't settle for the conditional question, "*Supposing* we do have moral knowledge, what is it like?" We can instead investigate a body of knowledge we are fairly confident exists. We can ask, without qualification, "How is our very real moral knowledge best described and explained?"

Nevertheless, before plunging into an examination of moral skepticism, I want to give you some sense of the field's more constructive aspects. This will help dispel the impression that moral epistemologists are unduly fixated on skepticism, and give us a glance at the many interesting debates that continue to litter the field.

To begin constructing even the most rudimentary theory of moral knowledge, we must have in mind some item of moral knowledge that needs explaining. We must assume, that is, if only for the sake of discussion, that someone, somewhere, knows some moral fact. But which example should we choose? Should we examine someone's knowledge of a *general* claim, like the claim that adultery is wrong? Or should we instead look at knowledge of a *particular* claim, say the average man's knowledge that Senator Ensign acted immorally when cheating on his wife with his aide's spouse? Suppose we split the difference. We begin with knowledge of a particular case and examine the claim that knowledge of particulars always stems from knowledge of some more general moral principle.

We can take as our point of departure Charles Dickens' widely beloved *David Copperfield*, a work that contains a host of details drawn from the author's own troubled childhood. Early on in the tale, Copperfield is sent to Salem House, a boarding school run by the despicable Mr Creakle. Copperfield's assessment of the man's cruelty bears repeating in full.

> I should think there never can have been a man who enjoyed his profession more than Mr. Creakle did. He had a delight in cutting at the boys, which was like the satisfaction of a craving appetite. I am confident that he couldn't resist a chubby boy, especially; that there was a fascination in such a subject, which made him restless in his mind, until he had scored and marked him for the day. I was chubby myself and ought to know. I am sure when I think of the fellow now, my blood rises against him with the disinterested indignation I should feel if I could have known all about him without having ever been in his power; but it rises hotly, because I know him to have been an incapable brute, who had no more right to be possessed of the great trust he held, than to be Lord High Admiral, or Commander-in-chief: in either of which capacities, it is probable that he would have done infinitely less mischief. (Dickens, 1849–50/1997, 85–86)[7]

We will have ample opportunity to return to this case in what follows. For now, I want to consider, in brief, the frame of mind Copperfield evinces as he comes to appreciate the sadistic motives that led Creakle to inflict so much suffering on his wards, and moves from this realization to a belief in the headmaster's cruelty and immorality. We are assuming, for the sake of inquiry, that Copperfield here *knows* that Creakle acted in a cruel and immoral fashion. But just *how* does Copperfield manage to acquire this knowledge?

According to one school of thought, Copperfield can just *see* that Creakle is acting immorally. That is, Copperfield knows that Creakle's actions are wrong without drawing this conclusion from distinct premises of any kind. Consider that many (if not most) epistemologists think we can know what we are feeling and thinking by simply introspecting. I don't need to infer that I am in pain from distinct premises or supporting evidence. Instead, the knowledge is wholly *non-inferential*. A smaller but still substantial number of epistemologists think of our perceptual knowledge in the same way. I just know by looking that there is something red in front of me. I needn't argue my way to this conclusion from other things that I know, or supply additional reasons to support my perceptual belief. I can just see that there is something red there. A growing number of philosophers would add certain instances of moral knowledge to this class of judgments. According to this group, just as I know by simply looking that there is something red in front of me, Copperfield knows by simply observing Creakle's actions that the headmaster is acting immorally. We will discuss this perceptual model of moral knowledge in section 4.2.

An instinct more prevalent among moral epistemologists is to depict Copperfield as inferring Creakle's immorality from the value-neutral facts of the case. That is, we might think of the boy as: (a) first using his observations of Creakle's behavior, and his observations of its effects on the students, to verify that the headmaster enjoyed causing the boys to suffer; and as then (b) using his knowledge of a general fact detailing the "defining essence" of cruelty to infer that the man acted cruelly. We can model this two-step inference as follows:

1   Creakle enjoyed causing others to suffer.
2   Someone acts cruelly just in case he takes enjoyment in causing others to suffer.
Therefore,
3   Creakle acted cruelly.

Now let us suppose, if only for the sake of discussion, that Copperfield's observations really do provide him with knowledge of the ways in which he and the other chubby boys have suffered at Creakle's hand; and that these same observations provide Copperfield with knowledge of the frame of mind in which his teacher delivered the lashings. These assumptions allow us to conclude that premise (1) is not only true, but that it is also known to be true by Copperfield. And yet it would seem that knowledge of premise (1) is not yet moral knowledge. Instead, it is the kind of knowledge philosophers and psychologists label "knowledge of other minds" (see 8.1 for discussion).

But let us now also assume that "cruelty" is accurately defined by the *Oxford English Dictionary* as something like "enjoying causing another to suffer." This allows us to conclude that premise (2) is in fact *true*: indeed, that it is true by definition. But we must still ask, as epistemologists, how Copperfield manages to *know* its truth. Surely, Copperfield's knowledge of (2) is not "based on" observations in the same way, or to the same degree, as is his knowledge of (1). It isn't as though Copperfield first learns what cruelty is by fixing on Creakle's motives. Instead, he seems to bring this item of knowledge to the case at hand. So how does he know the fact in question? According to some philosophers, though Copperfield will not have non-inferential knowledge of *particular* evaluative facts like (3), he can have non-inferential knowledge of *general* evaluative facts like (2). Just as we know, by "reflecting on our concepts," that bachelors are unmarried and vixens are foxes, Copperfield knows, by reflection alone, that it is cruel to relish the infliction of suffering. Theories of this kind are also discussed in section 4.2.

But there are other options here. According to a distinct set of epistemologists, Copperfield's knowledge of Creakle's immorality is inferential, but the premises of the inference needn't include moral facts that Copperfield knows in an intuitive or non-inferential way. Instead, the boy knows that Creakle has acted immorally by inferring as much from a set of wholly non-moral or value-neutral premises that he knows. On this view, Copperfield infers an "ought" from an "is." Indeed, some would argue that the requisite inference will prove *deductive* in form, that the value-neutral premises of Copperfield's inference will *entail* its value-laden conclusion. These deductive models of moral knowledge are the topic of chapter 5.

Other philosophers would reject altogether the deductive inference that we presented above as (1)–(3). To their way of thinking, Copperfield needn't deduce (3) from his knowledge of (1) and (2), as the boy's knowledge of Creakle's immorality is in fact *abductive* in nature. According to these accounts, Copperfield infers Creakle's immorality as the *best explanation* of the man's behavior, even though he knows that other explanations are possible. Abductive moral knowledge is discussed in chapter 6.

Epistemologists have also asked questions about (a) the causal origin of our moral beliefs, and (b) the differing roles that reflection and emotion play in generating moral knowledge like Copperfield's. We have observed that Copperfield's knowledge of premise (1) – that Creakle enjoyed striking the boys – is based on observation in a fairly direct way. And we remarked that Copperfield's knowledge of premise (2) – the general fact that someone acts cruelly when he relishes the infliction of suffering —differs in this regard, as Copperfield brings this item of knowledge to the scenes of corporal punishment Dickens describes. But is Copperfield's knowledge of the nature of cruelty *wholly* independent from his experiences?

When writing the definition of "cruelty" the compilers of the *OED* were trying their best to report common usage of the term, usage that is guided by the ordinary English speaker's beliefs about which people and actions are cruel and which are not. How, we might ask, does a speaker arrive at a fully general belief in the cruelty of taking enjoyment in the infliction of pain and harm? Is this knowledge similar to our knowledge of mathematics in its reflective or a priori nature? Or does it more closely resemble our knowledge of those scientific laws we establish through experimentation and observation?[8]

In the *Meno*, Socrates repeats a theory he had heard spoken among "priests and priestesses," a story repeated by Pindar, "and many others divine among the poets," a tale apparently embraced by Plato in the *Republic*.

> As the soul is immortal, has been born often and has seen all things here and in the underworld, there is nothing which it has not learned; so it is not surprising that it can recollect the things it knew before, both about virtue and other things. (81c)

And, though the *doctrine of recollection* here described is no longer taken seriously, there is fairly substantial evidence that certain aspects of a normal human being's capacity for empathy and sympathy are innately specified or genetically encoded. Indeed, there is at least some evidence that non-human primates possess a sense of fairness, however crude in nature (de Waal, 2006). We will discuss these matters in chapter 7.

Moral nativists go beyond the data we have at present to posit not only innate emotional capacities, and innate modes of inference, but a body of innate moral beliefs (Dwyer, 1999; Harman, 2000a; Hauser, 2006; Mikhail, 2008; cf. Kamm, 1993). The purportedly innate aspects of our ability to use and comprehend natural language provide the moral nativists with their model – a comparison that can be traced to Rawls (1971). Noam Chomsky (1957, 1986, 1988, 1995) has posited an innate universal grammar that enables children to learn a natural language – like English, Japanese, or Spanish – from the limited data presented to them during infancy. Similarly, nativists suggest, there is an innately known set of moral principles that enables children to acquire a moral competence from the limited instructions of their parents, teachers, and peers. Consider then Copperfield's understanding of the cruelty inherent in relishing the infliction of harm, or his grasp of the immorality people display when indulging in cruelty. Mightn't this understanding constitute one part of his innate knowledge of our shared "moral grammar?"

Critics of the nativist approach point to the range of moral disagreement and the differences among moral codes that we find at different times and places. Chomsky's hypotheses are supported by the common principles to which all natural languages conform. In contrast, anti-nativists argue, there are no universally accepted moral principles, or if there are some common moral rules, they are either empty or nearly empty in content (Sripada 2008a,b; Prinz 2008a,b).

There is at present very little empirical work that would move a neutral observer to favor either account of moral competence over its opponent. Indeed, it would seem that the controversy's resolution must await further articulation of the rules or principles that would constitute a universal "moral grammar" were one to exist (Harman, 2000a). But some of the issues relevant to the debate are broached in chapters 2 and 7 below.

Notice, though, that even if we go beyond the data and posit not only innate emotional capacities and innate modes of inference, but a body of innate moral beliefs, we won't have yet demonstrated or explained the existence of moral *knowledge*. Cognitive psychologists have uncovered a number of areas in which natural, nearly universal ways of thinking consistently lead us into error (Kahneman, Slovic, and Tversky, 1982; Kahneman and Tversky, 1996). So the innate specification of a cognitive structure is no guarantee of its truth or reliability. Nor is the nearly universal acceptance of an opinion sufficient to establish the justification with which we hold it, or the rationality of its retention. What, then, do we need to learn about Copperfield to figure out whether he truly *knows* what it is for an action to be cruel? And if, as we have been assuming, he does know premise (2), how did he arrive at this knowledge? Similar questions might be asked of a normal person's belief that it is unfair to break covenants on a whim or unjust to lie for monetary gain. Is it rational to persist in these beliefs? In virtue of what do they constitute knowledge?

Mathematics and science are commonly regarded as paradigm routes to knowledge. So attempts to compare various aspects of Copperfield's knowledge of immorality to our most fervently held mathematical and scientific beliefs are natural enough. But which (if either) is the more appropriate comparison? Is Copperfield's moral knowledge relevantly like our knowledge of math? Is it wholly based on abstract reflection? Or is it more like our knowledge of science? Did past encounters with sadism and hypocrisy play an essential role in its genesis?

Moral rationalists like Kant argue that we can know general facts like premise (2) in a wholly reflective manner: a way of thinking that resembles mathematical thought in its *a priority* or independence from experimentation, observation, and experience. *Moral empiricists* like Hume argue, in contrast, that moral knowledge depends for its existence on our emotional experiences, and is therefore *a posteriori* in nature. This historically important debate informs much of chapters 4–7.

We have asked whether Copperfield's knowledge of the immorality or cruelty of Creakle's actions is arrived at or sustained with an inference, or whether it is instead non-inferential in genesis; we have asked as to the nature of the inference that might support Copperfield's belief; whether it might be deductive or non-deductive in nature; how Copperfield might know its premises; whether his knowledge of its premises might be innate or learned; and whether this knowledge might be grounded in pure reflection, or must instead depend for its existence on his emotional or affective experiences. But once we have some sense of how Copperfield has arrived at his moral views we will also want to inquire into the *reliability* of the process. We have supposed that Creakle did in fact act immorally when whipping the boys placed in his care, and this supposition entails that Copperfield's opinion of his headmaster's actions is accurate in relevant respects. But is the truth of Copperfield's belief a matter of luck? Does the method by which he comes to believe in Creakle's immorality always issue in true or accurate judgments? And if, as seems plausible, the method Copperfield employs is not infallible, when does it break down and why does it do so? How large and varied is the range of cases in which Copperfield arrives at the truth when reaching moral conclusions in the manner Dickens has here described? Do the successes greatly outnumber the failures? And are the successes sufficiently common to warrant our self-consciously retaining the form of moral reasoning Copperfield here employs? We will return to these questions in chapter 7.

1.5 Chapter summary

Moral epistemology consists in the study of whether and how we know right from wrong along with a host of related topics. The field is therefore extraordinarily difficult to circumscribe. Philosophers have yet to agree on definitions of key moral and epistemological terms such as "knowledge," "justification," "virtue," and "immorality." The Socratic definitions of "knowledge" that once held sway were refuted by Gettier's counter-examples; and alternative analyses have proven controversial. Nevertheless, there is nothing barring us from launching into an investigation of moral knowledge and related phenomena without first having definitions of "knowledge" and "morality" in place. We can rely on our common understanding of these terms.

Moral epistemology is best pursued using the method of levels. Zero-level inquiry consists in a description of our moral beliefs; first-level inquiry consists in a description of our differing epistemological evaluations of our moral beliefs; and second-level inquiry consists in an evaluation of the epistemic evaluations uncovered at the first level. Coherence is the most powerful tool used by philosophers pursuing second-level moral epistemology, but there may be other ways to rationally revise common thinking about our knowledge of morality and related matters.

Defensive epistemology attempts to respond to skepticism; constructive epistemology assumes the existence of knowledge and tries to explain its nature and genesis. Though we begin our study in earnest with defensive moral epistemology, it is helpful to first give some sense of the constructive issues that have engaged researchers in the field. Theorists disagree over whether our knowledge of particular moral facts is inferential or non-inferential in nature. Those who think our knowledge of particular moral facts is inferential disagree over the nature of these inferences and our knowledge of their premises. Some theorists argue that moral inference is deductive; some that it is abductive. Some argue that our knowledge of general moral principles is innate; some that it is acquired. Some argue that this knowledge is based on reflection or understanding alone and is therefore a priori in nature, whereas others argue that moral knowledge is a posteriori because grounded in emotional experience. Theorists also differ in their opinions of the reliability of those processes that give rise to our most basic moral beliefs. Some think that our common methods of moral reasoning are too unreliable and must be supplanted with novel, more trustworthy ways of thinking. Some disagree.

1.6 Further reading

There are a number of excellent anthologies of work in analytic epistemology; these include Ernest Sosa and Jaegwon Kim, *Epistemology: An Anthology* (2000) and Matthias Steup and Sosa's *Contemporary Debates in Epistemology* (2005). Gettier's short paper "Is Justified True Belief Knowledge?" (1963) is indispensable, and Robert Shope's *The Analysis of Knowing* (1983) does a fine job of describing the differing sources of dissatisfaction with post-Gettier analysis of "knowledge." Timothy Williamson's influential *Knowledge and Its Limits* (2000) argues for a conception of epistemology that would preclude reductive analyses of "knowledge," and William Alston's *Beyond "Justification"* (2005) urges a non-reductive treatment of other important epistemic concepts.

W. V. O. Quine's "Epistemology Naturalized" (1969) pictures a reduction of epistemology to psychology, an approach criticized by Jaegwon Kim in his "What Is 'Naturalized Epistemology'?" (1988). The more nuanced method of levels described above has its origins in the drive to reflective equilibrium introduced by Nelson Goodman in *Fact, Fiction, and Forecast* (1955) and applied to ethical inquiry by John Rawls in his monumental work *A Theory of Justice* (1971). Norman Daniels discusses variations on the method of reflective equilibrium in his *Justice and Justification* (1996), and Stephen Stich warns against its uncritical use in both "Reflective Equilibrium, Analytic Epistemology, and the Problem of Diversity" (1988) and *The Fragmentation of Reason* (1990).

Robert Audi's "Moral Knowledge and Ethical Pluralism" (1999a) provides a nice overview of the issues that have divided constructive theorists of moral knowledge, and the collection of essays *Moral Knowledge?* (1996), edited by Walter Sinnott-Armstrong and Mark Timmons, contains a representative sampling of the field. Debates over the existence of innate moral principles take center stage in Sinnott-Armstrong (ed.), *Moral Psychology*, vol. I, *The Evolution of Morality: Adaptation and Innateness* (2008a) and Peter Carruthers, Stephen Laurence, and Stephen Stich (eds.), *The Innate Mind*, vol. III, *Foundations and the Future* (2007).

2

MORAL DISAGREEMENT

2.1 Disagreement and skepticism

We initiate our discussion of moral skepticism with what is perhaps the skeptic's most historically influential argument. For as long as theorists have reflected on our ethical practices, the existence of deep, persistent moral disagreement has induced skepticism. Even after all the "facts" are in, skeptics like to say, paradigmatic social conservatives continue to believe in the immorality of abortion, euthanasia, stem cell research, homosexuality, pornography, and atheism, whereas liberals believe in their moral permissibility. Doesn't nihilism or skepticism offer the best explanation of this state of affairs? Doesn't persistent disagreement about morality provide us with good grounds for thinking that there is no fact of the matter where morality is concerned, or that any moral view is just as rational as any other?[1]

To begin to get a handle on the skeptic's argument from disagreement, we need to isolate the kind of divergence in moral opinion that would challenge the truth or justification of our moral beliefs. We can then mount an empirical inquiry into how much conflict of this kind really exists.

First note that moral disagreements are often discerned against a background of shared moral principle. Alasdair MacIntyre (1981/2007) describes how Benjamin Franklin's list of virtues differed from Jane Austen's, whose list differed from Aristotle's, whose list, we might note, differed from Confucius's. Aristotle's virtue *magnificence* strikes the left-leaning MacIntyre as an aristocratic vice, and Confucius celebrated *obedience*, its polar opposite.[2] Austen thought being *agreeable* a virtue, whereas Aristotle thought it a sign of artifice or social calculation; and when Franklin celebrates *frugality* and *ambition*, MacIntyre sees greed or the vice the Greeks called *pleonexia*. Nor need we turn to the past to find important differences in moral view. Richard Miller (1985) tells us of violent actions deemed morally praiseworthy by the clannish Yanomamo — actions that we, in the developed world, consider morally abhorrent (Chagnon, 1974, 1977).

But *indiscriminate* cruelty, selfishness, avarice, injustice and cowardice are deemed vices by the majority populations of communities the world over. As Christopher Peterson and Martin Seligman (2004) note, there is significant overlap in the lists of virtues to which different cultures subscribe. Though it is hard to quantify these things, it seems that there is at least as much moral agreement as disagreement out there.

And then there are those philosophers who claim that all *possible* human moralities must share an essential core. According to Strawson:

> When all allowance has been made ... for the possible diversity of moral systems and the possible diversity of demands within a system, it remains true that the recognition of certain general virtues and obligations will be a logically or humanly necessary feature of almost any conceivable moral system: these will include the abstract virtue of justice, some form of obligation to mutual aid and to mutual abstention from injury and, in some form and in some degree, the virtue of honesty. (1961, 15)

Even MacIntyre, the great critic of rationalist, universalist moral theorizing, argues that justice, courage, and honesty must be counted virtues by any community sufficiently complex to engage in social practices of some sort and adopt standards of excellence internal to those practices (1981/2007, 179–81). If the persistence of disagreement is an argument for patches of nihilism or ignorance, why isn't widespread agreement an argument for the existence of at least some moral knowledge (Nagel, 1979; Parfit, 1984, 452–53)?

Moreover, persistent disagreement over an issue is not always best explained through nihilism or skepticism. Consider, for instance, why so many people continue to believe the Genesis creation myth in the face of ample geological evidence to the contrary. (Almost 50 percent of US residents, according to the latest polls.) Surely, irrational ignorance on the part of the religious orthodoxy does a better job of explaining disagreements over the Earth's origin than do the skeptic's hypotheses. The creationist curriculum at Bob Jones University is not best explained by denying the existence of geological facts, or hypothesizing that geological knowledge will forever evade our grasp. Epistemic irrationality can be both deep and intractable (Shafer-Landau, 1994, 2003).

Furthermore, as Hume (1751/1998) noted, some of the apparent disagreement in our ethical beliefs can be explained as the differing application of shared principles, as a single moral rule will demand different actions in different environmental circumstances. For example, universal agreement on a moral principle like "One should sacrifice human life only when it is necessary for the survival of the community" might explain why infanticide and the suicide of the elderly was a culturally acceptable response to famine among the Inuit in what is now northern Canada, while people observe univocal prohibitions against these practices in more hospitable climes. And a single trait might be aptly considered a virtue in some environments but not others. When economic conditions have advanced beyond a certain basic stage, a tendency to "bookish" reflection can help us generate laws, institutions, and agricultural practices all will regard as improvements. But when basic survival is at issue, the traits may constitute a vice, the promotion of which would actually detract from the general welfare (Bloomfield, 2001).

In Western societies all but the strictest utilitarians allow as morally permissible (if not obligatory) the favoring of family members over non-kin, though we consider certain forms of nepotism unjust, and would decry as patently immoral someone's lying under oath to protect a cousin. Similarly, most of us would condemn the vigilante killing of one's brother's attacker. But there are communities like the Tiv of Nigeria (Bohannan, 1968; Miller, 1985) in which lying under oath is considered a duty of fidelity, and people like the Baluch of the southeastern Iranian peninsula, who think non-state violence in defense of family often justifiable.[3] Does this mean that we have a fundamental, irresolvable disagreement with the Tiv over whether it is morally permissible to lie under oath? Do the Baluch and we irreconcilably disagree over the morality of vigilante justice? Perhaps we can find substantive (first-level) agreement on this much: if people are expected to lie under oath to protect members of their family or tribe, and other people are protecting their families and tribes by lying in this way, it may very well be disloyal for you not to lie in service of your family. Of course, we would need to explain how this practice came to exist and persist among the Tiv in Nigeria, when similar practices do not exist in the West. But once the convention is in place, we can allow that the demands of virtue will be affected by its prevalence. Similarly, if clans are perpetrating violence against your family members, and this violence will not be mitigated through non-violent or supposedly neutral (state-controlled) means, your family will denounce your efforts to turn the other cheek as weakness.[4] Loyalty and benevolence demand different things in different environmental and social contexts, and a proper discursive representation of their demands will have to take this into account. But an acknowledgment of this form of context-sensitivity is not tantamount to skepticism or epistemic relativism. Perhaps we all know that one should not lie under oath to promote the interests of family members unless it is an expected practice followed by all parties to the court; and perhaps we all know that one should leave law enforcement to the police unless there is no appropriately neutral and appropriately effective police force willing and able to do the job. Or it may be that a radical (second-level) critique will impugn these beliefs, and effectively argue that we are all bound by an unconditional obligation to testify honestly and practice pacifism no matter what the likely negative consequences for those we love. In any event, the existence of moral knowledge should not be held hostage to the philosopher's attempt to formulate simple, fully general, exceptionless moral principles. If most moral facts are complicated, then most moral facts will be difficult to know. But difficulty is not yet impossibility.[5]

We should note too that a great deal of moral disagreement would be resolved if we could only correct factual errors that are not baldly moral in nature (Boyd, 1988). For example, the belief that Africans are akin to non-human animals in their intellectual and emotional capacities may have led some nineteenth-century Americans to believe in the moral acceptability of slavery. (Almost all of us think that it is okay to use beasts of burden as instruments of labor, so why not the "beast-like" slave?) It was only after extensive interaction provided ample evidence against the more extreme versions of this hypothesis that halfway rational people were forced to switch course. Thus, we find the effective orator Stephen Douglas pandering to the greed, fears, and political self-interest of the white community when arguing that slavery should continue despite its palpable immorality. Indeed, though Douglas' political opponent, Abraham Lincoln, clearly knew that slavery was immoral, there is evidence that even he could not fully abandon the false belief in the innate intellectual inferiority of black people that led many of his detractors to disagree (Reynolds, 2006).

> I agree with Judge Douglas, he [the black man] is not my equal in many respects – certainly not in color, perhaps not in moral or intellectual endowment. But in the right to eat the bread, without the leave of anybody else, which his own hand earns, he is my equal and the equal of Judge Douglas, and the equal of every living man. (Debate at Ottawa, Illinois, August 21, 1858; full text online at: www.bartleby.com/251/12.html.)

These words may arise from epistemic irrationality on Lincoln's part, or he may have been pandering to his audience for political reasons, or it may just reflect the difficulty we all have in separating the cognitive "endowment" of a person from the conditions in which she has been brought to intellectual maturity.

It is also worth remarking that the existence of vagueness does not preclude the existence of moral knowledge and may even explain certain moral disagreements (Brink, 1984, 1989; Boyd, 1988; Railton, 1992; Shafer-Landau, 1994, 2003). Consider, for instance, Sideshow Bob, the acerbic clown whose hairless top is ringed with a puffy crown of red. There may be no fact of the matter as to whether Bob is a genuine, honest-to-God bald man. Or perhaps there is a fact one way or the other, but we cannot know which (Williamson, 1992). In either event, the vagueness infecting Bob's situation doesn't preclude us from knowing that Jessie Ventura, the entirely hairless former governor of Minnesota, is indeed bald, and that the bouffant-sporting rock star Jon Bon Jovi is not. Now it may be that vagueness induced by our concept of a *person* accounts for at least some of the current disagreement over the morality of abortion. Most of us know that it is immoral for a parent to abandon a healthy infant if her only reason for doing so is the inconvenience of childcare. And those who are not blinded by religious myth know that it is perfectly fine to use the morning-after pill soon after intercourse. But at what point prior to birth does a fetus become a person? At what point is an abortion more like abandoning one's needy child than ridding oneself of a largely undifferentiated mass of cells? There may be no fact as to exactly when a fetus acquires a right to his parents' aid, or such facts may be forever beyond our ken, and this may explain why we cannot know exactly when abortion for the sake of convenience becomes immoral.

Now the skeptic's claim must be that there are some moral disagreements that cannot be explained through ignorance of non-moral fact, vagueness, poor reasoning, special pleading, and the like (Mackie, 1977), as only disagreements of this special kind would even suggest nihilism or global moral skepticism. But is the persistence of disagreement so described supposed to be obvious? Is there an a priori way to figure out whether there are rationally irresolvable disagreements over well-framed moral theses? It seems that we must instead work our way through each ethical debate currently in play, size up the arguments on each side, and only then try to figure out whether one or more of the parties to the dispute has overlooked some fact, made some mistake, or ignored the vagueness endemic to our ordinary concepts.[6]

Indeed, the skeptic would make things too easy for himself were he to concentrate exclusively on hot-button issues like abortion and so-called moral dilemmas. Consider, for example, the case – often discussed in Ethics 101 – in which a white woman is killed in a small southern town in the early-to-mid twentieth century, and members of the white citizenry are poised to lynch the town's hundred or so black residents in an unjust act of racially motivated retribution (Rawls, 1955; Nielsen, 1972; McClosky, 1963; Smart and Williams, 1973). Suppose that pinning the murder on an innocent drifter locked in the town jail for vagrancy is the only way that you, the town's sheriff, can prevent these horrible crimes from occurring. Is charging the innocent man morally permissible? Do you have a moral obligation to do so? A skeptic might say that there is no fact of the matter as to the right answer to one or both of these questions.[7] But even if the skeptic were correct about scenarios where justice and utility conflict, this would not establish the complete absence of moral knowledge. We may all know both that it is immoral to knowingly accuse a man of a crime he did not commit, and that we are obliged to prevent great death and suffering when we can, even if none of us know what we should do when these moral obligations cannot be conjointly satisfied. (At some point the horrible consequences of maintaining justice must demand its sacrifice, but the point at which this occurs may be unknowable.) Admittedly, if we can *never* weigh competing moral considerations against each other to arrive at all-things-considered judgments as to the right thing to do in a particular circumstance, moral skepticism of a rather substantial sort would result. But the existence of hard cases needn't impugn the decidability of easy moral problems, and, at any rate, to establish a genuinely global moral skepticism, the skeptic must focus on the premises we employ in our reasoning, not the conclusions of moral deliberation.

Culturally, economically, and politically homogeneous communities tend to agree in their basic moral convictions, so skeptics almost always turn to cultural anthropology to find the kind of inter-community divergence in fundamental morals that they need to make their case. But even here it is important to find truly basic moral conflicts, where disagreements over particular practices will almost never prove sufficiently basic to establish the skeptic's conclusion (see Bloomfield, 2008, 341). Consider, for instance, Jesse Prinz's (2007) arguments for moral subjectivism that emphasize cultural differences in our beliefs as to the morality of female circumcision, polygamy, and cannibalism. In a psychological study conducted on Western subjects, Murphy, Haidt, and Björklund (2000) describe a hypothetical case in which a researcher decides to cook and eat an unused piece of a human cadaver donated to her lab for study. Most subjects say the act is immoral, but can find no good rationale with which they might defend their judgments (cf. Haidt, Koller, and Dias, 1993; Haidt, Björklund, and Murphy, 2000). And in contrast, Prinz argues (2007, 223–29), cannibalism was the norm in many societies of old. Does this show that we have a basic belief in the immorality of cannibalism, a belief that conflicts with the basic beliefs of cultures past, where this disagreement is best explained by there being no fact of the matter as to whether cannibalism really is immoral?

Now it seems, as a purely causal or psychological matter, that most people think cannibalism is morally wrong because they find it disgusting (cf. Nichols, 2004). And, one might argue, disgust is not the kind of experiential basis that can adequately justify a moral belief. Disgust is perhaps too obviously pliable and variable, and we can, perhaps, too easily see that we are disgusted by many morally permissible acts for disgust to provide us with a reliable guide to moral truth. (Think of drinking a cup of your own spit, eating live bugs, or handling feces. Most of us find these acts disgusting. But would this justify us in judging them immoral?) Nevertheless, the lack of basic (non-testimonial) justification with which the common man believes in a blanket moral prohibition on cannibalism would only impugn the justification with which we hold our most fundamental beliefs in the immorality of cruelty, selfishness, and injustice if we are also led to embrace the latter by disgust alone. And this is a highly implausible claim. I don't think John Edwards' adultery was selfish or Neville Chamberlain's policy of appeasement cowardly because they disgust me, nor do my general beliefs in the immorality of gross selfishness and cowardice have this foundation. Exactly what leads me to hold these beliefs is, as we will see, the subject of some controversy, but every serious hypothesis will have to employ resources beyond mere disgust.

Indeed, it may be that through reflection, the ordinary subjects studied by Murphy and his colleagues could be led to conclude that cannibalism is

fine in certain circumstances. As is the case in Murphy's scenario, the cannibalized man mustn't have been killed for the purpose of ordinary consump-
tion; but the act must also avoid indignity, imprudence, and callousness
– it mustn't be contrary to the wishes of the cannibalized man and his
family, dangerously unhealthy, or part of a general disregard for human life.
It is instructive to consider, by way of comparison, the change in attitudes
toward homosexuality that we are currently witnessing (Persily, Citrin, and
Egan, 2008, ch. 10). Perhaps the typical subject who judges homosexuality
immoral does so because the idea of homosexual sex fills him with disgust.
(We here put to the side those who explicitly invoke religious testimony
in defense of their prejudicial beliefs.)[8] But if a rational man knows that
he has no further reason for thinking of homosexuality in this way, he
will feel pressure to re-examine his views. This is particularly true if he is
cognizant of the pliability of reactions like disgust, and the distress that
homosexuals must experience at being thought of as immoral. Admittedly
when a person has been brought up to think that homosexuality is morally
abhorrent, it will often be impossible to get him to admit that his belief is
based on nothing more than disgust, that disgust is a variable and unreliable
guide to moral truth, and that negative moral judgments adversely affect the
judged. Instead, people tend to "confabulate" by formulating more substantive justifications on the fly (Haidt, Björklund, and Murphy, 2000).[9] Yet if he
can be brought to these realizations, a rational person would not react with
indifference, but would re-examine his convictions instead.

Similar things might be said about female circumcision and polygynous
forms of polygamy. If disgust were all we had to motivate our conviction
in the immorality of these practices, we would be wrong to label them
immoral. But suppose, instead, that we believe that every woman's right
to pursue happiness gives her a right to the unimpaired use of her sexual
apparatus. And suppose we think that a woman's right to autonomy or self-
determination gives her the right to play a full and equal role in her marital
partnerships. And suppose, too, that our beliefs in the right to autonomy
and the pursuit of happiness are not themselves wholly grounded in disgust
over their privation. Then we needn't regard our prohibitions on female
mutilation and polygamy as unjustified or arbitrary. Instead, we need to
know if and why foreign cultures disagree about the rights of women or
the implications that these rights hold for the morality of female circumcision and polygamy. In the end, if our disagreement over these matters does
not endure because of religious prejudice, it will almost certainly involve
at least one party's ignorance of non-moral matters. Perhaps the defender

of polygamy is ignorant of the abilities of women, or its detractor fails to recognize the utility or necessity of the practice in certain conditions.[10]

It seems, then, that the argument from moral disagreement must be buttressed with an independently motivated account of moral disagreement's sources. There may be fundamental, irresolvable moral disagreements, but their existence is not a priori guaranteed.

In the end, then, disagreement does not provide us with a quick route to moral skepticism. To impugn the rationality of our moral beliefs and our claims to moral knowledge, the skeptic must examine the causal origin of our most basic moral convictions. If our most basic moral judgments are generated by nothing beyond disgust, or if Karl Marx (1818–83) was right in assigning these beliefs to propaganda spread by the powerful, or if John Locke (1632–1704) proves correct in attributing them to a now-discredited form of religion, then a good case can be made for moral skepticism. (We will examine some of these claims below.) But if inquiry into the developmental origin of our most basic moral views reveals something like a reliable mechanism for distinguishing right from wrong, the skeptic will be left in an extraordinarily weak position.

2.2 Moral contextualism

I have argued that the mere creepiness of cannibalism does not justify our belief in its immorality. At the very least, it seems, such justification as can be provided by reactions like disgust and revulsion will stop well short of that necessary for moral knowledge. Of course, we may know that cannibalism is wrong in some distinct way, as we may learn it via the testimony of a reliable source, or infer its immorality from the health risks it purportedly poses, or the disrespect for human life it supposedly imbues. But the heebie-jeebies are, in any case, an insufficient basis for moral belief (Moore, 1912, 66–67).

The same would seem to go for female circumcision, polygamy, and even certain varieties of incest (Wolf and Durham, 2005). Suppose two mature siblings, who are incapable of reproducing, knowingly engage in consensual intercourse. Studies show that most people living today in the developed world will describe the act as immoral despite their having no good argument they can offer in support (Haidt, Björklund, and Murphy, 2000). Now it may be that however much two siblings consent to a sexual relationship, it will always be fraught with power inequalities and emotional strains sufficient to render it unwise, imprudent, or even immoral. (There is a good case to be made that parent–child incest is always wrong for at least these reasons.) But if grossness is all that can be cited against an affair between consenting, adult siblings, then, I think, we must re-examine our belief in its immorality.

Admittedly, there are those who take an opposing view, and allow that disgust is sufficient to justify moral belief (Prinz, 2007, 31–32 and 238). Since disgust can presumably warrant belief in the *disgustingness* of an action or practice in suitable circumstances, we must examine the view of morality that would result were we to think of immorality in these terms. Suppose, then, that grossness is good evidence of immorality, and that the inference from "x is disgusting" to "x is immoral" is correspondingly kosher. Because reactions of disgust are exceedingly pliable and variable, people from different cultures find different things disgusting. How then might we resolve a dispute between someone who thinks all forms of incest are immoral precisely because they are revolting and a member of a distant culture who does not find certain forms of incest off-putting and therefore thinks of them as perfectly permissible? And if we could not resolve this dispute, would the best explanation for our failure involve skepticism or nihilism regarding both disgustingness and morality (Joyce, 2001, 164–65)?

There is an alternative view worth exploring: *moral contextualism* (Dreier, 1990; Unger, 1995 and 1996, ch. 7; cf. Arrington, 1989). Contextualism, as we will understand it here, is a semantic or linguistic thesis: the contextualist claims that some of our ordinary moral terms shift their reference and/or sense from one context of use to another. Consider, for instance, the English sentence "It is raining." When Thomas utters this sentence in London he will use it to assert that it is raining in London, but when Chad utters the very same sentence in Santa Barbara, he will use it to assert that it is raining in Santa Barbara. "It is raining" is *context-sensitive* in that its standing, conventional meaning dictates that it be used to assert different things in different contexts, and speakers of English employ this fact to discern what someone has used the sentence to say in any given context. In the most basic cases, I figure out what you have said when uttering, "It is raining," by finding out where you are, and inferring that you've asserted that it is raining there.

Most important, given our interests here, is the possibility of *merely apparent disagreement* arising from ignorance of the meaning or denotation of certain context-sensitive expressions. The mere illusion of disagreement can result if I do not really understand a context-sensitive expression, or if I grasp its standing meaning, but do not know who is speaking, when and where she is, or toward which thing she is pointing. Genuinely *cognitive disagreement* is precluded by purely semantic or interpretive mistakes of these kinds.

> *Cognitive disagreement*: after S has knowingly asserted P because she believes P, S*≠S asserts not-P because she believes not-P and intends to deny the very proposition she knows that S has asserted.

Suppose, for example, that while Thomas is in miserably gray London, his friend Chad calls from sunny Santa Barbara to gloat, "It sure is sunny," over the telephone. Thomas displays gross ignorance of the standing meaning of this English sentence if he knows where Chad is and has no beliefs as to the weather in Santa Barbara, but retorts, "No, it's not" because of the gloom in London. And Thomas makes a fairly extreme interpretive error if he says, "No it is not," because he thinks that Chad is in London with him. (In this case, Thomas understands the standing meaning of "It is sunny," but because he doesn't know where Chad is, he cannot use this understanding to infer that Chad has asserted that it is sunny in Santa Barbara.) Semantic ignorance of both these varieties precludes substantive debate or genuinely cognitive disagreement. Cognitive disagreement results only if Thomas utters, "No, it's not sunny," because he knows what Chad has asserted – namely, that it is sunny in Santa Barbara – but thinks (contrary to fact) that it's really cloudy in Santa Barbara. Only then will we have a disagreement about "the facts" rather than mere miscommunication.

Now contextualism of the distinctively *moral* variety claims that sentences like "Incest is wrong" resemble sentences like "It is raining" in their being properly used to assert different things in different contexts, where the contextual variation results from a difference in the sense or reference of some item of moral vocabulary.

> *Moral contextualism*: one or more moral expression is properly used to denote or express different things in different contexts of utterance. As a result, sentences containing that expression will be properly used to assert different things in different contexts.

So, to continue with our examination of incest, we might suppose that Lucy, a born and bred citizen of the United States, is on the phone with Nalubutau, a Trobriand Islander who has recently married his first cousin on his father's side. When Lucy says, "What you did is incest, and incest is immoral," Nalubutau replies, "No it isn't." A contextualist account of this discourse might claim that because "immoral" varies in its denotation, Lucy and Nalubutau haven't really disagreed with one another – instead, they've used the single sentence "Incest is immoral" to assert different propositions. Just as Chad uses "It is sunny" to assert that it is sunny in Santa Barbara, and Thomas uses "It is not sunny" to assert that it is not sunny in London, Lucy uses "Incest is immoral" to assert that knowingly having sex with your first cousin is immoral given the cultural practices prevalent in her community, whereas Nalubutau uses "Incest is not immoral" to assert that such behavior is not immoral given the standards assumed in the Trobriands. As a result, Lucy and Nalubutau have no more contradicted each other than have Chad and Thomas.[11]

Remember that if Chad and Thomas go back and forth with "It is sunny" and "It is not sunny," they are really just confused. They should both agree that it is sunny in Santa Barbara, but not sunny in London. And the moral contextualist might claim something similar for "Marrying your first cousin is fine." If Nalubutau and Lucy go back and forth with "Incest is fine" and "Incest is immoral," they are just confused. They should both agree that incest of the variety in question is immoral given Lucy's moral standards and perfectly okay given Nalubutau's. There's sunny in Santa Barbara and sunny in London, but there's no such thing as just being sunny, *full stop*. Similarly, there's immoral for the Americans, and there's immoral for the Pacific Islanders, but there's no sense to be made of something's just being immoral, *full stop*. Of course, this doesn't rule out cases in which it is sunny at every spot on the Earth facing the sun, and it doesn't rule out acts that are immoral on every culture's reckoning. But even in such cases, the moral facts will be *relational* in form. Immoral according to everyone is still an instance of "immoral according to *x*". It is not quite full-stop immorality or immorality simpliciter.

Though there is a deflationary element to the account, the contextualist's view of moral discourse would actually help reconcile a non-skeptical moral epistemology with what look to be fundamental moral disagreements between cultures (Harman and Thomson, 1996). For instance, the contextualist can say that Lucy expresses *knowledge* when she says, "Incest is immoral," because if the contextualist is right, what Lucy knows here is that incest is immoral according to standards operative in her society. And this does not rule out Nalubutau's also expressing knowledge when he says, "Cousin incest is morally fine." (Compare: Thomas expresses knowledge when he says, "It's not sunny," and so does Chad when he says, "It is sunny." Chad knows that it is sunny in Santa Barbara; Thomas knows that it is not sunny in London.) The lesson is that moral facts are easier to know when they are construed as relational in form. Apparent moral disagreements pose no threat to relational moral knowledge, but can instead be diagnosed as symptoms of semantic misunderstanding.[12]

But how plausible is the contextualist view of moral discourse? David Kaplan, one of the first theorists to supply a rigorous logic for context-sensitive expressions, supplied an open-ended but limited list.

> The group of words for which I propose a semantical theory includes the pronouns "I", "my", "you", "he", "his" "she", "it", the demonstrative pronouns "that", "this", the adverbs "here", "now", "tomorrow", "yesterday", the adjectives "actual", "present", and others ... What is common to the words or usages in which I am interested is that the referent is dependent on the context of use and the meaning of the word provides a rule that determines the referent in terms of certain aspects of context. (1989, 489–90)

But the phenomenon is now thought to be much more widespread (though see Cappelen and Lepore [2005] for resistance). Tense clearly introduces context sensitivity, as do quantificational expressions and gradable adjectives. If Mary says, "The leaf is green" in May, Sam does not contradict her in saying of the same leaf "It is red (not green)" in October. If Frank says to himself, "There is nothing in the refrigerator," because there is no food to be found there, Sam, the cleaner, who has asked his assistant, Murray, to empty the fridge of all its parts, does not contradict Frank when saying, "Murray, the shelves and drawers are still in the refrigerator." If Usain, a resident of impoverished Jamaica says, "Evander is rich," when comparing him to other Jamaicans, the wealthy UAE businessman Amir need not contradict him by saying, "Evander is not rich," when comparing him to residents of his own nation. Instead, we say that Mary asserts that *the leaf is green in May*, and Sam does not contradict her in asserting that *it is not green in October*. Frank asserts that *there is nothing to eat in the refrigerator*, and Sam says nothing to the contrary in asserting that *the refrigerator still contains removable parts*. Usain asserts that *Evander is rich for a Jamaican*, and Amir can agree, while saying, further, that *the man is not rich for a member of the UAE*.

But what about "disgust"? Suppose that while Maria loves cilantro, it tastes like soap to Kathy. Kathy sincerely says, "Cilantro is disgusting," whereupon Maria replies, "No it is not." Is there a genuinely cognitive disagreement here, or has Kathy asserted that cilantro is disgusting to her (Kathy), while

Maria has asserted that it is not disgusting to her (Maria)? Well, there are several possibilities that Maria might entertain: perhaps Kathy has only ever eaten old, near-rotten cilantro and has never had it washed and prepared properly, or perhaps she always refuses to try new things out of fear or xenophobia and would enjoy cilantro were she to consume it with an open mind. And Kathy might have a few hypotheses of her own: maybe Maria has just gotten used to the soapy tang of cilantro and would actually prefer the taste of her dishes were they purged of the ingredient. We might say, in an anti-contextualist vein, that Maria and Kathy actually disagree with one another over the taste of cilantro: if Maria's hypotheses are correct, she speaks truly when telling Kathy that cilantro is simply not disgusting; and if Kathy turns out to be right, cilantro really is disgusting.

But let us suppose, instead, that there is a genetic explanation for why cilantro tastes like soap to a limited but still substantial portion of the population – a group that includes Kathy but not Maria among its numbers. And suppose Kathy and Maria both know this, and know, moreover, that the taste of soap disgusts us all. Then, if they continue going back and forth with "Cilantro is disgusting" and "Cilantro is not disgusting," we must conclude that they are either massively confused or mistaken about the meanings of their words. Kathy should simply assert that cilantro tastes disgusting to *her* (and others like her); and Maria should limit herself to the claim that cilantro is not disgusting to *her* (and those like her). There is just no point to disagreeing about whether cilantro really is simply disgusting. We know ahead of time that cilantro cannot be disgusting (or delicious), full stop.

Still, given the wholly semantic nature of moral contextualism, we can ask whether its truth would really matter to us given our role as moral epistemologists. And it seems that if we restrict ourselves to things judged immoral simply because they disgust us, a contextualist account of moral discourse will have much the same practical upshot as would an "invariantist" account like the one I've suggested – an account that insists disgust is an insufficient basis on which to judge something immoral. According to the contextualist, Lucy cannot coherently persist in saying, "Incest is immoral," in the hopes that she will therein assert that incest is simply immoral. Instead, the conventional meaning of this sentence dictates that she use it to assert that incest is immoral given her standards (or those operative in her community). In partial contrast, the invariantist thinks the standing meaning of "Incest is immoral" is such that Lucy can use it to assert that incest is simply immoral. But if the invariantist joins us in thinking that disgust is an insufficient basis for moral judgment, she will still insist that Lucy's assertion is unjustified. In either event, then, Lucy will be subject to criticism of a fairly strong form for continuing the argument with Nalubutau. Either the contextualist is right and Lucy cannot use "Incest is immoral" to assert something that contradicts what Nalubutau has asserted, or the invariantist we have described is right, and she can only contradict Nalubutau in an unjustified or unwarranted manner. On both accounts, Lucy cannot rationally or coherently condemn the Trobriand Islanders' marital practices as immoral.

Of course, Lucy would come out as both coherently using "Incest is immoral" to assert that incest is simply immoral and as being justified in this assertion, if an invariantist account of her utterance is correct and her community's reactions of disgust really are good evidence of incest's *simple* immorality – evidence that is superior in kind to the evidence for incest's moral permissibility provided by the reactions of the Trobriand Islanders. But it is hard to see how mere disgust could be regarded in this light. I have claimed that because disgust is fairly obviously either uncorrelated with immorality or only very weakly correlated, it cannot provide Lucy with even *prima facie* justification for believing in incest's immorality. But even if I am wrong, and her feeling of disgust does justify Lucy in thinking of all incest as simply immoral, it is fairly certain that this feeling cannot provide good enough evidence of incest's immorality to justify her in persisting in that belief in the face of Nalubutau's contrary experience and testimony. As a rational person exposed to a contrary practice, Lucy needs some reason to think that her reaction is a more reliable guide to incest's immorality than is Nalubutau's, and without evidence for the immorality of cousin incest that goes beyond mere disgust, no such reason will be forthcoming.

Nevertheless, as we will see, theorists as different in approach as Hume and Kant have argued for basic – non-inferentially grounded – moral beliefs that are generated by reactions other than disgust. And it remains to be seen whether we might justifiably retain at least some of these beliefs by rejecting the contradictory claims of foreign cultures or communities. Again, we must look for an account of the genesis of our most basic moral judgments if we are to assess their reliability and the epistemic credentials of the beliefs we ground in them. The devil is in the details.

2.3 Chapter summary

Some theorists argue for nihilism or epistemic moral skepticism from the supposed depth and ubiquity of moral disagreement. There are a number of ways to resist this line of reasoning. There is, of course, a great deal of moral diversity; but justice, courage, honesty, and some form of mutual aid are valued the world over. A single moral principle will demand different kinds of behavior in different environmental circumstances, and moral disagreements often arise from ignorance of non-moral fact. Vagueness in our ordinary concepts may make certain disagreements irresolvable without impugning our knowledge in cases where these concepts clearly apply. Epistemic irrationality explains why we continue to disagree about religious claims – such as the Genesis creation myth – that have nothing to do with morality: claims that should have been dispelled to everyone's satisfaction long ago. And the same might be said of moral disagreements regarding homosexuality and immodesty that also have a religious cause.

Some judgments are caused by disgust alone, and it is fairly clear that disgust cannot justify our moral beliefs or supply us with moral knowledge without the help of good arguments or more reliable methods of belief formation. But this would impugn our most basic moral beliefs only if they were also grounded in nothing beyond disgust. And they are not. We must further investigate the causal origin of our belief in the immorality of cruelty, selfishness, and injustice to discover whether these beliefs are reliably held. There is no quick route from disagreement to skepticism.

Moral contextualists argue that cross-cultural moral disagreement is often merely apparent. We use "wrong" to assert that polygamy is wrong according to our lights; the members of certain foreign cultures use "wrong" to assert that the practice is not wrong according to their lights. We are therefore just confused if we continue going back and forth with "Polygamy is wrong," and "No, it is not wrong." Our disagreement is illusory.

Moral contextualism is implausible when it is applied to our central moral beliefs in the injustice, selfishness, and cruelty of certain practices. We argue against the morality of polygamy from beliefs regarding the rights and capacities of women, arguments that our polygamous interlocutors cannot rationally dismiss as irrelevant to the truth of what they believe. But when contextualism is relegated to moral judgments sustained by nothing more than disgust, its truth would be of little epistemological importance. We are either unjustified in arguing for such beliefs in the face of contrary views, or we cannot cogently contradict the views of foreign cultures on such matters. In either event we can be criticized for insisting on the immorality of an action others find acceptable when nothing beyond disgust lies behind our assertions.

2.4 Further reading

Chris Gowans (ed.), *Moral Disagreements* (2000) anthologizes important readings on the subject, as does Paul Moser and Thomas Carson (eds.), *Moral Relativism: A Reader* (2001). Recent discussions emphasizing the depth and extent of our differences on moral matters include Gilbert Harman, *Explaining Value* (2000b), David Wong, *Natural Moralities* (2006), and Jesse Prinz, *The Emotional Construction of Morals* (2007). Discussions that emphasize actual and potential agreement include Russ Shafer-Landau, *Moral Realism* (2003) and Michael Heumer, *Ethical Intuitionism* (2005). Richard Miller's important essay "Ways of Moral Learning" (1985) aims at a middle position.

The most nuanced and influential versions of contextualism are found in the literature on knowledge in general. These include Stewart Cohen, "Knowledge and Context" (1986), David Lewis, "Elusive Knowledge" (1996), and Keith DeRose, "Assertion, Knowledge and Context" (2002). Peter Unger develops the moral case in "Contextual Analysis in Ethics" (1995) and in the final chapter of his *Living High and Letting Die* (1996). Criticisms of contextualism include Jason Stanley's *Knowledge and Practical Interests* (2005), and the more wide-ranging indictment mounted in Herman Cappelen and Ernest Lepore, *Insensitive Semantics* (2005).

3

MORAL NIHILISM

3.1 Moral skepticism characterized

The existence of moral disagreement shouldn't blind us to our customarily non-skeptical ways of viewing moral judgment. For we typically assume that all normal, well-functioning adults know right from wrong in basic measure, and that so long as our children are born without extreme psychological handicaps, they too can be taught how they ought to behave. The *moderate moral skeptic* challenges this way of thinking by arguing that we have no moral knowledge, whereas *the extreme skeptic* claims that none of our moral beliefs are even justifiably held. In this chapter we aim to describe and assess additional arguments on behalf of these skeptical claims.

We begin by noting that moral skepticism does not simply consist in someone's doubting our ordinary attributions of moral knowledge. As René Descartes (1596–1650) remarked (1641/1993), a patient in an insane asylum may irrationally think that he is made entirely of glass, but this does not seriously challenge our claim to know that he is really flesh and bone. Similarly, a crazy man may become convinced that there is nothing wrong with killing old ladies for their money. In and of itself, this does nothing to undermine our belief to the contrary.[1]

What would indeed challenge our belief in the existence of moral knowledge, warranted moral belief, and the like is someone who had *good reasons* for thinking our attributions of these false or unwarranted. The skeptic with whom we must be concerned, then, would not only doubt or disbelieve our claims to have knowledge in moral matters, he would also be justified in adopting this stance. But what could ground radical skeptical doubt? Given the sophisticated, reflective nature of the skeptic's critique, it is unlikely that he could be directly or *non-inferentially* justified in doubting the ordinary claims to knowledge that we have uncovered. The skeptic's doubt is therefore unlike the kinds of arguably non-inferential knowledge I grant you when I allow that you know, simply by introspecting, that you are in pain, and know, simply by looking ahead, that there is something red in front of you, or know, simply by grasping the concepts involved and their logical relations, that $4 + 4 = 8$. Instead, it seems, the skeptic must have some *argument* for his position – an argument that would lead a rational person to doubt or reject the existence of the kind of moral knowledge that he regularly attributes to himself and the adult members of his community. His argument may consist in nothing beyond the bold assertion that we have no good reason to believe what we do about morality, along with the tacit assumption that we do not know or cannot rationally believe things for which we lack good reasons. But he has to offer something that might motivate us common folk to doubt what we take to be common wisdom.

Such arguments come in two stripes. The *nihilist* argues that there are no moral truths to be known and thus no moral knowledge. In contrast, the *purely epistemic moral skeptic* argues that whether or not there are moral truths, any evidence, reasons, or grounds we have for our moral beliefs must prove insufficient to provide us with moral knowledge or even justified moral belief. We begin our discussion with skepticism of the first kind.

3.2 The death of god

In traditional societies, moral instruction is decidedly religious in tone. But parents and religious-school teachers continue to intertwine moral learning and theological precept in even those Western states whose laws and constitutions enshrine a separation between church and state. Does moral truth require the existence of god? And if so, might a skeptic convince us that we lack moral knowledge with an argument placing god's existence in question? Dostoyevsky's (1880/1990) character Ivan Karamazov concludes (if not in exactly these terms) that if god does not exist, everything is morally permissible. If Ivan is right, and god does not exist, there will be no facts of moral obligation to know.

Indeed, the most convincing arguments for moral skepticism focus in on the concept of *permissibility* featured in Dostoyevsky's work – on our conviction that we are morally *obligated* to perform certain actions and refrain from others. It hardly needs saying that children are prone to selfishness and can be quite cruel to one another. (Though the "natural" badness of children is often overstated.) To bring the next generation to maturity in a responsible manner, we must reprimand them for such behavior and encourage generosity and kindness in its stead. Now, when we try to warn our children off cruelty and selfishness, we quite reasonably assume that they will be motivated to do what they know they must to get what they want. If they want their parents' love and approval more than the toys they are hogging or the sense of power they derive from teasing their playmates, our telling them that we want them to share or play nicely – because it would be wrong not to do so – will have its intended effect. And if they are not sufficiently concerned with our wishes or how we feel about them, we will have to resort to punishments and rewards of a cruder kind. But how can a child's parents get her to keep on sharing when they are not around? How can they ensure that she will continue to act kindly when they have passed away and she either doesn't need the approval of those aware of her actions or can get away with her misdeeds undetected? Perhaps the child can be made to want the approval of an eternal god who knows all things. Or perhaps she can be convinced that whatever she wants most, god will deny it to her should she act immorally. Fear or love of god can be made to serve as an "internal" moral sanction.[2]

Now if our child's beliefs about her moral obligations have this kind of theological underpinning, they are vulnerable to metaphysical doubt. The skeptic holds his sword over the souls of our children as follows:

1   *The authority of moral obligation*: if you are morally obligated to refrain from cruelty, then you ought not be cruel all things considered.

2   *The supremacy of instrumental rationality*: if you ought not act cruelly all things considered, there must be something that you want that you can get by refraining from cruelty, where you want this more than whatever you can get by acting cruelly.

Where principles (1) and (2) together entail:

3   If you are morally obligated to refrain from cruelty, there must be something that you want that you can get by so refraining, something you want more than whatever you can get by acting cruelly.

Of course, the skeptic admits, the existence of the kind of god that the child's parents have described would make (3) true in all cases. God, as the enforcer of morality – or the "executive branch" of the moral realm – would ensure that you always get what you want when you fulfill your moral obligations, but that you cannot ultimately succeed in your aims when you shirk your responsibilities. In Locke's words:

> Good and evil are nothing but pleasure or pain, or that which occasions or procures pleasure and pain in us. Morally good and evil then, is only the conformity or disagreement of our voluntary actions to some law, whereby good and evil is drawn on us, from the will and power of the law-maker; which good and evil, pleasure or pain, attending our observance, or breach of the law, by the decree of the law-maker, is what we call reward and punishment. (1690/1991, §183)[3]

But if Locke's god does not exist, (3) will prove empirically false in many cases. As it happens, some of the immoral people out there at least seem to prosper from their immorality at least some of the time. (Though the degree to which this occurs is also often overstated.) If these immoral people are not *really* getting what they want through their misdeeds; this can only be because their rewards are replaced by punishments in the world to come. However, since a god of Locke's description does not exist, and divine rewards and punishments are not to be had, it is in fact sometimes instrumentally *irrational* to fulfill what you thought were your moral obligations.

4   Sometimes, there is nothing that you want that you can get by refraining from cruelty, or at least nothing that you want more than what you can get by acting cruelly instead.

And (3) and (4) together imply an intermediate skeptical conclusion:

5   Sometimes, you are not morally obligated to refrain from cruelty. In particular, you are not morally obligated to refrain from cruelty when, as sometimes happens, cruelty will get you what you (on balance) desire.

But we, who are listening to all this skepticism, cannot accept that our child ought to refrain from cruelty only when this will satisfy her on-balance desires. After all, as Kant (1785/2002) argued, moral obligations are supposed to be *categorical* in nature, and they distinguish themselves from other kinds of obligation in precisely this manner. Suppose, for instance, that no one would suffer from your failing to show up for work, but that doing so is a condition on your continued employment. Then it seems that you are only obligated to show up for work if you want to keep your job, where you might or might not have this desire. And this, one might think, is enough to show that the obligation in question is not a distinctively *moral* one. If you were in fact *morally* obligated to show up for work, this could not depend on your wanting to remain employed. You can *opt out* of certain non-moral obligations, but morality binds you come what may (cf. Foot, 1981; Wiggins, 1995; Herman, 2008).

Now the skeptic can join us in these reflections. Of course, *he* doesn't think that our child ought to remain upright even when she can best satisfy her ends through immorality. But he will happily join us in a conditional claim: if our child really were morally obligated to refrain from such things as cruelty, this could not depend on what she happens to want.

6   *The categoricity of morality*: if you were *morally* obligated to refrain from cruelty in any case, your being so obligated would not depend on your happening to have a desire (or desiderative structure) that you might lack.

And when taken together with our previous argument, (6) allows us to infer:

7   You are never morally obligated to refrain from cruelty.

Clearly, there is nothing (save incarceration) that could keep the skeptic from giving similar arguments to people other than our girl, and nothing to keep him from shifting his focus from cruelty to selfishness, deviousness, or any one of the other ways of acting we deem morally impermissible. Thus, because he chose his target audience and deed with full neutrality, the skeptic can claim to have established a somewhat general conclusion.

8   We have no moral obligations.

In this way, loss of belief in god can leave someone vulnerable to moral skepticism of a rather radical kind – a truly existential crisis.[4]

Now, though the skeptic's reasoning is not without its attractions, each one of his premises can be coherently doubted. Against (1) we might claim, for example, that Paul Gauguin was morally obligated to provide for his wife and children, but that he nevertheless did what was the all-things-considered right thing for him to do in moving to Paris (and then the Pacific) to paint his masterpieces (Williams, 1981; cf. Wallace and Walker, 1970, 11). Of course, we think of moral considerations as more important than aesthetic considerations generally speaking, but some thinkers have nevertheless maintained that the latter can trump the former (Nietzsche, 1886/1966). Against premise (6) we might argue that morality is a system of hypothetical imperatives, albeit imperatives rooted in deep human needs or desires. And mightn't our moral obligations be real enough even though they only bind sympathetic, properly raised individuals, or those who have voluntarily signed on to the moral enterprise (Foot, 1972; cf. Wong, 2006)? And, of course, premise (4) would be denied by those who believe in Locke's god.

But by far the most questionable premise in the skeptic's argument is its second. Surely there is something irrational in failing to do what you know you must to get what you want. (Indeed, the psychological incoherence involved can be compared to remaining confident in the premises of a valid argument while refusing to accept what one knows is its conclusion.) As a fully general matter, we can say, one ought to either execute (or try to execute) those actions one knows one must in order to get what one wants, or revise one's preferences. But it is far from clear that the kind of instrumental rationality enshrined in this dictum is *supreme* in the sense claimed by premise (2). Indeed, let us suppose that morality is commonly assumed to be categorical in the sense defined by premise (6), and thought to be such by even those who lack belief in Locke's god. Then I will feel comfortable in telling you that you ought to refrain from cruelty all things considered, even when I know that cruelty will get you what you want most, and you will say the same to me. What could then prevent me from adopting your perspective on my own actions? What could stop me from judging that I ought not be cruel in the case on hand even though – at least prior to my making this judgment – I cannot get what I most want by doing what I know I ought?

3.3 Mackie's queerness

We will return in the discussion to come to the important question of whether instrumental rationality is sufficiently supreme to generate nihilism from the death of god. But we need to first discuss a related argument that has proven even more influential within analytic philosophy: John Mackie's (1977) famous argument from "queerness."

The common man, Mackie says, thinks of his moral obligations as both "objective" and "intrinsically prescriptive" (1977, 33).[5] Let us put to the side for the moment the question of what objective, intrinsic prescriptivity is supposed to be. For whatever it is, Mackie thinks we have good reasons to conclude that nothing actually has this quality.[6] Why? Because we would have no plausible story as to how we could come to know objective, intrinsically prescriptive obligations, and no plausible story of how the fact that we have these obligations might be related to other, more ordinary sorts of facts. Could it be that we have moral obligations, but that they are not both objective and intrinsically prescriptive? Mackie thinks not, as our concept of moral obligation has become so enmeshed with the assumption of objective, intrinsic prescriptivity that nothing could be a moral obligation unless it had this character. We must therefore conclude that there are no moral obligations. No one is really morally obligated to do anything.

The overarching structure of the argument can be represented as follows:

9   An assumption of the "objective, intrinsic prescriptivity" of our moral obligations has become so integral to moral thought that there can be no moral obligations unless they have this quality.
10   There is nothing that is objectively, intrinsically prescriptive.
Therefore,
8   We have no moral obligations.

To make some headway in interpreting Mackie's view we clearly need to know what he has in mind by "objective, intrinsic prescriptivity" (1977, 35). What are these features? And why does Mackie think that the common man believes his moral obligations must have them? Unfortunately, Mackie does not do what he must to answer these questions. He makes almost no effort to reveal the assumptions of objectivity and intrinsic prescriptivity being made in the course of daily life. Instead, he argues that morality is not objective and necessarily compelling in the way that Plato, Aristotle, Price, Kant, Sidgwick, and Moore took it to be (15–33). Plato, Mackie argues, was wrong to think that the Form of Goodness is "such that knowledge of it provides the knower with both a direction and an overriding motive; [that] something's being good both tells the person who knows this to pursue it and makes him pursue it" (40). Aristotle was wrong to think that each man has an "objective" function, where fulfilling this function is impossible in the absence of virtue or excellence of character (45–48). And Kant was wrong to think that there is a valid or veridical "categorically imperative element" in our judgments or assertions as to who is morally obligated to do what (29). Morality is objective and intrinsically prescriptive according to the leading characters in the history of moral philosophy, and they are all dead wrong.

But even if we suppose, as is far from obvious, that in one short work Mackie successfully undermines many of the most important claims of many of the most important thinkers in the history of ethical theory, we will still be left to wonder what all this has to do with our ordinary judgments. Consider, for instance, the common conviction that Governor Spitzer knew that he was morally obligated not to cheat on his wife. If Spitzer knew that his cheating was immoral, he must have had an obligation to refrain from such behavior, and an obligation to fidelity must exist in this and like cases. Do we think of this obligation as an abstract idea attracting all rational agents to the cause of justice with its supernatural magnetism? Do we think that Spitzer incompletely grasps the Form of the Good, and that a full comprehension of it would render him impervious to the attractions of well-groomed young women? The suggestion strains credulity (Gibbard, 1990, 154). Even Socrates' most pliable interlocutors balk at the wilder flights of Plato's fancy.

Moreover, even if we were to grant Mackie that some or all of our ordinary thinking about moral obligation *incorporates* Platonic assumptions, this would be insufficient to establish Mackie's crucial premise (9). That is, one could agree with Mackie's claim that "ordinary moral judgments include ... an assumption that there are objective values," where these values are "action-directing absolutely, not contingently ... upon the agent's desires and inclination" (1977, 29) while denying that this assumption is a referential presupposition of our use of moral terms. For one might deny that objective, intrinsic prescriptivity is, in Richard Joyce's (2001, 3) terminology, a "non-negotiable" element of our moral thinking.

Consider, for instance, the ordinary glass of which windows and drinking vessels are made. We commonly think of glass as solid in state, but scientists tell us that it is really a highly viscous liquid, or that it is neither solid nor liquid in form (Brill, 1962). But this discovery does not lead us to conclude that there is no glass. Should it? Similarly, we can ask, even supposing that the assumption of morality's objective, intrinsic prescriptivity really is as widespread as Mackie claims it to be, is it sufficiently central to our thinking that its abandonment would lead us to conclude that Spitzer has no moral obligation to fulfill his wedding-day vows? And if it did not do so, might Mackie argue that it should?

To argue that it probably would, the nihilist of Mackie's stripe might try to assimilate our concept of *moral obligation* to concepts like *dragons* and *witches*

(Joyce, 2001). *Dragon* looks to be a species concept, and there probably was a time at which the majority of people believed in dragons. But we now know that there is nothing of the kind; dragons don't exist. Notice that we do not say that there are or were dragons, and that upon closer investigation these creatures turn out to be dinosaurs or monitor lizards. And we do not say that medieval peasants were right about the existence of dragons, but were dramatically mistaken about the properties of the animals in question. Thus, it seems we say that glass exists even though it is dramatically different from what we assumed it to be, and we go the other way on the dragon issue. But is there a principled difference to be made between *dragon* and *glass*? And how plausible is Mackie's claim that the link between the existence of our moral obligations and their purported objective, intrinsic prescriptivity more closely resembles the connection between dragons and their supposed magical powers than it does glass and its alleged solidity?

One possibility here is that *dragon* is not a zoological concept, but a wholly mythological or fictional one (Walton 1973, 1978; Evans, 1982, ch. 10). Perhaps talk and thought of dragons were initiated through works of fiction – myths – that were known to be fiction by those producing them. This would distinguish the concept *dragon* from the concept *glass*, which most likely originates in honest attempts to sort, classify, and investigate the materials we encounter in daily life.

But if he took this line, Mackie could only assimilate our concept of *moral obligation* to *dragon*, *unicorn*, *witch* and the like if he could successfully show that moral instruction was originally a kind of yarn-spinning. It must be that, somewhere along the line, what were intended to be fantasies for the youth were somehow mistaken for realities by young and old alike. Of course, in creating myths we are not trying to assert what is literally true, so the truth of a myth – if, as is doubtful, it ever happens – is always to some degree accidental.[7] This is particularly true of the at once derogatory and mythical use of "witch," when liars bent on limiting female empowerment and apostasy deployed it for their own vicious ends. (In contrast, the notion of a *kind witch* – when it is not equivalent to *grumpy but well-meaning old lady* – is "merely" fantastical in character.) Indeed, the allegation of witchcraft still provides cover for horrible child abuse in parts of Angola, Congo, and the Congo Republic, as each year thousands of children are starved, blinded, cut, banished from their homes, and even killed on the charge (Bearak, 2009). Thus, in arguing that the etiology of our concept of moral obligation is like that of our mythical concepts, Mackie would be forced to provide empirical support for a *debunking explanation* of our moral beliefs and concepts. Clearly, though, a demonstration of morality's unreliable origins in myth-making, story-telling, or persecutory propaganda would put the truth of our moral judgments and the applicability of our moral concepts in doubt quite independently from any purported connection they have to assumptions of objectivity and intrinsic prescriptivity. Absent a compelling debunking genealogy of our moral concepts, Mackie's argument would be nothing more than a bald assertion of epistemic skepticism. We are simply being told that our moral beliefs have an unreliable origin, and are therefore unlikely to constitute knowledge of moral truths. The real action would be found in history, anthropology, and developmental psychology. Until we had figured out how we came to possess and retain our most basic moral beliefs, we would not be able to assess Mackie's skeptical allegations of unreliability.

Alternatively, we might allow that the concept *dragon*, like the concept *glass*, was introduced or given verbal expression in the course of a good-faith attempt to categorize and explain the material world. But how could this be? How could good-faith efforts to taxonomize the animal kingdom result in the admission of flying lizards and fire-breathing serpents? This is particularly hard to imagine when we consider that belief in dragons is a feature of ancient Semitic, Persian, Chinese, and European cultures. (Though the stories seem to have migrated from some regions to others, there are differences in the myths that suggest two or more different points of origin.) How could the zoologists of old make the very same errors in seeming independence from one another? Surely the role of myths known to be such by those relating them must have played some role. But is it not also possible that some of the original users of "dragon" and its synonyms were doing their best to account for "visions" of some kind? Might they have introduced "dragon" to refer to what *looked* to be fire-breathing lizards and winged serpents? (We might compare *dragon* with *witch* in this regard, and the accidental concurrence of a child's bad behavior with the death of crops.) If so, another principled distinction between *dragon* and *glass* can be drawn. Since hallucinations – rather than monitor lizards, dinosaurs, or real dragon-like creatures of some other stripe – played the central role in regulating use of "dragon" and its synonyms, we do not think of any real creatures as falling under its extension. In contrast, "glass" continues to refer to glass despite the substance's shocking liquidity, because the term was introduced (and its usage maintained) through interactions with glass.[8]

But, again, if he were to try to establish that *moral obligation* is more like *dragon* than *glass* in this respect, Mackie would have to isolate the relevant range of "moral hallucinations" in the etiology of our beliefs in moral obligation. The argument from queerness would require supplementation from an independently motivated debunking explanation. The queerness of our assumptions regarding the force and scope of our obligations could do no more than raise suspicion that some such story might be true.

Mightn't Mackie have a different comparison in mind? Consider the term "phlogiston," which can be traced to Johann Becher's (1635–82) attempts to explain combustion. What makes things burn? Becher hypothesized that flammable substances contain phlogiston: a colorless, odorless, massless substance that burned compounds released into the atmosphere when reverting to a "calx," their true form. Eventually, the experiments of Mikhail Lomonosov (1711–65) and Antoine-Laurent de Lavoisier (1743–94) refuted phlogiston theory and in so doing demonstrated that phlogiston does not exist. So, we can ask, mightn't moral obligations go the way of phlogiston? Mightn't our concept of obligation figure in our ancestors' radically mistaken attempts at explanation? Modern theories of combustion eschew all talk of phlogiston. Similarly, Mackie might suggest, a better, more modern understanding of the universe would eschew all talk of moral obligation.

Still, to argue for this position, Mackie would have to establish two non-trivial claims: (1) that our concept of "moral obligation" is a theoretical concept and (2) that the theory in which this concept figures is radically false. To begin with an assessment of the first of these tasks: is "moral obligation" a theoretical term? Unlike "phlogiston," the term was not introduced into our vocabulary with a scientific treatise akin to Becher's *Physical Education*. Instead, "obligation" (along with its synonyms in other languages and their etymological ancestors) has a more organic origin in the thought and talk of the population at large. Mackie must therefore argue that our moral concepts constitute an *implicit theory* – a web of shared beliefs that would look like a scientific theory were their assumptions adequately articulated. Moreover, the role that "obligation" plays in this implicit theory must itself be rather theoretical. Consider, for instance, that on our second account of the term "dragon," it was introduced in an ineffectual attempt at folk zoology. And yet when we adopted this account we had to posit hallucinations – or equivalent failures of observation – to explain how "dragon" could fail to pick out anything real. Why? Because we supposed folk zoologists used "dragon" to categorize (what they took to be) *observable* entities – in this case animals. Thus, even if "obligation" were introduced with an implicit moral theory, if the term's main role within that theory rested with the categorization of observable actions, the falsity of our implicit morality would not yet impugn the existence of moral obligations. It is useful to compare "obligation" with "glass" in this regard. Suppose we think of "glass" as a theoretical term, and we think of the implicit theory in which it figures as a rather difficult to articulate "folk chemistry." So conceived, folk chemistry turns out to be false in rather dramatic respects. (For instance, as we have seen, glass is not a solid.) But the failures of folk chemistry don't tempt us to infer that there is no glass. Why? Because the role that "glass" plays within this supposed folk chemistry is not particularly theoretical. Instead, we primarily use the term to classify an observable material. To really conclude that there is no glass, we would have to posit widespread hallucinations or comparably radical errors in the observations guiding our deployment of the term "glass." In sum, Mackie must argue that "obligation" is *doubly* theoretical; the concept must play a largely theoretical role in a largely bankrupt implicit theory.

Now Mackie does nothing to motivate these assumptions, and his arguments for nihilism are correspondingly deficient. But let us suppose, for the sake of argument, that an empirical investigation into the matter would reveal that "obligation" is indeed a doubly theoretical term. Let us suppose, that is, as is far from obvious, that psychological investigation would reveal that folk morality is a widely shared but largely implicit theory, and that the role "obligation" plays within this theory is rather remote from observation. Still, we can ask, is folk morality a *false* implicit theory? And if the theory does contain inaccuracies, is moral thinking so *radically* false, and false in precisely those *ways* that would preclude knowledge of our moral obligations? For we might compare "obligation" with terms like "solidity" and "density" and the role these two concepts play in what we might suppose is an implicit folk physics, or we might compare moral terms with "memory," "belief," and "desire" and their role in what we might suppose is an implicit folk psychology. Folk physics and folk psychology have their inaccuracies (McCloskey, 1983; Holland *et al.*, 1986), but we don't conclude from them that nothing is solid or dense, or that no one has memories, beliefs, and desires. Why think that "obligation" must go the way of "phlogiston" rather than "solidity, "density," "memory," "belief," or "desire"? These are the questions to which Mackie's arguments against our obligations must speak.[9]

3.4 Motives internalism

We are forced, then, to return to the question of what "objective, intrinsic prescriptivity" is supposed to be. Commentators on Mackie have interpreted the phrase in two main ways. According to some, a moral obligation has this quality just in case its recognition must always constitute a *motive* for respecting it – a state of mind that will lead one to fulfill the obligation in the absence of countervailing motives. According to others, a moral obligation is objectively intrinsically prescriptive just in case knowledge of it always supplies one with a *reason* for respecting it – a consideration in favor of fulfilling the obligation that, in the absence of considerations against so acting, would make fulfilling the obligation the thing one has most reason to do.[10]

> *Motives internalism*: if a person consciously or explicitly knows that she is morally obligated to x, then she has a motive for x-ing, and therefore will x unless prevented by contrary motives or external impediments.

> *Reasons internalism*: if a person consciously or explicitly knows that she is morally obligated to x, then she must have some reason for x-ing, so that in the absence of substantive reasons against x-ing, x-ing will be what she has most reason to do.

Admittedly, many philosophers think that "moral knowledge" should be replaced with "moral judgment" in at least the first of these characterizations (Darwall, 1983, 1995; Joyce, 2001; Sinnott-Armstrong, 2006). After all, they reason, if Huckleberry Finn is fully convinced that he has a moral obligation to repatriate Jim, the runaway slave with whom he is traveling, this will have as much impact on his decision as would the recognition of a genuine moral obligation. Huck cannot *know* that he is obligated to return Jim, if he is not so obligated, but the *truth* of what Jim believes should be irrelevant to what he is going to decide to do. All that matters here is the strength of his conviction, not its accuracy.

But I think it is probably best to resist these calls to recast our Socratic formulation of motives internalism. That is, we should insist on examining what David Brink calls "hybrid internalism," on which moral knowledge is supposed to be conceptually linked to motivation, rather than "agent internalism," on which the existence of the obligation is supposed to be sufficient, or "appraiser internalism," on which the moral judgment is supposed to be enough (1986, 27).

Why do we focus on hybrid internalism? Well, for one thing, some philosophers have argued that knowledge differs from even justified, true belief in its motivational or explanatory properties (Williamson, 2000). Consider that, as Mark Twain tells the story, Huck keeps Jim from being captured out of feelings of sympathy and friendship. Huck thinks that he is acting against the force of obligation, but the modern reader knows that he is doing the right thing (MacIntyre, 1957; Bennett, 1974). It may be that were Huck to have instead known that he was obligated to prevent Jim's escape to the North, conflicting feelings would not have swamped his sense of obligation, if they had been present at all.[11] At any rate, if moral knowledge incorporates moral belief, the internalisms we have described above will be entailed by their judgmental analogues. If the internalist is wrong about the motivational or reason-providing powers of moral knowledge, he will be wrong about moral belief as well.

Arguments for nihilism that begin with the attribution of motives or reasons internalism share the form of Mackie's attempted demonstration. The view in question must be both false and a "non-negotiable" presupposition of moral thought.

9'   An assumption of motives or reasons internalism has become so integral to moral thought that there can be no moral obligations unless knowledge of them always supplies someone with a reason or motive for fulfilling them.
10' There are no such things such that knowledge of them always supplies one with a reason or motive for fulfilling them.
Therefore,
8   There are no moral obligations.

It is a bad sign for the nihilist, then, that so many philosophers have carefully reflected on our moral thinking and continued to deny one or more of these premises. Those who continue to subscribe to some form of motivational and reasons internalism include both neo-Kantians such as Thomas Nagel (1970) and Christine Korsgaard (1996a,b), and neo-Aristotelians such as John McDowell (1979, 1985), and David Wiggins (1991). According to this camp, the nihilist may be right that knowledge of one's moral obligations must bring reasons or motives in its wake, but in the final accounting there is nothing queer about the suggestion that they do. Those who deny the nihilist's claim that motivational or reasons internalism is a non-negotiable aspect of common moral thinking include many externalist moral realists, such as Peter Railton (1986), Richard Boyd (1988), and David Brink (1989). According to this camp, we have moral obligations, but we don't "intuitively" think that our awareness of them need always move us toward their fulfillment or provide us with reasons (of a substantial sort) for doing so.

We can begin with motives internalism, as it is by far the clearer of the two positions in question. How do we ordinarily think of the relation between moral knowledge and moral motivation? We first note that it is a commonplace that those who know right from wrong do sometimes knowingly act immorally. Indeed, the demonstration that someone was ignorant of the immorality of her misdeed is commonly taken to remove or mitigate the blame that would otherwise be appropriately sent her way. Thus, a wrongdoer's ignorance of the obligation she violated is thought of as a special circumstance, not a necessary condition for her having done what she did.

There are two features that those who would defend a common assumption of internalism can play with here: the kind of knowledge involved and the kind of motivation (Deigh, 1995). The strongest form of internalism would claim that *minimal* knowledge of an obligation yields an *unimpeded* motivation toward its fulfillment even when the knowledge is wholly inexplicit.

> *Radical motives internalism*: anyone who can be credited with knowing that *x* is morally obligatory will always have an unimpeded motive to *x* so long as she retains this knowledge.

Surely, radical internalism is not a commitment of common sense. Aristotelian virtue is incompatible with a motive to vice, and if Aristotle is to be taken seriously, there is a special kind of knowledge or wisdom sufficient for it: *phronesis*. But Aristotelian wisdom features as an ideal in our thinking, as we commonly allow that the "merely continent" man can know that he is obligated to keep his word even if he is tempted to break it for monetary gain. So perhaps it is a priori knowable (or even definitional) that Aristotelian wisdom precludes any serious temptation toward immorality. And we can wonder with Mackie whether anyone actually has such wisdom or whether it is even attainable. But our answering in the negative would not lead us to say that no one knows what he is obligated to do. Should it?

Let us suppose not, and that an *unimpeded* motive to morality is not needed for run-of-the-mill moral knowledge. Is an *overriding* motive still thought necessary? This too is implausible, as a conflicted person can know that what she is doing is wrong, and even come to regret her misdeed upon reflection. So maybe moral knowledge just requires *some* motivation, as our characterization of motivational internalism stipulates: the person who knowingly acts as she knows she mustn't has to be conflicted in some way. But it is unclear whether common sense even endorses this thesis. Common sense says that Spitzer knew that he was acting immorally; but are we to suppose the governor conflicted even while in the throes of carnal ecstasy? If we suppose that he wasn't at all torn, and wholeheartedly thrust himself into the deed instead, must we say that he temporarily forgot the immorality of adultery? Surely not. According to common thought, *inexplicit* run-of-the-mill knowledge of a moral obligation is compatible with full-throttle immorality.[12]

What is perhaps both true and commonsensical is that consciously contemplating, or, better still, *dwelling on* the moral impermissibility of a deed, will provide or even constitute a motive against its performance. Though much here depends on what we have in mind in speaking of someone's *dwelling* on how wretched the act is or would be. If Spitzer is thinking of his wife and how awful his betrayal of her really is, and if he is in this way contemplating the viciousness of adultery, it is hard to see how he could at the same time debauch with full vigor.

Admittedly, there may be some cases in which conscious knowledge of one's own immorality needn't impede one's actions in the least. Gerald Wallace and A. D. M. Walker ask us to:

> Suppose a child's parents are brutally murdered before his eyes; he vows he will take revenge and eventually does so without subsequent pangs of conscience or feelings of repentance. He says of the episode: "I know [or believe] that what I did was wrong; nevertheless I would do it again." Is the thesis we are examining so strong that we can simply conclude he does not believe that what he did was wrong? (1970, 16)

But it may be that the child's hatred and anger block him from fully contemplating the kind of injustice he has perpetrated and the reasons why he should not give in to the thirst for vengeance he expects others to resist. Perhaps, that is, were he to suitably meditate on the need for impartial mechanisms for executing justice he would be at least conflicted in motive.

At any rate, if we think of dwelling on the known immorality of the act as actively "perceiving" its immorality, we might here affirm what Stephen Darwall has called "perceptual internalism," the truth of which is compatible with the falsity of Darwall's "judgment internalism" (1983, 54–55; 1997, 306–10; cf. Watkins and Jolley, 2002, 79).

But if perceptual internalism – or a suitably minimal internalist thesis of another stripe – is all that the nihilist can attribute to common sense, her demonstration of its falsity will prove much more difficult. What is so queer about our thinking that vivid, conscious appreciation of an act's immorality is motivationally efficacious?

At this point, defenders of the nihilist line turn to purportedly "Humean" arguments for the motivational impotence of reason. Either dwelling on the immorality of an act is the product of reason, or some passion, emotion, or appetite must be involved. If the state of mind in question is the product of pure reason, it might amount to knowledge, but then it won't be able to dissuade one from performing the immoral act unless it is helped along by some desire. On the other hand, if dwelling on the immorality of the deed is thought to include sadness, despair, or self-censure as a constituent part or aspect, then it may be sufficient to motivate someone toward the right course. But then it won't be the agent's bare knowledge of the immorality of her action that is doing the motivating, but its emotional or desiderative concomitants instead (Smith, 1994, 2004; Dreier, 1997). Thus, it isn't Spitzer's knowledge that he is putting his wife's happiness in jeopardy that accounts for the lack of enthusiasm he is showing in the pursuit of vice tonight, nor are abstract thoughts about the injustice of his breaking his nuptial promise properly implicated. Instead, some sadness or despair coextensive with – but distinct from – these thoughts must be credited.

But why should we think reason and passion are always distinguishable? Humean arguments for a "real distinction" between the two come in both bottom-up and top-down varieties. The bottom-up approach leans on special examples. When a typical person is consciously focused on the fact that she is morally obligated to do something, she will be motivated to do it to at least some extent. But in certain extreme cases, we seem to see knowledge and motive come apart. The depressed mother may know she is morally obligated to prepare food for her hungry children while entirely lacking the will to do so (Stocker, 1979). And the psychopath's cold, unemotional knowledge that it is immoral to kill the innocent will fail to impact his decisions in one way or the other (Brink, 1986; Smith, 1994, 2004). Cases of this kind can lead us to question whether moral knowledge is itself a motive even in typical cases where people do what they know they must. For consider the complete set of those psychological elements that motivate us to fulfill our moral obligations and lead us to feel conflicted when we knowingly act immorally. If the depressive and amoralist know their moral obligations in the absence of moral motivation, they must be missing at least one of the elements in this set. And, as the presence of these missing elements seems to be a necessary condition on one's doing what one knows one must, it is tempting to say that these elements are the *real* causes of moral action – and that this is so even in the typical case in which moral knowledge is accompanied by moral motivation. To resist this temptation, we must seemingly deny that the depressive and the amoralist really have knowledge of their moral obligations, or insist that they must have some motivation – an unconscious or deeply implicit inclination to do what they know is right that is somehow blocked or held down by aspects of their pathology (Sidgwick, 1874/1981, 5; Dancy, 1993, 25; Jackson and Pettit, 1995).

In contrast, the top-down approach to arguing against motives internalism begins with the defense of a *teleological* scheme for constructing a scientific psychology. Non-mental organs are perhaps best individuated or classified according to their functions. For example, the function of the heart is to supply oxygen-depleted blood to the lungs and to pump its oxygen-enriched issue to the rest of the body's cells. Indeed, one might argue, what it is to be a heart is to be something that has circulating blood as its function, and, in consequence, something is a heart just in case it pumps blood (or does so when functioning properly). Perhaps, then, the best scientific practice is to individuate mental organs or *psychological modules* in the same way. Perhaps, for example, the function of the visual faculty is to accurately represent the visible aspects of one's environment, and the function of the kind of appetitive conativity that issues in feelings of thirst and hunger is to initiate actions that satisfy an organism's primal needs. What then is the function that individuates the moral faculty? To answer, the Humean argues, we must pursue one of two mutually exclusive options. Either the moral module is like vision and has accurate representation or *truth* as its function, or it is like appetite and has *successful action* (e.g. moral, prudential, or fitness-enhancing behavior) as its function. If the first choice is made, the moral faculty can issue in knowledge or true beliefs, but these will not motivate on their own, as motivation will be the job of a distinct set of faculties. If the second choice is made, the moral module can issue in motives, but they won't be assessable for accuracy and so won't constitute knowledge or true belief. In neither event can we think of someone's consciously dwelling on the immorality of a prospective course of action as both moral knowledge and moral motive.

Something like this argument may be found in Hume's claim that pure reason cannot motivate because "reason must be considered as a kind of cause of which truth is the natural effect" (1739–40/2000, 1.4.1.1), whereas the products of our motivational faculties fail to "contain" any "representational quality" that "renders them copies" so that these faculties cannot have truth as their "natural effect" (1739–40/2000, 2.3.3) (cf. Zimmerman, 2007). But modern formulations that are decidedly behaviorist in tone have received more extensive discussion. When Michael Smith (1994) says that someone's belief that p "aims at the truth" of p, he is saying, roughly, that perception that p induces or reinforces the state of mind in question. When he says, in contrast, that someone's desire that p "aims at satisfaction" or bringing it about that p, he is saying, roughly, that perception that p eliminates or quiets that state of mind. Since no mental state could interact with perception in both these ways, no state of mind could have both directions of fit. As a result, Smith argues, moral knowledge cannot itself constitute a moral motive. There are no hybrids of belief and desire. There are no "besires" (Smith, 1994).[13]

In response to these arguments, the internalist can point to other, more mundane psychological faculties that seem to have a *dual* function. The psychological module that issues in feelings of physical pain seems to function so as to: (a) provide an organism with information about bodily damage and (b) initiate behaviors aimed at mitigating and avoiding both pain and the damage it indicates. For instance, the fairly intense pain I am experiencing in my left foot right now is an accurate representation of what is going on just in case I indeed have a left foot and there is indeed something bad for me occurring there. (On this way of thinking of things, phantom limb pain and "referred" pain – as in sciatica – are both inaccurate representations.) But it is hard to see why a representationalist view of my pain is supposed to be incompatible with allowing the sensation a central role in motivating, causing, or explaining my subsequently hopping onto my right foot (Pitcher, 1970). How can we be so sure that the moral faculty will not also turn out to be individuated by a dual function? Why cannot feelings of self-censure, sentiments of disapprobation, or judgments of unfairness constitute "besires" of a sort?[14]

We will have more to say about these Humean arguments in the chapters to come. It is enough here to note that determining the truth or falsity of the moderate form of motives internalism correctly attributed to common thought is a highly abstract theoretical matter. To resolve it, we would seem to need an empirically plausible account of depression and psychopathy and a well-grounded scheme for individuating the mind's faculties or modules. Our concepts of moral knowledge and moral motivation – and the at times hazy "intuitions" about extreme cases that they generate – are not entirely set in advance of these empirical studies. Hopefully, they will solidify as decisions about classification and categorization are made in the course of further inquiry.

Indeed, suppose that a review and development of empirical psychology proves the externalist right. Suppose, that is, that the best – most explanatory and predictive – theories of mind that we can develop will hold that conscious, explicit moral knowledge does not motivate us to act morally without the addition of dissociable emotional or desiderative states of mind. It might still turn out that paradigmatic or *canonical* (Lewis, 1989) moral knowledge is always held within a frame of mind that inclines us toward the right course. For instance, we might suppose that a cold man's knowledge of the need for charity will prove inert when it is acquired from a leaflet sent him in the mail. It is compatible with this that the sensitive man, who labors for the charity, has firsthand (non-testimonial) knowledge of the same need: intimate knowledge of those who are suffering that motivates him to work hard on their behalf without much in the way of monetary compensation. It is far from clear that this result would conflict with ordinary thinking, much less that it would so drastically clash as to render commonly held criteria for the existence of moral obligations unsatisfiable.

3.5 Reasons internalism

We turn then to the argument from reasons internalism and its twin claims: (a) that according to common thought, knowledge of a moral obligation must always bring a reason to respect that obligation in tow, where (b) nothing actually meets this condition. The first of these two claims must be interpreted before it can be evaluated. For though "reason" is not nearly as obscure as Mackie's "objective, intrinsic prescriptivity," its use is sufficiently flexible to lend reasons internalism an unhelpful degree of imprecision (cf. Audi, 1997a).

First, "reasons" can be used to denote the brute (non-psychological) causes of a phenomenon, as when we speak of the reasons apples fall from trees or the reasons the Earth continues to spin on its axis. Though this usage may reflect a history of anthropomorphization wherein our ancestors thought of celestial bodies as acting upon deliberation, we can now speak of the reasons why non-conscious, inanimate objects behave as they do without asserting or implying that they have minds or rationales. To do so is to speak of *reasons qua brute causes*.

But when we think of the reasons why a person acted as she did, we often have a different kind of explanation in mind. For instance, we might say (however falsely) that the reason why President Bush ordered the invasion of Iraq was that he thought they had weapons of mass destruction and wanted to rid the region of the threat that these weapons posed. And despite our knowledge that Iraq did not have these weapons, we might even speak here of *Bush's reasons* for doing what he did. "Bush's reason for invading Iraq was that he thought they had WMD and wanted to eliminate the threat – though, as it turns out, he was wrong about the WMD." Now we can contrast this description with a not-too-fanciful case in which Cheney hypnotizes Bush and gets him to initiate the war without any rationale at all. Though much depends on how such hypnotism is supposed to work, we might imagine Bush sending in the air strikes in a zombie-like, detached state all the while wondering why he is doing what he is doing. If we describe the scenario in this way, we will speak of *Cheney's* reasons for initiating war and *Cheney's* reasons for hypnotizing Bush. But we will not speak of *Bush's* reasons for doing what he did even though we know his actions have a proximate neurological cause. Instead, we will say that our hypnotized Bush ordered the invasion even though he had *no reasons* for doing what he did – he caused the invasion without reason. It seems, then, that when looking for the reason why someone did what she did, we often have in mind a particular kind of explanation of the action. We are looking to explain the action in a way that "rationalizes" or makes sense of its occurrence by establishing a certain kind of connection between the agent's frame of mind when acting and the action performed (Davidson, 1984). We can therefore speak here of *reasons qua rationalizers*.[15]

But there is a third use of "reasons" that comes to the fore when we deliberate before acting and advise others as to how they should act. Suppose, for instance, that Dr Jack Shephard is deciding whether to use his medical training to help relieve the physical suffering rampant in an impoverished rural area or to instead remain in a culturally diverse, intellectually lively city in which he will have a much more enjoyable existence. It would not be out of character for Jack to set out the "pros" and "cons" of each option and have someone advising him also construct such a list. Here it is natural to speak of the items in the "pro" column as *the reasons* why Jack should take the job in question (at the time in question) and the items in the "con" column as *the reasons against* his doing so.

Joining Doctors Without Borders

Pros	*Cons*
(a) Helping those in dire need	(d) Less money
(b) Taking part in a new culture	(e) Missing out on friends and family
(c) Feeling righteous and purposeful	(f) Feeling ungrounded or "at sea"

When we speak of reasons in the context of an agent's thinking up, writing down, or communicating such a list, we regard reasons as something like the premises in an argument for why the agent should or should not adopt the course of action under review. Of course, we do not think of such reasons as a set of sentences; nor we do not think of them as anyone's state of mind. Instead, in contexts of advice and deliberation we think of reasons to act in a somewhat abstract way, as a set of propositions or facts. The first reason in favor of Dr Shephard's joining Doctors Without Borders is the purported *fact* that it would enable him to help those in dire need, and the first reason he should not take the job is the purported *fact* that it would leave him with much less money than he would otherwise earn. Thus we arrive at a third, distinct range of cases in which "reason" is used. Sometimes "reasons" denotes neither a mindless cause nor a rationalizing frame of mind, but considerations for or against an agent's adopting a particular attitude or course of action (Skorupski, 1997; Scanlon, 1998; Parfit, 2001). Philosophers often use the term "normative reasons" or "justifying reasons" to denote the class in question, but to more clearly distinguish it from the second use of "reason" that we have identified, we will here call them *reasons qua relevant considerations*.

Now it should be clear that the first of the three uses of "reason" we have identified cannot be supplied when interpreting our characterization of reasons internalism, as doing so would reduce the doctrine to the kind of motives internalism we have already surveyed. Consider, for example, Will Jimeno, a rookie cop who had been recently assigned to New York City's Port Authority Bus Terminal when two airplanes crashed into the city's World Trade Center on September 11, 2001. On the bus ride down to the site of the collapsing buildings, Jimeno had ample time to experience fear for his own life and to entertain thoughts of what would happen to his pregnant wife and unborn child were he to perish in the wreckage. But he rushed into the building anyway, only to be trapped by its collapse, and then pulled from the rubble thirteen hours later.[16] Now we can suppose that Jimeno correctly surmised that joining in the rescue attempt was his duty as a police officer and that fulfilling this duty was a moral obligation he must not shirk. And we can ask whether this knowledge was a *reason qua cause* why he decided not to flee the scene. But to ask this question is to simply re-examine the matter of whether moral knowledge can motivate, and to ask whether, if it cannot, it is nevertheless labeled "intrinsically motivational" by common-sense moral thought.

But what of the second use of "reason"? Suppose we admit that Jimeno's knowledge of his duty did lead him to act and that he would not have acted as he did if he hadn't thought of entering the building as a moral requirement. Can we question whether the state of knowledge rationalizes or makes sense of Jimeno's behavior? Might Jimeno have done the right thing, but for no reason at all? Surely, the reasons internalist will say, we cannot compare the heroic Jimeno to Dick Cheney's hypnotized pawn. If Jimeno did what he did because he knew it was his duty, his knowledge was his reason in the second use of "reason" on offer.

To challenge this description of the case, the reasons externalist must adopt some variation on the Humean arguments with which we are already familiar. We must distinguish, says the externalist, between Jimeno's purported knowledge of his duty on the one hand and, on the other, his fear of being ostracized by his fellow police officers, his anticipation of feelings of guilt or shame at not doing his duty, his desire for a hero's fame, his sympathy for the people trapped inside the building, or even just his bare desire to do what he thinks he must. Mental states in this latter grouping cannot be properly thought of as constituents (parts or aspects) of Jimeno's moral knowledge; and at least one of these distinct states of mind must be present to rationalize his action. Thus, far from its being the case that knowledge that some act is morally obligatory always lends a rationale to the knower's performing it by providing her with a reason to do so, knowledge that an act is obligatory never rationalizes that act on its own. If Jimeno knew that going into the building was his duty, but had no distinct desire to do his duty, did not anticipate feeling guilt or shame at removing himself from the scene, felt no sympathy for the people trapped inside, and so on, his going in would "make no sense." Without augmentation with some distinct passion, emotion, or desire, moral knowledge cannot rationalize action, and this is so even on the assumption that moral knowledge can motivate or cause action on its own.

Recall that the nihilist is arguing that reasons internalism is a false, common-sense presupposition. So it must be common sense that Jimeno acts in a rationally explicable way when he is led by moral knowledge alone to attempt the rescue, and there must also be some reason to think that common sense errs in making this assumption. Indeed, the assumption must be so central to our thinking about morality that its falsity establishes the nihilist's conclusion.

Admittedly, the nihilist's first claim here is hard to dispute. As Kant (1785/2002) points out, though it is difficult, if not impossible, to be certain that someone has acted from duty alone, we do hold this up as a kind of moral ideal. This is not to agree with Kant's claim that it is always better to act from obligation than from tender emotion, or that one deserves praise or respect only when one does so, much less that the will operative in an act of pure duty is the greatest good or the source of all the value in the world. But it does seem right that were the ordinary man to become convinced that Jimeno acted from duty alone, he would not treat the act as incomprehensible, nonsensical, or irrational. Those who struggle with and regularly fail to meet their moral obligations might regard the rookie with something like awe were they convinced that he embodies the Kantian ideal. But awe is not the kind of incomprehension the nihilist has in mind.

But what of the nihilist's second claim? Why is he so sure that the common man is wrong to think that moral knowledge can rationalize an action without the aid of a contingently connected emotion, sentiment, or desire? It is hard to see how the skeptic could argue for this suggestion without invoking the supposed supremacy of instrumental rationality that we have already surveyed. According to the instrumentalist, what one ought to do all things considered is what one knows or thinks will best satisfy one's desires. And, says the instrumentalist, if this is what one ought to do all things considered, failing to do it will be irrational or incoherent. If Jimeno wants to flee more than he wants to run into the trembling struc-ture – if everything in his mind save his knowledge of his duty inclines him in this direction – then fleeing is what he ought to do, obligation be damned. If his morals lead him to do otherwise (as we are now supposing is possible), he is a dunderhead – a dunderhead we'd like to keep around, but a dunderhead nonetheless.

We will again discuss the claim that instrumental reason is "supreme" below. For now we can just note the potentially destructive effects of a skeptical argument built upon it. Suppose the case is like this: Jimeno thinks that he ought to enter the tower despite his not wanting to, simply because it is his moral duty to do his duty as an officer. And he is convinced that he is morally obligated to fulfill his professional obligations only because he thinks that it is *rational* to do your duty even when everything else in you is screaming for you to do otherwise. Then a demonstration that acting in this way is foolish or incoherent will undermine his belief that he ought to enter the tower. If the skeptic could then convince Jimeno that the very existence of moral obligation in any case depends on moral knowledge making moral action coherent in those special cases where no other motive is forthcoming, Jimeno will have been converted to the skeptic's cause.

It remains, then, to examine reasons internalism when it is interpreted as a claim about reasons qua relevant considerations. There are two ways to address the issue. First, we can discuss the doctrine from the perspective of an advisor. According to the internalist, I can always properly cite the obligatory nature of an action as a consideration in its favor when I am convinced that the agent contemplating it will know – if only upon hearing my advice – that the action is indeed morally obligatory. (Again, the skeptic insists that this is our practice, while also denying its coherence.) Second, we can discuss the doctrine from the perspective of the deliberator herself. According to the internalist, when I know that an action is morally obligatory, the fact that it is obligatory must always find its way into the "pro" column I construct when deliberating. The common man thinks that it is impossible for me to know that an action is morally obligatory without my giving some positive "weight" to this consideration in my deliberations, but according to the skeptic, this cannot be right.

The controversial nature of these claims comes to the fore when we reconsider the nature of various forms of psychopathology and amoralism. Surely, the psychopath is capable of deliberation, and most people think he can know right from wrong (Nichols, 2002). But must the psychopath give moral considerations any weight in his deliberations? When deciding whether to rob, cheat, and steal to further his selfish ends, must he include the moral impermissibility of these actions – or the facts that make them morally impermissible – as entries in his column of "cons"? Shifting now to the advisor's perspective, can we properly tell the psychopath not to rob, cheat, and steal? Can we truly say that the moral impermissibility of the actions he is considering gives him a reason to refrain from their performance? Could we truly say this if we knew that his knowledge of their impermissibility would not factor into his deliberations?[17]

Consider, in this light, the Mafia hitman discussed by Harman (1977, 1984) and Joyce (2001). The hitman Harman describes is not without moral motives of a kind, as he values loyalty to his "family" and would look down upon his victims were they to betray the "families" to whom they have sworn allegiance. But he is still a sociopath who doesn't care about the suffering of his victims. Now suppose he tells us of his plans to take out a pesky cop whose incorruptible stance is cutting into the mob's profits. And suppose, for the sake of argument, that though he knows the act is immoral, he doesn't see any reason why he shouldn't go through with it. Do we speak truly when we insist that he should not go through with the assassination, because it would do irreparable harm to an innocent man and his family? Do we report *the facts* in arguing that the harm and injustice of the deed outweigh the mix of clannish and self-interested reasons that he has cited in its favor? We will surely insist that these are "non-negotiable" cons. Indeed, as more or less moral people we won't give the man advice or counsel unless their status as cons is assumed in the context of deliberation.

Killing the incorruptible cop

Pros	Cons
(a') Helps the mob's situation	(e') Might get caught and jailed
(b') It's been ordered by the boss	(f') Death of an innocent man?
(c') Increases prestige	(g') Suffering of a fine family?
(d') Big payday	(h') An unjust act?

Now some philosophers – of a roughly "internalist" bent – will insist that we have asserted something true in telling the hitman that (f')–(h') are good reasons for him not to carry through with his plans only if we can make him care about the harm and injustice we have identified through something like *rational argumentation*. Suppose we force the thug to adopt the perspective of his victims and their families by vividly imagining the consequences of his crimes. Suppose we get him to think about his life in general and to examine whether his acts of violence cohere with the other ends and projects he has set for himself. Suppose we make him think about the rules of conduct that could be rationally endorsed by both his victims and himself. Suppose, to speak more generally, that we get him to undergo what Richard Brandt (1979) calls a course of "cognitive" psychotherapy. If we do all this, and yet he *still* has no desire to refrain from his crime, then, some will say, we cannot truly claim that he has any moral reasons not to kill for profit, and we must strike (f')–(h') from our list (Williams, 1981). Of course, if we must say that the hitman lacks moral reasons to refrain from murder, the reasons internalist will insist that we revise our assumption that he *knows* his murders are morally impermissible. And, if we revise this assumption, the skeptic will offer a nihilistic explanation for why we have been forced to do so. We have concluded that the hitman does not know that he is morally obligated to refrain from carrying out his hits because he really isn't so obligated. There are no moral obligations.

In answer, the non-skeptical philosopher can either abandon reasons internalism or try to save it from its nihilistic consequences. Mightn't defects that cannot be corrected through rational argumentation or cognitive therapy still make a man "blind" to the reasons why he should change his ways? Of course, we all think that there is something wrong with the hitman. Since he isn't moved by his victims' suffering, he must be horribly cold and uncaring. Why can't we think of his defects in sympathy or humanity as inducing a kind of ignorance, a failure to appreciate the very real reasons why he should not proceed on his current course (McDowell, 1979, 1985)? In particular, it may be that sympathy is needed to really know one's moral obligations or to truly appreciate the reasons one has to fulfill these obligations. Or it may be that humanity or fellow feeling is necessary if we are to move from an abstract appreciation of these obligations and reasons to a perspective within which they can play an active role in our deliberations and decisions.

The issue is rife with controversies – controversies that will re-emerge in the chapters to come. But we can here note two important features of the debate: First, questions about a psychopath's deliberations and decisions are not entirely unlike questions about his motivations; both are somewhat empirical in character. (Indeed, if we overly intellectualize the matter and think of having a motive to x as treating some consideration as a reason to x, the questions will collapse into one another.) We must therefore try to join psychologists and criminologists in investigating how psychopaths actually deliberate. In the end, we may uncover important respects in which a psychopath's understanding of his obligations differs from the knowledge possessed by a healthy person. And the differences in question may explain why the psychopath does not treat an action's moral impermissibility as a reason against its performance when he is deciding what to do. It is far from clear that this result would shock common sense, much less jar it to so great an extent as to rob us of all belief in moral obligation. The philosopher might hope to argue immorality out of existence, but the common man puts his faith in law enforcement and social sanction.

Second, it is not at all obvious that we are best served by adopting the psychopath's immoral perspective when advising him as to what he should do. We can insist that the cruel and unjust nature of his crimes are reasons for him to change his ways, even if we know that — as he lacks moral ends and cannot be made to adopt them through "cognitive" forms of psychotherapy alone — our advice is unlikely to move him. Ignoring his immoral goals may be somewhat paternalistic, and he may experience "estrangement" from the reasons we are trying to force down his throat (Joyce, 2001). But the evils of our browbeating will pale in comparison to the evil of his crimes. There may be times when paternalism is the appropriate stance to take — times when estrangement from one's deliberative framework brings one closer to the truth about the value of one's actions.

3.6 Chapter summary

Moderate moral skeptics claim that we have no moral knowledge; extreme moral skeptics claim that we are not justified in retaining any of our moral beliefs; and nihilists claim that there are no moral truths to be known.

Some think that moral obligations depend for their existence on the existence of a god who will punish those who act immorally and reward those who do not. If there is no such god, then we have no reason not to act in supposedly immoral ways when this will get us what we on-balance desire. But if it is permissible for us to act in these supposedly immoral ways, then doing so cannot be truly immoral, as it is a non-negotiable feature of common thought that we ought never to act immorally. We can respond to this argument by affirming the existence of a god that enforces moral strictures, or by allowing that those with immoral ends are right to act immorally, or by insisting that we ought not act immorally even when doing so is a necessary means to the satisfaction of our desires. The last of these responses denies the supremacy of instrumental rationality.

Mackie argues that moral obligations would have to be objective and intrinsically prescriptive to exist, and, as nothing actually has these features, we have no moral obligations. But we can allow that we commonly think of our moral obligations as objectively, intrinsically prescriptive; and allow that Mackie is right in thinking that nothing has these properties; and yet still insist on the existence of moral obligations. The supposed objective, intrinsic prescriptivity of our moral obligations might be like the supposed solidity of glass. Though we would perhaps be surprised to discover that our obligations do not have these features, we might nevertheless ration- ally retain our belief that obligations exist in the wake of the discovery. Of course, if Mackie could show that our moral concepts originated in myth or hallucination, he could indeed impugn the reliability of our core moral beliefs. But neither he nor anyone else has ever supplied the historical data needed to substantiate a debunking genealogy of moral concepts. Mackie must show that "obligation" plays a largely theoretical role in a commonly held implicit moral theory and that this theory is mistaken in relevant respects. He does nothing to establish the first of these claims.

There are two interpretations of Mackie's overall argument: (i) it is a non-negotiable aspect of common thought that moral knowledge supplies an agent with a motive inclining her to moral action, but moral knowledge does not have this feature; (ii) it is a non-negotiable aspect of common thought that moral knowledge supplies a deliberator with a reason in favor of pursuing the moral course, but moral knowledge does not in fact do this. On the first interpretation, "motives internalism" is a deep, commonly held conviction and yet wholly mistaken; according to the second interpretation, "reasons internalism" is similarly entrenched and similarly false. There are many different versions of these two doctrines, but it is far from clear that any single version can both be assigned to common thought and refuted.

The version of motives internalism most plausibly assigned to ordinary thinking says that dwelling on the immorality of an action always provides an agent with some aversion to it. Whether this thesis is true depends on the nature of psychopathy, the nature of amoralism, and the best classificatory scheme with which to pursue psychology. If the moral faculty has the dual function of representing what is bad and motivating us to do what is good, a weak form of motives internalism may turn out to be true. But even if moral belief (or representation) and moral desire (or motivation) are always dissociable, this realization may not be sufficiently shocking to impugn the very existence of morality.

Reasons internalism suffers from the extremely flexible way in which we use "reasons." "Reasons" can denote brute causes, an agent's frame of mind when acting, or the pros and cons cited in contexts of advice and deliberation. If we suppose that we can act from moral knowledge alone, we might then wonder whether doing so is horribly naïve and confused. To deny that it is, is to once again deny the supremacy of instrumental rationality. On this way of thinking, it is sometimes rational for us to fulfill what we know are our moral obligations even when we know that we have no distinct desires that might be served by our doing so.

Whether knowledge of an action's immorality always supplies those contemplating that action with a "con" depends on the proper ways of deliberating and giving advice. We might allow that the immorality, disutility and injustice of an unrepentant hitman's actions do not really supply him with reasons to change his ways, and claim that only those with moral ends should take moral factors into consideration when deliberating. Or we might insist that the hitman ought to take these considerations into account even though his pathological lack of concern for his victims presents a considerable obstacle to his doing so. The nihilist must insist that the first stance is ruled out by our shared conception of morality and that the second stance is irrational or mistaken. But an argument for this conclusion is not to be found in Mackie, and it is far from obvious that nihilists of more recent vintage will prove successful in their attempts to supply one on his behalf.

3.7 Further reading

The extinction of belief in the Judeo-Christian god and the event's consequences for morality are central themes in early existentialist thought. Walter Kaufmann (ed.), *Existentialism from Dostoevsky to Sartre* (1956/1975) contains representative sources. The route from atheism to skepticism is explored in greater detail in Zimmerman, "A Conflict in Common-Sense Moral Psychology" (2009).

Economists – and other social scientists – often just assume that instrumental rationality is "supreme" in the sense described above, as classical models of rational decision and action are instrumentalist in nature. James Dreier, "Humean Doubts about the Practical Justification of Morality" (1997) is one of the best attempts at a philosophical defense of the view. Jean Hampton argues against instrumentalism in *The Authority of Reason* (1998), as does Christine Korsgaard in *Creating the Kingdom of Ends* (1996a). One of Korsgaard's essays, "Skepticism about Practical Reason" (1986), has been particularly influential, as have Thomas Nagel's *The Possibility of Altruism* (1970) and *The View from Nowhere* (1986). Bernard Williams, *Moral Luck* (1981) and Derek Parfit, *Reasons and Persons* (1984) argue that preferences are subject to rational evaluation.

Mackie's skeptical arguments can be found in *Ethics: Inventing Right and Wrong* (1977). They have received discussion in a great deal of subsequent work on the nature of morality. Stephen Darwall has done more than most to distinguish different varieties of moral internalism and externalism; his *Impartial Reason* (1983) and *The British Moralists and the Internal "Ought"* (1995) are two good sources. Robert Audi's work in this area is also noteworthy, including his *Moral Knowledge and Ethical Character* (1997b). Parfit's "Rationality and Reasons" (2001) draws the necessary distinctions with exemplary clarity and care.

Bernard Williams' "Internal and External Reasons" (1979) is the classic defense of reasons internalism, and John McDowell's reply to Williams in "Might There Be External Reasons?" (1995) has proved equally important. Jonathan Dancy, *Moral Reasons* (1993) rejects so-called Humean theories of motivation and reasons for action outright, whereas Michael Smith's *The Moral Problem* (1994) tries to combine a Humean theory of motivation with a nuanced, highly hedged form of the claim that our reasons for action depend on what we want. In contrast, Gilbert Harman, *The Nature of Morality* (1977) and Richard Joyce, *The Myth of Morality* (2001) argue from Humean constraints to full-blown skepticism about universally shared reasons to act morally. In "Externalist Moral Realism" (1986) and *Moral Realism and the Foundation of Ethics* (1989) David Brink avoids moral skepticism by rejecting the varieties of internalism on which, he argues, it is typically premised.

The nature of psychopathy and its relation to various forms of internalism are debated in the essays that form chapters 3 and 4 of Sinnott-Armstrong (ed.), *Moral Psychology*, vol. III, *The Neuroscience of Morality* (2008c). The volume's bibliography references the relevant experiments and their varying interpretations.

4

THE SKEPTIC AND THE INTUITIONIST

4.1 The Pyrrhonian problematic

In arguing for nihilism, Mackie and his heirs set their sights higher than is necessary. For the skeptic needn't argue that there are no moral facts, he need only show that we have strong reasons to doubt their existence, reasons strong enough to rob us of moral knowledge or even justified moral belief. These purely epistemic arguments for moral skepticism can be sorted into two categories: those that are specific to morality and those that have a more general application.

A fully general skeptical line of attack is provided by the *epistemic regress argument* or the *Pyrrhonian problematic* (Sextus Empiricus, 1562/1949; Chisholm, 1964; BonJour, 1985; Audi, 1993; Fogelin, 1994; and Sinnott-Armstrong, 2004). To know something, you must be justified in believing it. (Knowledge lies beyond substantive epistemic criticism.) But, says the skeptic, to be justified in believing a proposition, you must have some good reason for believing it, where this reason must be some distinct proposition or propositions – some evidence or supporting facts – that show what you believe to be sufficiently likely. Moreover, continues the skeptic, the distinct supporting propositions in question cannot provide you with good reasons to hold your initial belief, unless you are justified in believing them. But to be justified in believing them, you must have still further reasons for belief – a second body of evidence that entails or provides good reasons for believing the body of purported fact supporting your initial belief. The regress is off and running.

The skeptic's initial argument has three premises:

1   If S knows p, then S is justified in believing p.
2   If S is justified in believing p, then S must have some reason to believe p.
3   S's having a reason to believe p must consist in S's justifiably believing some q≠p.

Repeated application of these premises generates the epistemic regress and leaves those who accept (1)–(3) with three possibilities. Perhaps *circular reasoning* can confer justification on one's belief in a proposition; or perhaps people are in principle capable of generating an *infinite series* of non-circular defenses of what they believe; or if, as the skeptic maintains, neither of these options is acceptable, perhaps we really neither know nor justifiably believe anything at all.

> *Minimal coherentism*: S can be justified in believing p by accepting a series of distinct reasons $q_1{\neq}p$ ... $q_n{\neq}p$ for believing p, even though at least one of her reasons for believing one or more of q_1 ... q_n is p itself.[1]

> *Infinitism*: S can be justified in believing p by having some distinct reason $p_1{\neq}p$ for believing p, where S is justified in believing p_1 because she has some distinct reason $p_2{\neq}p_1$ for believing p_1, ... where S is justified in believing p_n because she has some distinct reason $p_{n+1}{\neq}p_n$ for believing p_n for all $n>2$.

> *Radical skepticism*: no one is ever justified in believing anything.

A notable defense of the minimal coherentist route is provided by Laurence BonJour in his early work (1985); Peter Klein (1999) is equally remarkable for adopting the infinitist course; and general skepticism (of a sophisticated, contextualist kind) is embraced by Peter Unger (1975).

But what are we to make of the skeptic's premises themselves? Perhaps it is a priori knowable that knowledge requires justification, and perhaps it is a priori knowable that you cannot be justified in believing something if you have no good reason to believe it. (Though each of these claims has its detractors.) But, the *foundationalist* asks, why must all of our reasons be inferential in the way asserted by premise (3)? The rejection of premise (3) provides us with another important response to the regress argument.

> *Minimal foundationalism*: S's having a reason to believe p needn't consist in S's justifiably believing some $q \neq p$. (For example, the fact that p might itself constitute a good reason to believe p, or S's having a suitable course of experience might itself provide S with a good reason to hold this belief.)

I know that I am in pain. So my believing that I am in pain must be justified – that is, it mustn't warrant serious epistemic criticism. But why think that my introspective belief can be appropriately criticized so long as I have no *distinct* evidence or supporting grounds for believing its truth? Surely, this is not our practice. Instead, we think that the fact that I am in pain is itself a good reason for me to believe that I am in pain. As A. J. Ayer points out:

> It would clearly be absurd to ask anyone how he knew that he was thinking about a philosophical problem, or how he knew that he was in pain. For what could he answer except that this was what he was thinking about, or that this was what he was feeling? Our knowledge of our thoughts and feelings accrues to us automatically in the sense that having them puts us in a position and gives us the authority to report them. All that is then required is that the reports be true. (1968, 34)[2]

Premise (3) is not even believed by the common man, much less known prior to substantive argument or investigation. The skeptic needs to argue for this crucial premise, and it is hard to see how the premises of any such auxiliary argument could be thought to warrant belief in its radical conclusion.[3]

Still, the foundationalist's reply to the Pyrrhonian problematic has its limits. My belief that I am in pain is the product of introspection, my belief that there is something red in front of me is the product of visual perception, and my belief that $2 + 2 = 4$ is (arguably) the product of pure conception or understanding. We typically treat these faculties as sources of non-inferential knowledge and justified belief, where non-inferentially justified beliefs can, it seems, halt the skeptic's attempted regress of reasons. But what happens when we turn from the generalized form of the epistemic regress argument to a version directed at morality in particular? A broadly foundationalist reply that focuses on the rejection of premise (3) will seem plausible in this arena only if we can establish one or more of two very controversial claims. To defend a foundationalist conception of moral knowledge we must either: (a) identify a class of non-inferentially justified moral beliefs, or (b) show how we can infer moral propositions from non-moral propositions that we are non-inferentially justified in believing.[4] In the section that follows we will tackle (a) head-on by asking whether there might be any non-inferentially justified moral beliefs. Option (b) and coherentist responses to moral skepticism are addressed in chapters 5 and 6 respectively.

4.2 Non-inferential moral knowledge

In the section above we pointed out that common sense allows for non-inferential knowledge of various kinds. A typical person knows, without either argument or inference, that he is in pain. He need only introspect. Similarly, you probably can know, by simply looking, that there is a book or computer in front of you right now. Perhaps you could argue for this conclusion from premises describing how reliable visual perception most often is. (Though you would clearly have to use your senses to establish their reliability in this way.) But must you mount any argument at all to know what you can so clearly see? Don't you have knowledge of the color and shape of this book or computer before reasoning your way to what you knew all along?

Similarly, we can know by reflection, or understanding, or simple comprehension that $2 + 2 = 4$. Perhaps you could argue for this fact from set-theoretic definitions of the integers and arithmetic operations involved. But does knowledge of $2 + 2 = 4$ await the proof of its truth? And what of the definitions and set-theoretic axioms themselves, like the axiom that something is a set just in case it has members or is empty? Surely no argument is needed for knowledge of this fact; you need only reflect on what is involved in being a set.

Of course, introspection is itself a psychological process subject to examination and assessment. And it must be allowed that we do not yet know much about its nature, as psychologists and neuroscientists are busy constructing theories of it and other mental phenomena: theories they can then test with experiments. What will our best theories of introspection say about the processes that occur when you focus on your own sensations? Though it doesn't *seem* to you as though you must infer that you are in pain from distinct premises that you know or believe, mightn't scientists wind up positing a set of wholly unconscious inferences of this sort?

Though it seems unlikely, perhaps they will. Still, the inferences scientists might posit to explain your awareness of your own mind will remain inaccessible to you. Indeed, they are so remote from what you can now think and feel as to hardly warrant our attributing them to you at all. Maybe some part of you – or some part of your mind or brain – reasons to the conclusion that you are in pain. But for you, the path from the sensation of pain to your belief in its existence is as direct as direct can be. You might have to turn your attention away from other things to truly consider how you are feeling right now. But if you do this, and closely focus on your feelings, you won't have to reason your way to the conclusion that you are or are not in pain. If you do form a judgment on the matter, it will constitute a phenomenologically immediate reaction to the sensation under review.

The same might be said of your knowledge that 2 + 2 = 4. There was a point at which you didn't know much of anything about addition. Your parents or instructors had to teach you the concept – or bring it to salience – with a variety of examples.[5] At some point, though, you could successfully add novel sums – sums you had not encountered during the course of your instruction – and your teacher became justly confident that you understood "+," "addition," "sum," and similar terms. She became convinced, that is, that you adequately grasped or understood the concepts with which these expressions are associated.[6] Now it seems that once you reached this point, and sufficiently understood "+" and the other numerical concepts of equality and plurality brought to mind by "2 + 2 = 4," you became absolutely certain of the equation's truth. And your certainty did not rest on distinct propositions that you knew or believed to be true. Indeed, if you now reconsider whether 2 + 2 might not equal 4, this will only deepen your conviction that it must.

Of course, we cannot rule out the possibility that the process by which you came to believe that 2 + 2 = 4 is best modeled as an inference of some sort or other. And perhaps an inference of some kind generates the further conviction in the equation's truth that you experience when you reflect on it at present. But these inferences – if they do in fact exist – are so removed from your experience as to be properly attributed to sub-personal components of your mind or brain. For you, the path from comprehending "2 + 2 = 4" to believing that 2 + 2 = 4 is as direct as direct can be.

Nor do we commonly regard this as an epistemological shortcoming on your part. We do not ask, "What convinces you that 2 + 2 = 4?" in an attempt to assess your reasons for thinking the equation holds. Nor do we ask ourselves for evidence of the equation's truth nor criticize ourselves for failing to come up with any. In contrast, if you believe a complicated mathematical theorem, cannot cite the testimony of a mathematician on its behalf, and can give no argument in its support, then we will conclude that you do not know the theorem in question. (And this is so even if *we* know that the theorem is true.) Simple equations are not like this. Understanding 2 + 2 = 4 typically generates belief in its truth in a phenomenologically direct or immediate manner. And the resulting belief is typically said to constitute knowledge even when we know its possessor can neither explain nor argue for its truth (Ginet, 1975).

Locke was not skeptical of these common-sense claims. Unlike the full-blooded Pyrrhonian skeptic described above, Locke was willing to grant us non-inferential knowledge of certain basic truths. But Locke thought that moral facts are importantly different from the simple introspective and intellectual facts we have cited. To know or justifiably believe *moral* propositions you must have substantive arguments or a substantive body of evidence supporting your moral convictions.

For instance, on Locke's favored account, you can deduce that you ought not lie from: (a) your purported knowledge that god wants you to be honest and will bring you great pain and suffering if you fail to tell the truth, and (b) your knowledge of the self-evident claim that you oughtn't do what you know will bring you great pain and suffering. On Locke's view, our non-inferential knowledge of a non-moral norm of prudential reason helps us reason our way to knowledge of morality.

Some would accuse Locke of confusing the "ought" of morality with the "ought" of prudence. Others would claim that (b) is not self-evident. We must infer that we ought to act prudently from other things we know. And, of course, many would reject the knowledge of god's policies claimed by (a). But more important, given our current focus, is Locke's negative thesis. For Locke claims that in the absence of his inference or some other, your moral beliefs would be *baseless*, and would therefore fall short of knowledge (cf. Hare, 1952). In Locke's words:

> He would be thought void of common sense, who asked on the one side, or on the other side went about to give a reason, *Why it is impossible for the same thing to be, and not be*. It carries its own light and evidence with it, and needs no other proof: he that understands the terms, assents to it for its own sake, or else nothing will ever be able to prevail him to do it. But should that most unshaken rule of morality, and foundation of all social virtue, *That one should do as he would be*

done unto, be proposed to one, who never heard it before, but yet is of capacity to understand its meaning: might he not without absurdity ask a reason why? And were not he that proposed it, bound to make out the truth and reasonableness of it to him? (1690/1991, §157)

But moral intuitionists would deny Locke's assertion. Perhaps Locke was right in arguing that the golden rule must be supported with arguments if its truth is to be known. After all, as Henry Sidgwick (1838–1900) pointed out (1874/1981, 380), the golden rule isn't even true when it is interpreted in full generality. The sadomasochist shouldn't beat you, even though he would have you do this "unto" him. And there is nothing at all wrong with your buying skis for a skier, even if skiing leaves you so cold and bored you would hate having the cumbersome equipment bought for you. But mightn't there be moral facts that can be known directly?

> *Moral intuitionism*: we have a body of non-inferentially justified moral beliefs or non-inferential moral knowledge.

Let's set the golden rule, the Ten Commandments, and similarly influential dicta to the side for the moment. For while belief in non-inferential knowledge of fully *general* principles like these is perhaps more common than belief in non-inferential knowledge of *particular* moral facts, there are a number of theorists who embrace the latter class as well.

First, many historically important philosophers have hypothesized that belief in particular propositions regularly precedes belief in generalities in the course of a person's cognitive development. (Though see Hooker [2002, 174] for resistance.) An eminent representative would be W. D. Ross (1877–1971). Speaking of promises in particular Ross describes what C. D. Broad (1930, 214) would call an "intuitive induction."

> We see the *prima facie* rightness of an act which would be the fulfill-ment of a particular promise, and of another which would be the fulfillment of another promise, and when we have reached sufficient maturity to think in general terms, we apprehend *prima facie* rightness to belong to the nature of fulfilling a promise. What comes first in time is the apprehension of the self-evident *prima facie* rightness of an individual act of a particular type. From this we come by reflection to apprehend the self-evident general principle of *prima facie* duty. (Ross, 1930, 33)[7]

And Bertrand Russell (1872–1970) endorsed the view in its full generality.

> In all our knowledge of general principles, what actually happens is that first of all we realize some particular application of the principle, and then we realize that the particularity is irrelevant, and that there is a generality which may equally truly be affirmed. (1912/1997, 70–71)

The view of immediate knowledge these passages convey is noteworthy in a number of respects. But there is first an interpretive matter. Ross speaks of our initially seeing the "prima facie" rightness of a particular act of fidelity. But what is the legal term "prima facie" supposed to mean in this context?

On one possible interpretation, what we immediately know in the case Ross describes is that the honoring of a promise *seems* right to us. I raise this reading to salience, only to dissuade anyone tempted by it. For it has Ross simply reiterating the widely accepted thesis that introspection delivers non-inferential knowledge. You keep a promise, or witness someone else doing so, and it "strikes you" that this was the right thing to do in the case on hand. On the interpretation we are considering, Ross is reporting that you will be aware of having been "struck" in this manner, where this awareness is not the end product of an inference. Just as you needn't reason to the conclusion that you are in pain, you can know in a direct or non-inferential manner when things seem good or right. Since the knowledge in question is compatible with things failing to be as they seem, it is not moral knowledge. The nihilist can accept all of the facts that you know in this way.

According to a more promising interpretation of "prima facie," what Ross thinks we directly know in the case he describes is not that the act of promise-keeping *seems* right to us; but nor do we directly know, without the aid of inference, that the act of promise-keeping is *in fact* right. Instead, Ross is claiming that we know, in a direct or non-inferential manner, that the keeping of the promise is in fact right *unless* some one of a limited number of exceptions to the morality of fidelity obtains in the case. Perhaps you know, in an immediate fashion, the following proposition: that the promisor is acting rightly in keeping his promise unless: (i) the promisor knows that keeping his promise is going to produce great suffering; (ii) the promisee coerced the promise; (iii) in keeping his promise the promisor is breaking a more weighty promise; and so on. On this reading, Ross is granting us non-inferential knowledge of the highly *conditional* virtuousness of instances of promise-keeping and other varieties of moral behavior.

Contemporary philosophers often restrict the term "prima facie wrongness" to denote what would seem wrong to a rational observer in a given context. The distinct term "pro tanto wrongness" is used for those acts that will be wrong so long as one of a number of exceptional circumstances fails to obtain. Let us adopt this convention. Then, if Ross is correct in allowing that you can know in a non-inferential manner that a particular act of fidelity is pro tanto right, and if you can also know – in either a non-inferential manner or some other – that none of the particular exceptions to the rightness of promise-keeping exists in the case, you will be able to infer that the act is *simply* right or right *all things considered*.

1   That act of promise-keeping was pro tanto right.
2   None of the exceptions to the rightness of promise-keeping was present in the case.
Therefore,
3   That act of promise-keeping was right all things considered.

But just how do you know premise (2)? Ross would argue that your knowledge of this sort of fact is also non-inferential in nature. There is, some say, no way to articulate all of the legitimate exceptions to the general prohibition on promise-breaking that might be offered. Thus, a good moral judge does not (and perhaps cannot) infer that (2) is true in the case on hand in an exhaustive fashion from her prior knowledge of the exceptions to the rule and her on-the-spot knowledge of their absence. She does not infer (2) from her knowledge: (a) that z is an exception to promise-keeping, but it is not present in the case, (b) that y is an exception to promise-keeping but it is not present in the case, (c) that x is an exception to promise-keeping, but it is not present in the case, and so on. Instead, good moral judges have a kind of "sensitivity" to the exceptions that might be justly given to the rule against breaking promises: a sensitivity they can use to directly apprehend the truth of (2) in favorable circumstances.

You know that you should keep promises. And, though you cannot articulate them, you perhaps know most – if not all – of the legitimate exceptions to this rule. (Do you remember the exceptions (i)–(iii) that I listed above? Did you know them before reading them? Is this a part of your innate "moral grammar"?) According to the intuitionist, you can use this ineffable knowledge to verify that none of the legitimate exceptions to promise-keeping are present in the case before you, and therein infer that the promisor did right in keeping his promise in that case.[8]

Another thing to notice about the two passages quoted above is the *multiple sources* of knowledge they depict. Russell and Ross embrace both inferential and non-inferential knowledge of moral generalities. Our realization that some particular moral fact is true, when wedded to our knowledge of a series of similar truths, initially grounds our belief in a moral generalization. But then, at some point, Ross and Russell say, the particular instances are justly regarded as irrelevant.

To illustrate the view, let us suppose that little Abe realizes that his uncle Bob did wrong in lying to his aunt a month ago, that his aunt Cathy did wrong when lying to his grandma last week, and that his best friend David shouldn't have told the teacher that his dog ate his homework. Eventually, Abe comes to realize, by somehow generalizing upon these encounters, that lying is (pro tanto) wrong.

To complete the story we must also posit some process by which Abe acquires the sensitivity to exceptions mentioned above. He tacitly knows that one shouldn't lie *unless* it's necessary to maintain a surprise party planned for months; or necessary to thwart a great evil; or necessary to maintain the confidence entrusted to you by a dear and noble friend; and so on, for most if not all of the legitimate exceptions that might be made to the rule.

At this point, Ross says, we can suppose that Abe's knowledge of the pro tanto immorality of lying *depends on* his knowledge of the immorality inherent in the particular lies he has observed. When we say that Abe's knowledge of the generality "depends on" his knowledge of these particulars, we mean at least this: if some critical mass of these particular judgments weren't knowledge, neither would Abe's belief in the hedged generalization be.

And yet as time moves on we can suppose that the boy's thinking matures. He begins to contemplate the general prohibition on lying in the abstract. He thinks about what it is to lie: the nature of assertion, the nature of honesty, and their relation to other important activities, traits, and concerns. Eventually, Ross claims, Abe's knowledge that lying is pro tanto wrong will loosen itself from its roots in the boy's evaluation of particular lies. For at this stage in his development, Abe's knowledge of dishonesty's immorality is no longer based on his assessment of the particular lies he has observed. Importantly, he would still know that lying is wrong even if his uncle hadn't really lied to his aunt; his aunt did no wrong when lying to his grandma; his friend's homework really was eaten by the dog; and so on. There is a single proposition that Abe knows throughout this process – that is, that lying is pro tanto wrong – but Abe's knowledge of that fact shifts its evidential or justificatory basis from induction to *reflection*.

Thus, as Audi (2004, 29) rightly points out, Ross credited us with both inductive knowledge of intermediate moral principles – such as "One ought not lie" – and the kind of non-inferential, understanding-generated justification for believing these principles that marks our relation to facts like 2 + 2 = 4 – facts we find self-evident. Audi's own (2004) moral epistemology then adds to these two sources of knowledge the further justification theorists obtain when they conduct a deduction of these same intermediate general principles from the *formula of humanity* iteration of Kant's categorical imperative, "Act so that you use humanity, as much in your own person as in the person of every other, always at the same time as end and never merely as means" (1785/2002, 46–47 [Ak 4:429]).[9]

Suppose again that Abe begins to form beliefs about the immorality of lying by thinking that Bob did wrong when lying to Cathy, that Cathy did wrong when lying to grandma, that David did wrong when lying to the teacher, and so on. The boy then generalizes in the way Ross and Russell describe – while developing the sensitivity to exceptions he must have – to arrive at a belief in the pro tanto immorality of lying. Similar inductions lead him to believe in the exception-riddled immorality of adultery, extortion, theft, cruelty, exploitation, and so on. But now imagine further that Abe enrolls in a course on Kant's ethics in which the categorical imperative is explained to him. First, reflection on cases convinces him that the principle is extensionally correct in large measure. That is, he thinks about the cases in which we fail to treat humanity as something valuable in and of itself; and he thinks about the actions he thought were immoral before enrolling in the course; and he finds, upon reflection, that these classes correspond to one another in large part. Of course, the correspondence is not exact, as Abe finds that there are certain actions he had previously thought of as immoral that do not in fact involve a failure to treat humanity as intrinsically valuable. But he now finds himself doubting whether most – if not all – of these actions really are immoral after all. ("Perhaps," he thinks to himself, "I only thought they were immoral because I found them disgusting. Or maybe I was wrong to rely so heavily on the Bible.") In contrast we have those actions Abe had thought of as immoral that (he now realizes) *do* involve the denigration of self or other. And we find that Abe's conviction in the immorality of these actions only grows when he thinks of them in a Kantian light. Indeed, as a convinced Kantian, Abe now claims to finally know *why* these acts are wrong. They are immoral precisely because they disrespect those parts of us most worthy of esteem. Immoral acts deny humanity the dignity it is due.

If we extrapolate Audi's model to the case on hand, we might say that:

(a) Abe is initially justified, to a substantial degree, in believing his friend David acted in a pro tanto immoral fashion. (Abe directly "apprehends" the fact in question.)

(b) Abe's justification then grows in strength when he has deduced this same fact from the inductively justified, and then non-inferentially (reflectively) known general claim that lying is pro tanto immoral.

(c) Abe's belief in the pro tanto immorality of David's lie then attains an extraordinarily robust form of justification when he deduces the intermediate generality in question from his theoretical knowledge of the principle of utility, the categorical imperative, or some other "first principle" of morality.

Of course, as intuitionists, the theorists with whom we are currently concerned think that moral knowledge is already present at the first of these stages: the direct apprehension of immorality asserted by (a). It need not await the greater justification provided by one or both deduction from general principles.[10]

According to the intuitionist theories just surveyed, moral knowledge begins with an immediate or direct grasp of the immorality of a particular action. But do we typically allow that someone can know, in a direct or non-inferential way, that something wrong is happening before her eyes? Should we? Though a recent slate of theorists have joined Ross in endorsing precisely this proposal, the account remains controversial even among those who would eschew moral skepticism.[11]

To be honest, I should admit up front to my own skepticism of the view. Perhaps reflection can earn us knowledge of moral generalities comparable to certain truths of arithmetic or geometry; or perhaps the imaginative engagement of our sympathies can give us knowledge of the same. On these matters, I am undecided. But I don't see how someone can really just "apprehend" the immorality of a particular act.

Since, on many accounts, sensory perception provides us with non-inferential knowledge of particular facts regarding the shapes, colors, and locations of the objects in our immediate environment, we can call the view under consideration the "perceptual model" of moral knowledge. And we can begin its evaluation by considering a fairly basic example of Harman's, an example that is often used by the defender of the perceptual model in arguing her case.

> If you round a corner and see a group of young hoodlums pour gasoline on a cat and ignite it, you do not need to *conclude* that what they are doing is wrong; you do not need to figure anything out; you can *see* that it is wrong. (1977, 4)

Let's acknowledge that the immorality of what is being done to the cat will be obvious to all but the most skeptical observer. But do we see, *without drawing a conclusion from some premise or set of premises*, that an immoral act is perpetrated in the scenario? Though we would commonly *say* that you just see that what the hoodlums are doing is wrong, ordinary language is not a particularly helpful guide here, as we quite commonly use perceptual idioms to describe knowledge that is obviously inferential in both origin and epistemic pedigree. We say that the teacher can just see that an apple has been placed before her, and that you can similarly see that there is a book (or computer) in front of you right now. But we also say that John can see that his neighbors have stayed home from work even though we know he has inferred this in a more or less conscious way from his observation that their cars remain parked in the driveway and the relevant background assumption that they haven't arranged for alternative transport (Siegel, 2005; Väyrynen, 2007). We even say, in a common, entirely felicitous manner, that Richard can see that Sarah is upset and that he can see that she has put a lot of effort into her work, when he has clearly inferred her emotions from her behavior and reasoned from the quality of her work (and his knowledge of the difficulty of the task) to the amount of labor involved.

Harman's case is similar to these last two. For while there is a sense in which we may be said to "see" that the hoodlums are doing something wrong, it is fairly clear that we can only see that this is so by executing a chain of non-trivial inferences. We infer the immorality of the act from the sadistic torture we judge present in the case; we infer that the act is sadistic or cruel from an appreciation of the cat's suffering horribly unto its death and our knowledge of the excitement the children derive from causing this to happen; and we infer that the children are excited by their deed from an evaluation of their devilish expressions and celebratory behavior. Thus it seems we really do conclude that the action is wrong – we draw this conclusion from cognitively distinct assessments of the motives and immediate consequences of the action under review.

Admittedly, it might be argued that our knowledge of the motives of the actors involved in a morally fraught scenario plays a role in grounding our moral judgments that is importantly similar to the role perceptual experience plays in grounding our perceptual judgments. And the same might be said of our knowledge of the act's consequences. On this way of thinking, your knowledge that the cat is suffering and your knowledge that the children are taking pleasure in causing this to happen *directly* justify you in thinking that the act is immoral. The claim, then, would just be that you don't need an *additional* supporting argument to justly infer the immorality of the act from your knowledge of the cruelty or sadism involved.

4   The boys are enjoying torturing the cat.
Therefore,
5   The boys are acting immorally.

We might consider a similar treatment of Ross' case. You infer that David lied from the improbability of his excuse and your knowledge of his likely motive (i.e. to escape the punishment he would otherwise receive for having failed to complete the assignment). And you directly infer the pro tanto immorality of what has been done from your knowledge of the dishonesty involved.

But let us suppose for the moment that your knowledge of (5) is directly derived from your knowledge of (4) without the aid of additional premises or further reasoning. (We will consider challenges to the truth of this supposition in what is to come.) Even so, you still do not literally see, without an inference, what the various participants in the scenario are thinking and feeling. Moreover, your knowledge of their thoughts and feelings is not yet genuinely moral knowledge; you must, for example, infer immorality from sadism. Thus, you reason your way to knowledge of the value-neutral premise (4). And when you reason from "is" to "ought" in moving from (4) to (5), you therein execute a further inference.[12]

Nor are these psychological facts irrelevant to our assessment of your belief in the immorality of the hoodlums' crime. If common sense is to be trusted, you do not know (5) if you do not know (4). And if, as a general matter, knowledge of (4) does not adequately justify belief in (5), the inference we have articulated cannot provide you with moral knowledge. In consequence, the skeptic can challenge your belief in the immorality of what is being done to the cat by presenting evidence against the boys' supposed sadism or by arguing that knowledge of the suffering intentionally inflicted does not yet warrant belief in its immorality.[13]

Since we cannot have wholly non-inferential knowledge of *particular* moral facts, the intuitionist's only hope is to argue for non-inferential knowledge of *generalities*. As we saw, Ross thought immature thinkers come to know fairly abstract moral rules with an inductive inference. But he also thought we could arrive at a more sophisticated knowledge of these same principles through a non-inferential process he called "reflection." If we can gain general moral knowledge by reflection without the aid of induction, the fact that we cannot acquire non-inferential knowledge of particular moral facts needn't rule out non-inferential knowledge of general moral rules.

We must, then, turn our attention to the kind of reflection that might give someone like Abe non-inferential knowledge of the immorality of lying: knowledge that does not rest on the accuracy of his past evaluations of particular lies. But there is a preliminary matter that must be addressed. For it goes without saying that we cannot know moral generalizations in a non-inferential manner if we cannot know them at all. And it is equally true, and no less obvious, that we cannot know moral generalizations if they are not true. Indeed, this is what led us to agree with Locke's verdict on the golden rule. We cannot directly apprehend the truth of the golden rule because its discernible falsity prevents us from knowing it at all.

Thus, before we can evaluate the possibility of our knowing general moral principles in a non-inferential manner, we must first ask whether there are any true moral generalizations to be known. Are there moral laws? Or is moral knowledge wholly "particular" in nature?

Radical particularists are theorists who argue against the existence of true moral principles of any kind. For example, the particularist will allow that Copperfield knows that Creakle acted immorally in the case described in chapter 1. But the particularist will insist that Copperfield's evaluation of Creakle's actions must arise from a conception of immorality that resists codification into rules (cf. McDowell, 1979, 1994, 1998; McNaughton, 1988; Nussbaum, 1990; Dancy, 1993). Copperfield knows how to detect the immorality of those particular punishments that are immoral. But he does not do this by subsuming the case before him under a general rule describing which punishments are immoral and which are not. In other words, Copperfield *knows how* to detect the immorality of a given punishment without *knowing that* the genuinely immoral punishments are those with such and such further features. Moral knowledge is largely a matter of skill or ability.

Of course, it is not at all obvious that the particularist's conception of moral judgment is an accurate one. *Generalists* are those philosophers who would defend moral principles from the particularist's critique.

By definition, generalists are keen to retain a substantive role for moral generalizations. And yet many nevertheless allow that moral principles must be hedged in one way or another if they are to be saved from counter-examples (Anscombe, 1958; Holton, 2002; McKeever and Ridge, 2006; Väyrynen, 2009). According to this line of thought, though we might not be able to know an unconditional condemnation of lying, we can know that lying *tends* to be wrong, that dishonesty is *pro tanto* immoral, or that dissimulation is impermissible *all things being equal*. The most concessive version of the position would incorporate important elements of Ross' position: We know certain hedged moral principles in a wholly non-inferential manner (by reflection), and then deploy a non-inferential sensitivity to exceptions when mobilizing our knowledge of these hedged principles to issue verdicts about particular cases. Mightn't Ross have been right about at least this much?[14]

The question is obscured by debates over the substance of hedged principles. To bring the matter to light, let us suppose that you simply claim to know that lying is wrong. The skeptic objects that your belief in this principle is no better than a belief in the golden rule, as it is demonstrably false. After all, lying to save a life isn't wrong; your belief must be hedged. There are two possible lines of response you might pursue: (i) you can complicate your principle by claiming to know that lying is wrong *unless necessary to save a life*, or (ii) you can use a "catch-all" hedge and claim to know that lying is immoral *except in special circumstances*.

If you follow the first course, the skeptic will try to come up with exceptions to the more complex principle you have formulated. If someone loves surprise parties and you know as much, fibbing to instigate the ruse isn't immoral in the least. Thus, the skeptic points out, it isn't true that lying is wrong unless necessary to save life. You must further complicate your principle. Of course, if you can formulate all the legitimate exceptions to lying, you will arrive at a complicated but true moral principle, a principle you might then claim to know. (Indeed, if the principle isn't too long or complicated it might be an item of knowledge you actually *use* when figuring out whether some particular lie is immoral.) But if you leave some of the legitimate exceptions out, you won't even have a candidate for knowledge. In the event of your failure, the skeptic can legitimately reject your claim to know the immorality of lying; and he can do this without invoking the infinite regress argument, or raising any other doubts about your judgment's grounds. For it is admitted on all sides that you cannot know what isn't true.

Suppose, though, that you fall back on a catch-all hedge by claiming to know that lying is immoral except in special circumstances. There are two responses to this alternative tactic that the skeptic might make. First, he might argue that the knowledge you have claimed for yourself is really quite empty. After all, he asks, how is knowing that lying is immoral except in special circumstances different from knowing that lying is immoral except when it is not? The skeptic can allow that you know that lying is immoral except when it is not, as the truth of this proposition is compatible with the nihilistic claim that neither lying nor anything else is ever immoral.

To respond to this objection we must distinguish knowing that something tends to be immoral (or is immoral all things being equal, or is immoral except in special circumstances) from the morally irrelevant, wholly logical knowledge that each thing is either immoral or it is not. A comparison with seemingly non-empty hedges in the sciences might be thought to help us in this task. A thing needn't fall when dropped, as a sustained breeze from below might keep it suspended in place. What then was the general observation on which Newton premised his belief in gravity? He knew that things tend to fall when dropped, or that things fall when dropped all things being equal, where this substantive observation isn't equivalent to the wholly logical knowledge that things fall when dropped except when they don't.

Of course, the analogy cannot be exact, unless we are prepared to think of the relation between lying and immorality in causal terms. After all, we think that gravity attracts objects to the Earth's surface and that this causes them to drop in the absence of an opposing force. Do we want to say that lying "causes" immorality in the absence of opposing "moral forces"? When speaking of moral phenomena, can causal language be used in any but a figurative sense?

We could fall back on a bare claim about frequencies: lying is more often immoral than not. And we might allow that you learned this fact from your experience with liars. But we have seen that your knowledge of the immorality of particular lies must be inferential in form. So your inductively justified belief that lies are more often immoral than not is doubly inferential. It is an inductive generalization from facts known inferentially. It is not a moral intuition.

Let us suppose for the moment, though, that these objections to your having non-inferential knowledge of a moral principle modified with a catch-all hedge can be met. (We will return to related matters in chapter 5.) If the proposition that lying is pro tanto immoral is non-tautologous, then a skeptic bent on rejecting all moral knowledge must argue that you do not know that this proposition is true. But a slightly less ambitious skeptic might focus on your attempts to apply this knowledge to arrive at knowledge of the immorality of particular lies.

Consider, for instance, Bernie Madoff, the once respected Wall Street titan, who recently perpetrated the largest Ponzi scheme in the history of finance.

You know that Bernie lied about his use of the money invested with him. And we are now supposing that you know that lying is immoral all things being equal. But how do you know that all things *are* equal in the case on hand?

6   Bernie Madoff lied.
7   Lying is immoral except in certain special cases.
8   Bernie's lie was not one of these special cases.
Therefore,
9   Bernie acted immorally.

If he allows that (7) is substantive, the skeptic will argue that you cannot know this premise without inferring it from distinct facts that you know. (And he is willing to bet that no such inference will prove sufficiently cogent to supply you with knowledge.) But we are now supposing that the skeptic might allow that you do know this purportedly substantive fact, and nevertheless deny you knowledge of your conclusion, by denying that you know (8). And if you can do *nothing* to articulate the range of special cases in which, you think, lying is okay, we will be hard pressed to say why you are justified in thinking that Bernie's is not a special case. Can you, as the intuitionist might suggest, just *see* that no exception to the general prohibition on lying can vindicate Madoff? How is this view any better than the perceptual model of moral knowledge we rejected above, a model on which your knowledge of (6)–(8) is beside the point, as you can just *see*, without any reasoning at all, that Bernie acted immorally?

Perhaps we conceded too much to the skeptic when, under pressure from the exceptions that must be made to the immorality of lying, we took refuge in non-inferential knowledge of a lie's pro tanto immorality. After all, those of us who read the papers know a great deal about Madoff's fraud. And the fact that he lied is only one among many reasons we have for thinking the act immoral. There are, for instance, his motives. Madoff was propelled by vanity and greed. The intended beneficiaries of his dishonesty were himself and members of his family who were also aware of the fraud. If Madoff were a modern-day Robin Hood, stealing from the rich and giving to the poor, we might still condemn his acts as misguided. But our evaluation of the case would differ considerably.

And then there are the consequences. Madoff's fraud caused an enormous amount of pain and suffering; it undermined charities on which vulnerable people depend; and there was no compensating gain in happiness or well-being for anyone except the criminal and his cronies. If Madoff had saved the money invested with him, his financial statements would have remained dishonest. But if, in this event, the state had forced him to repay the sums with large penalties, our attitude toward the whole thing would be one of bewilderment rather than abject outrage.

Our adverse judgment of Madoff also derives much of its intensity from the seriousness of the lies and the character flaws they reveal. The deception was a wanton violation of laws and rules the man promised to respect. He betrayed friends, colleagues, and mentors, and in so doing showed complete disregard for relationships most of us think sacred. He is a wolf in sheep's clothing. A realization of our worst fears regarding those we trust.

My sense, then, is that doing justice to the complexity of a typical person's reasoning regarding even so simple a case of immorality as Madoff's would force us to seriously complicate the premises from which it proceeds. And it is also my impression that these complications must be in place if the reasoning is to issue in moral knowledge. Since I haven't done a serious (first-level) survey of "our" views on the matter, I can do no more than report my own: I would not feel comfortable asserting that someone truly "knows" that Madoff acted wrongly unless I first confirmed that she knew a fair amount regarding his motives, the seriousness of the lies, and the consequences they wrought. There are probably people who inferred that Madoff acted immorally simply upon learning that he lied. But I am tempted to accuse these people of having rushed to judgment.

Thus, while the "intuitions" on which the model is based may not be universally shared, I think the intuitionist is probably best served by depicting the average newspaper reader's reasoning as follows:

10 When lying about his use of those funds invested with him, Bernie was driven by his greed and vanity to knowingly defraud several charities and scores of hard-working people, while neither improving the life nor substantially mitigating the suffering of anyone not privy to his criminal scheme.
11 If someone lies out of vanity and greed in the commission of criminal fraud without substantially improving the situation of anyone unconnected to the scheme, he therein acts immorally.

Therefore,

12 Bernie acted immorally.

Note, that though premise (11) is rather complex, it is still a fairly general moral rule or principle. And this is precisely the sort of combination the intuitionist needs.

The *complexity* of the principle shields it from the accusations of demonstrable falsehood that threaten the extraordinarily simple golden rule. And this same complexity protects the premise from the accusations of triviality leveled at our even simpler (irreducibly) pro tanto prohibition on lying.

But the principle's *generality* preserves it as a candidate for non-inferential knowledge. As we saw above, knowledge of a *particular* moral conclusion – like (12) – must be inferred from knowledge of the act's motives and consequences, knowledge which is itself inferred from observations of the actor's behavior. But, for all our arguments have shown, inferences of this kind needn't play a role in supplying us with knowledge of a complex general truth like (11). So, we can ask, with the intuitionist, whether our knowledge of (11) might be direct or immediate – the kind of non-inferential knowledge that a foundationalist might use to halt a skeptic's attempts to induce an infinite regress of supporting reasons or arguments.

We must first decide whether the premise is true. And we can note, in this regard, the many bases it covers. Our principle depicts a self-important man; motivated by greed and vanity; who destroys the lives of many unexceptional people; in an incredibly disloyal manner; without any compensating gain in happiness for anyone innocent of the crime. It therefore describes the kind of act considered immoral by Kantians, utilitarians, virtue theorists, and lay-people the world over. So it is difficult to see how its truth could be denied without recourse to nihilism. In other words, if anyone ever does act immorally, then it would seem that Bernie actually did act immorally, so long as the events transpired in the way described by our newspapers.

We have, then, a first-level observation: if there really is a way that Bernie's fraud could fail to be immoral that is compatible with the journalistic details asserted by (10), we, who believe our premise (11), will insist on its description. Indeed, this is precisely the argumentative burden we discharged above when explaining how keeping a promise could fail to be praiseworthy and how intentionally lying could fail to be immoral. And it is the burden the nihilist seeks to discharge (in spades) when arguing that moral facts would have to be supported by divine sanctions that are not, in fact, forthcoming; or that we can only lie under a supposed set of moral obligations if our moral judgments are internally motivating or rationalizing, when, as it turns out, no judgments have these features. In sum, the skeptic cannot apply critical pressure to our belief in Madoff's immorality by just *saying* that (11) is false, he must *explain how* it could fail to be true.

We have already addressed the more general arguments for nihilism that a skeptic might deploy for this purpose. And I can think of no less general argument against the immorality of selfish fraud that might be mounted on the skeptic's behalf. In consequence, I can find no help for a skeptic who would deny the truth of our principle without an argument for nihilism. If the moral skeptic is to follow the wholly epistemic strategy we have described, he must allow for the sake of argument that (11) is true and argue that – even given this supposition – we cannot *know* its truth.

The infinite regress argument is supposed to secure precisely this result. For it is supposed to put the burden on us to explain *how* we know those moral principles we claim to know. And now that we are confronted with the argument, we do feel this burden. (At least I do.) But how can we support our claim to know that self-interested acts of fraud are immoral, when, by hypothesis, we do not have – or at least needn't have – a distinct set of reasons or evidence that we can offer in support of our claim?

The intuitionist tries to improve the situation by reassuring us that we can verify our premise with a non-inferential process of reflection: just reflect on (11) and you'll therein see its truth. But the skeptics out there – and I have heard them – typically reply with a chorus of dismissive scoffs. ("Reflection? Hah!") The argument between the two parties then grinds to a halt.

If we part ways with the pair at this stage in the dialectic, can we justly remain confident in our general moral opinions? We have already supposed that (11) is true: harmful acts of self-interested fraud are immoral. So let's now also suppose that the intuitionist is in fact right, and a reliable process of reflection really does generate and maintain a typical (non-philosophical) person's belief in the moral principle at issue. These suppositions might warrant our saying that *the typical person* knows that selfish acts of harmful fraud are immoral. For we might want to allow that typical people can know moral principles of this kind on the basis of reflection alone, even though they cannot show, and indeed do not know, that their beliefs are generated by this reliable process (Audi, 1998, ch. 10). Perhaps *reliability* is necessary for knowledge, but *knowledge of reliability* almost certainly is not.

And yet *we* are not typical people. We have actually considered the skeptic's arguments. And we have puzzled over just how we do come to know moderately complex, moderately general principles like (11). If *we* do not know – or cannot show – that we acquire belief in these principles in a reliable way, can we rationally persist in our belief that they are true? Can we continue to claim knowledge? Or do those of us who have advanced to this stage in the conversation need reasons to think that the intuitionist's view of the matter is superior to the skeptic's?

In point of fact, most intuitionists are not satisfied with the impasse we have identified. Instead, they try to say something about the kind of reflection that might provide us with knowledge of the immorality of fraud. Suppose, for instance, that the intuitionist can successfully compare the process through which we are supposed to acquire non-inferential knowledge of certain moral principles with the kinds of reflection that bring us non-inferential logical and mathematical knowledge. Suppose, that is, that a comparison can be made to the very kinds of non-inferential knowledge that Locke was willing to countenance. If the comparison rings sufficiently true, this will further increase our confidence in our powers of reflection and the moral beliefs to which they are supposed to give rise. Indeed, it might even convince the Lockean skeptic that we have non-inferential moral knowledge after all.

We must then turn to our knowledge of mathematics. On the one hand, we have the simple axioms of set theory; the simple arithmetical fact that 2 + 2 = 4; and Locke's maximally simple logical example: necessarily, whatever is, is. And, on the other hand, we have complex mathematical theorems that mere mortals cannot know without proof. But in the middle, we have a range of moderately complex examples like that proposed by Audi: that it takes four generations of people to produce a great-grandchild (2004, 49).

Apparently, some people cannot immediately see that it takes four generations to make a great-grandchild, but must think through the relation of child to parent, of parent to grandparent, and grandparent to great-grandparent: four generations in all. The moderate complexity of the principle ensures that many of us will not judge it true without forethought. And yet, Audi argues, the thought process that precedes belief in the case does not make the resulting knowledge inferential, because it does not move us *beyond* contemplating the proposition at issue. What we have here is a way of understanding the claim that four generations are necessary for great-grandchildren that *itself* justifies belief in its truth. The process of understanding involved in the case justifies belief quite apart from any inference *external* to that process.

> *Reflective basis*: your knowledge of P is non-inferentially grounded in reflection (or held on the basis of reflection) just in case: (i) you reason, in a wholly intellectual way, to a justified belief in P, where (ii) this thought process is internal to (or part of) your understanding of P.

Let's go through the account step by step.

Audi's zero-level claim is that our understanding or grasp of certain propositions includes, as a constituent part, certain ways of reasoning that result in our believing these very propositions.

His first-level claims are two. First, we treat these internal bouts of reasoning as warranting belief in the propositions that they help us understand. (If you think of the relation of child to parent, parent to grandparent, and grandparent to great-grandparent, we will not subject your subsequent belief that it takes four generations to yield a great-grandchild to substantive epistemic criticism.) Second, we treat a belief that is generated in this manner as knowledge so long as we are not aware of any evidence that runs contrary to the truth of what is believed, where this contrary evidence is something that the believer cannot (in turn) rationally rebut or dismiss. That is, we will allow someone knowledge of what she believes in the case unless we think there are "defeators" to her justification that she cannot "defeat" with further evidence or reasoning.

Finally, we have Audi's second-level claim: that the epistemic practices we have uncovered at the first level are perfectly fine. We are right to say that you know that it takes four generations to produce a great-grandchild even though we know that you cannot infer the truth of this proposition from any distinct propositions that you know.

Of course, our premise (11) is substantially more complex than the example we have been discussing. But the intuitionist might argue that this is a difference in degree, not kind.[15] Just as there is a process of reasoning by which you contemplate and come to fully understand the proposition that it takes four generations to make a great-grandchild, there is a reflective process by which you come to fully comprehend the claim that self-interested acts of harmful fraud are immoral. In both cases, the process is internal to your understanding, and yet justifies you in believing the item understood. And since no inference external to your grasp of the proposition need be executed, you can be said to know this moderately complex moral principle in a truly non-inferential manner. The intuitionist claims that your knowledge that Bernie acted immorally (if he did what the papers say) is grounded in substantive reflection. It more closely resembles your knowledge that it takes four generations to yield a great-grandchild than it does your knowledge of those mathematical theorems you must infer from axioms.

Though we have a fairly detailed, fairly intuitive description of the reasoning by which you "process" and therein come to know that it takes four generations to yield a great-grandchild, as of yet we have no account of the reasoning by which you come to believe in the immorality of selfish fraud. But the aptness of the analogy between the two examples – and the argument for adopting a single epistemic model of both – would seem to depend on precisely these details. Recall that when we described Ross' intuitionist theory above, we wrote rather abstractly of Abe's thinking of the nature of assertion and its relation to other practices when coming to non-inductive, reflective knowledge of the immorality of lying. But vague descriptions of this kind will do nothing to convince a Lockean skeptic that we have non-inferential knowledge of general moral principles like (11). Indeed, they will do little to deepen our conviction in these principles – principles we hope to save from skeptical assault. How, we want to know, is moral reflection supposed to work?

The challenge will prove difficult to meet. First, the intuitionist's account must be psychologically plausible. The intuitionist isn't explaining how a theorist like Kant might come to a reflectively justified belief in the immorality of lying, but how, at a given stage in his thinking, subjects like Abe really do come to this belief. An extraordinarily strong form of skepticism would be refuted by the mere possibility of reflective knowledge, but if most of us lack moral knowledge, this is itself a radically skeptical result.

Second, any inferences invoked by the account must be "internal" to the reasoning with which the typical subject "processes" the proposition. That is, the justification provided must be truly non-inferential.

But third, and finally, the process of reflection described must also be sufficiently substantive to supply us with knowledge of those moral principles we are supposed to understand with its aid. In consequence, the method of reflection must be a reliable one. Is it possible to satisfy all three of these criteria?

To my knowledge, intuitionists have not yet met the challenge on hand. Though moral theorists have advanced insightful accounts of the immorality of fraud, betrayal, and similar indiscretions, the justifications these accounts provide for believing in the immorality of dishonesty are fairly obviously inferential in nature. And the accounts on offer are usually not intended to explicate the reasoning that leads the non-philosophical public to their beliefs in the immorality of these behaviors. Most moral theories ensure a measure of accuracy through an even greater level of complexity. They are far too sophisticated to attribute to the common thinker.

What, then, is the thought process that leads a typical person to believe in the immorality of greedy deception? I will use my own powers of introspection to tell you what I can about my own case. Now, if I am to conform my reasoning to the rules of the intuitionist's game, I mustn't argue for (11) from distinct propositions that I believe. And if I follow this stricture,

I can do no more than mount an unsuccessful attempt to imagine counter-examples to the principle's truth. I believe that (11) is true because barring nihilism, I just cannot see how it could be false.

How closely does this resemble the method by which we have reasoned to the conclusion that four generations is necessary for a great-grandchild? Truth be told, the resemblance is not great. There is a *constructive* route to knowledge of the non-moral proposition Audi discusses. When we think through the parental relations involved, and count four generations in all, we consider factors that "show" or "reveal" the proposition's truth. In contrast, my failure to imagine how (11) could be false is wholly *negative* in nature. And it seems that "showing" or "revealing" (11)'s truth would require the use of distinct propositions that I know. It would require a derivation of the fact from some other items of knowledge. In other words, it would require an inference.

But, though negative in nature, mightn't the imaginative method that I employ when attempting to verify the immorality of self-interested fraud still be aptly described as "reflection"? Perhaps. But the reasoning on hand is different enough from the methods we employ to reach mathematical knowledge that we have as yet little assurance of its reliability. Just how good are my powers of imagination? Do they provide me with knowledge of the moderately complex moral principles to which I subscribe? Mightn't they lead to me overlook a range of legitimate exceptions to these principles?

It seems we have returned to the impasse at which we began. Because we have done little to assimilate our knowledge of (11) to our knowledge of mathematical truths, it is unlikely that we have done much to deepen our conviction in our knowledge of this moral principle. Nor have we done much to increase our confidence in the process of reflection through which we are supposed to know it. In the absence of a better, more detailed theory of reflection, the Lockean skeptic will remain unimpressed. He will continue to argue that we cannot know that acts of harmful fraud are immoral unless we can argue for this claim from distinct things that we know.

The intuitionist accounts that we have so far considered are forms of *moral rationalism*, as they compare the process by which we acquire non-inferential knowledge of moral principles to the processes by which we acquire mathematical or wholly "conceptual" knowledge (cf. Bealer, 1998; Greco, 2000; Heumer, 2005; and Peacocke, 2000, 2004).

> *Moral rationalism*: we can know, in a manner that resembles the methods of mathematics in its independence from experience, various substantive (non-trivial) moral truths.

To frame the thesis in more philosophically loaded language: the moral rationalist posits a body of substantive *a priori* moral knowledge.

But if our knowledge of moral principles depends on experience or observation in crucial ways it will prove importantly different from our knowledge of arithmetic. *Moral empiricists* think that experience really is necessary for moral knowledge. And, because of this, they reject the rationalist's comparison of morality to math.

> *Moral empiricism*: all knowledge of substantive moral truth depends for its existence on experience.

Of course, many empiricists join Locke in rejecting moral intuitionism altogether. But there is also an important empiricist strain of the intuitionist view: an intuitionism that posits non-inferential *a posteriori* knowledge of moral generalities. Hume's theory, on which passions and emotions are necessary for moral knowledge, has proved an influential example of this approach.

As we will see, Hume thinks we infer judgments of morality and immorality from judgments of virtue and vice. But we can get a sense of the general "Humean" approach by applying his account of basic moral judgment to our acceptance of moderately complex moral principles: the kinds of principles that our discussion of intuitionism has led us to treat as non-inferentially believed or basic.

So let's return, once again, to your belief in the principle that someone acts immorally if he knowingly perpetrates an extraordinarily harmful fraud for his own benefit. We can say that your knowledge of this principle is an a posteriori moral intuition if we: (i) persist in maintaining that you do not infer its truth from distinct things that you know, and yet (ii) allow your experiences an essential role in its genesis.

What role might your experiences play? Well, suppose that you imagine what it is like to be the kind of person who would perpetrate such an act: the ingratitude, deceit, and distrust that mar a life lived in this way. You imagine what it is like to be one of the man's victims: an old woman robbed of retirement funds she accumulated through years of hard work, or an orphaned child who can no longer afford schooling after a charity dependent on the fraudulent enterprise collapses into bankruptcy. And you imagine what it is like to be the relative or friend of such a person; the grief involved, the misery, fear, and anger. The overall effect of these imaginative acts is bound to be an emotional state negative in its polarity.

Now suppose that it is this frame of mind that induces your belief in the immorality of selfish acts of financial fraud. The Humean might then claim that a person could not be credited with *knowing* what you here believe if she were entirely cold or affectively barren. For instance, we might suppose, as an empirical conjecture, that certain psychopathic children – animal torturers perhaps – are not at all distressed when they imagine all this suffering. In the absence of the moral testimony of normal parents and teachers these children would then lack conviction in the immorality of even the cruelest murder (Hume, 1739–40/2000, 3.1.1.26 [SBN 468–69]).[16] Again, our knowledge of the immorality of selfish fraud would turn out to be a posteriori because it would depend for its existence on experience: albeit experience that is emotional rather than sensory in nature. We can say that knowledge of this kind has a wholly "empathetic" basis.

> *Empathetic basis*: your knowledge of *P* is non-inferentially grounded in empathy (or held on an empathetic basis) just in case: (i) you employ empathy in considering *P*, where (ii) your consequent emotional reaction leads you to believe *P* quite apart from any inference to *P* from distinct propositions that you know or believe.

Note, though, what happens if we say with Hume that the child can't even *understand* the proposition that harmful deceit is immoral unless she has the appropriate emotional reactions to suffering and betrayal. (The truly "congenital" psychopath uses the moral terms she only pretends to understand.) Then the normal man's belief in the immorality of fraud would be based on understanding alone and emotional experience, as emotional experience – or a disposition to such – will turn out to be part of his understanding of moral claims. In this event, all of Audi's intuitionist theses will hold with the exception of one: his claim that intuitive moral knowledge is typically a priori or wholly intellectual in origin. Instead, if any version of empiricist intuitionism proves correct, empathetic imagination will have provided us with a constructive route to knowledge of the immorality of dishonesty – an emotional path that is nevertheless internal to our understanding of deceit's impermissibility.

Though I haven't subjected this last issue to rigorous study, I would conjecture that common thinking on the matter is actually divided against itself. For years now I have asked my students if they can imagine a man who calls "moral" just those acts we call "moral" and calls "immoral" just those acts we call "immoral" – and who can apply these and related terms to novel scenarios without error

– but who feels nothing at all for the suffering and joys of others. Roughly half of the students claim that such a man would not truly grasp moral concepts and so would not know wrong from right; roughly half grant the man an understanding of moral terms; and a vanishingly small number say that the case is incoherent, as applying moral terms to the right actions itself depends on an emotional connection to others. It is my sense, then, that our shared concept of what it is to grasp moral concepts does not determine this issue one way or the other. We must look beyond folk psychology to succeed in our effort to develop the best account of moral understanding and its relation to our sentiments. And when we turn to experiments designed to test the psychopath's understanding of moral terms, we do indeed find some evidence of abnormality (see, e.g., Blair, Mitchell, and Peschardt, 1995; Blair *et al.*, 1997, 2001).

At any rate, whether or not empathetic experience is necessary for moral understanding and moral belief, the contemporary Humean maintains that it is an essential part of much of our knowledge of moral generalities. You must truly feel bad for others to know that intentionally harming them is wrong; and you must smile at their achievements to know that benevolence is virtuous. Either that, or you must rely for your knowledge on the testimony of someone who does have these experiences.

Moral rationalists reject this view, and their reasons for doing so are many and varied. One central worry concerns the psychopathic agents we discussed in chapter 3. Suppose the hitman feels nothing for others. Must the empiricist then say that the hitman doesn't really know that what he is doing is wrong? And if the hitman doesn't realize that he is doing anything wrong, how can we hold him responsible for his actions?

In 1843, Edward Drummond was murdered by Daniel M'Naghten, a man suffering from paranoid delusions. Though controversial, the subsequently formulated *M'Naghten Rules* admit a defense of "not guilty by reason of insanity" for any defendant who did "not know the nature and quality of the act he was doing; or if he did know it … did not know he was doing what was wrong." How many people lack the emotional sensitivity the empiricist thinks is necessary for moral knowledge? Can they all evade blame by invoking the moral analogue of the M'Naghten Rules? Do we need to know anything at all about a person's emotions to know that he can be properly punished for harming others with impunity?

There are a number of ways an empiricist might respond to these objections, but none is wholly uncontroversial. First, the empiricist might invoke moral knowledge acquired via testimony. We might suppose that the hitman's parents have normal emotions, and that they have conveyed the wrongness of killing to him. In such a case, the empiricist might say, the hitman will be sufficiently aware of the immorality of his actions to be blamed for them. Perhaps a full or perfect grasp of morality is impossible in the absence of other-regarding emotions. But a derived or minimal knowledge of morality might be thought sufficiently robust to preclude the M'Naghten defense. This depends upon whether it is reasonable to expect someone to conform his behavior to the minimal knowledge of right and wrong we are supposing testimony can provide.

But what if the hitman was born to outlaws and ruffians? Or what if, like Ishmael Beah (2007), he was kidnapped from his home in Sierra Leone at a young age, pressed into the service of a roaming militia, and conditioned to revel in all forms of vice, banditry, rape, and murder? According to Kant's brand of rationalism, there must still exist some way for the young soldier to reason his way to moral knowledge. And because this knowledge remains available to him, Beah can still be held responsible for his crimes. If he didn't know any better at the time, he should have.

Clearly, the empiricist cannot adopt this view of the matter, though whether we think this tells against his account will depend on our commitments in other areas. Should we level blame at the crimes of those whose emotions are completely shut off from the people with whom they interact? If the empiricist is right, this amounts to blaming those who don't truly realize that what they're doing is wrong. Isn't this an irrational practice?

We can put the rationalist's worries aside for the moment, to consider the skeptic's dissatisfaction with the empiricist's strain of intuitionism. The skeptic's complaints are rather different from the rationalist's, as the skeptic would actually go beyond the empiricist and deny moral knowledge to psychopaths and normal people alike. Instead, to rebut empiricism, the skeptic simply rehearses his criticisms of rationalist strains of intuitionism – criticisms that we have already encountered.

First, why should we think that we actually use empathetic identification when coming to accept moral principles? Is there a route from empathy to acceptance of moderately complex moral rules that at least some of us sometimes travel? Though controversial, the work of psychologists like Daniel Batson (1991), Jonathan Haidt and Craig Joseph (2007), and Haidt and Fredrik Björklund (2008) might be mobilized to support a positive answer to this claim. We will return to these matters in chapter 7 when discussing, in brief, a normal child's basic moral development.

But even if we suppose, for the moment, that the empiricist's method is psychologically real, why should we think that it's reliable? Why should we think that non-inferential processes of empathetic identification provide us with moral knowledge?

Since the empiricist rejects the comparison between morality and math, he will not argue for his method's reliability by comparing it to the wholly conceptual forms of reflection that the Lockean skeptic accepts. After all, our mathematical knowledge is not grounded in our feelings. And because the empiricist's method is supposed to be non-inferential, the resulting judgments cannot be compared to scientific knowledge. Scientific knowledge depends on both theory construction and observational tests. In consequence, the empiricist needs a wholly independent assessment of his method's reliability. He needs to leave the armchair to judge its performance in the field.

When we do this, and examine the historical record, we are immediately struck by the myriad cases in which empathy breaks down. The distorting effects of ennui, schadenfreude, and the objectification of others are far too common to be ignored. An incomplete understanding of people who look and act differently from us, and a lack of concern for the goals and interests of those people we do understand, too often leads to the acceptance of racism, sexism, paternalism, and extraordinarily pernicious ideologies that continue to be embraced by religious extremists and egomaniacal despots the world over.

But breakdowns in empathy represent defects in the application of the Humean method. They do nothing to show that the method produces false judgments when it is skillfully applied. Admittedly, in order to demonstrate that a particular person knows a given moral principle on an empathetic basis, we must show that she is good at understanding and connecting with others and has employed these abilities in coming to accept the principle in question. (The truth of her moral judgment must be no accident.) But to show that empathetic knowledge exists, we need only argue that this can and does happen.

Of more direct relevance to the empiricist's debate with the moral skeptic, then, is the reliability of the empathetic method when it is properly or skillfully employed. So let us suppose that a rather sympathetic person makes her judgments about which kinds of behavior are morally objectionable (and which are not) by both adopting the perspective of someone performing the behavior in question and by putting herself in the shoes of those people the behavior typically affects. (This is her method for "testing" principles to see if they are morally acceptable.) How likely is it that she will come to judge that a certain kind of act is immoral when it is in fact perfectly permissible? And how often will she use this same method to mistakenly judge that an act is permissible when it is really immoral? Is the empathetic method any more reliable than trying and failing to imagine exceptions to a principle's truth? Is the empathetic method sufficiently reliable to generate moral knowledge? Or must we confirm our empathetic beliefs with additional arguments or inferences?

As of yet, there is no consensus on these matters. We will discuss them further in chapter 7, when we focus our attention on the reliability of our moral beliefs.

4.3 Chapter summary

The epistemic moral skeptic does not reject moral truths outright. Instead, he would deny us knowledge of – or well-grounded beliefs in – any moral truths that might be thought to exist.

The Pyrrhonian argues that our beliefs cannot be justly held if they are not supported by distinct propositions that we know or rationally believe, and that this requirement altogether precludes justified belief. But Pyrrhonian skepticism pretty obviously flies in the face of our ordinary conception of basic introspective and mathematical knowledge.

A less ambitious skeptic would apply the Pyrrhonian's reasoning to morality alone. Perhaps we can know basic facts of math without argument, but we are only justified in holding our moral beliefs if we can support them with distinct propositions that we know. The skeptic completes his argument by rejecting infinitely regressive and circular arguments and by claiming that we cannot rationally infer moral conclusions from wholly non-moral premises.

The intuitionist rejects this form of skepticism by arguing, against Locke, that we have non-inferential moral knowledge.

Intuitionists have posited a number of different kinds of non-inferential moral knowledge. According to Ross, we have non-inferential knowledge of the pro tanto immorality of particular lies, knowledge from which we can inductively infer to the pro tanto immorality of lying in general. The fact that lying is pro tanto immoral can then be verified in a different way, by reflecting, in an abstract manner, on the nature of lying. Audi and others would add another source of knowledge to this picture: Those of us who know the validity of Kant's categorical imperative can use it to deduce the very same prohibition against lying.

Perceptualist forms of intuitionism grant us non-inferential knowledge of the immorality of particular acts. These accounts face a serious objection.

In the absence of testimony, we cannot know that a particular act is immoral if we haven't determined its motives and gauged its impact on the lives of those affected. We infer our way to knowledge of motives and effects. And we then infer the act's immorality from our non-moral knowledge of these motives and effects. Thus, we cannot have wholly non-inferential knowledge of the immorality of particular indiscretions.

We cannot know general moral principles if none are true. But the only general moral principles that are plausibly thought true are those that are either hedged with an "all things being equal" clause or complicated to include information about motives and consequences. The intuitionist's best bet is to argue that principles of one or both of these kinds can be known without inference.

An ambitious skeptic might argue that moral principles modified with an "all things being equal" hedge are empty; a more modest skeptic would argue that we lack the knowledge we would need to apply these principles to arrive at unqualified knowledge of the immorality of individual acts. To avoid these complications, we can turn our attention to moderately complex moral principles. Since these principles are only moderately complex, it is not wildly implausible that we often use them when judging particular acts immoral.

Rationalists compare our knowledge of moral principles to our knowledge of mathematical truths. Since the kinds of moral principles we might know are somewhat complex, our knowledge of them must differ to some degree from our knowledge of extraordinarily simple arithmetic truths like $2 + 2 = 4$. But there are moderately complex conceptual truths that we can know without argument. Our knowledge that it takes four generations to produce a great-grandchild is a plausible example. On Audi's account, the reasoning some people use to verify this principle is actually internal to the process by which they understand it. The knowledge that results is therefore non-inferential; it is based on reflection alone.

To be confident that a similar process of reflection leads us to knowledge of moral principles, we need a somewhat detailed description of the reflective reasoning that might lead us to accept these principles. Those who defend rationalist forms of intuitionism have not yet met this challenge. Introspection reveals that we cannot imagine exceptions to certain moral principles. But trying and failing to imagine how a moderately complex claim could be false is not an obviously reliable route to knowledge of its truth. It differs considerably from the constructive form of reasoning that convinces us that four generations are needed for a great-grandchild.

According to the empiricist, all moral knowledge depends on experience. Hume's theory weds this empiricist thesis to intuitionism. According to the Humean, we know that selfish fraud is immoral by imagining what it is like to be the kind of person who would do such a thing and imagining what it is like to be regularly affected by such a person's actions. The negative affect produced plays an essential role in justifying the resulting belief. In the absence of an aversive emotional response, we would need testimony to know that the contemplated act is immoral.

Rationalists are dissatisfied with the empiricist brand of intuitionism because it implies that many affectively barren people do not know right from wrong. And if they do not know right from wrong, it is hard to see how we can be justified in blaming them for the immoral acts they commit. The weight of this objection depends on the role best assigned to blame in our moral practices.

The empiricist cannot argue for the reliability of his method by comparing the beliefs it produces to our basic mathematical and scientific beliefs. Our basic mathematical beliefs are not based on emotion. And our basic scientific beliefs are supported with inferences from observation. The empiricist therefore needs an entirely independent assessment of empathy's reliability. This is an ongoing project, the success of which is uncertain.

4.4 Further reading

The Pyrrhonian problematic is most closely associated with the five modes of Agrippa and the skepticism of Sextus Empiricus, *Writings* (1562/1949), though the form of argument can already be found in Aristotle's *Posterior Analytics*. The history and cogency of this form of reasoning are helpfully discussed by Ernest Sosa, "The Raft and the Pyramid" (1980), "Philosophical Skepticism and Epistemic Circularity" (1994), and "How to Resolve the Pyrrhonian Problematic" (1997). Sinnott-Armstrong (ed.), *Pyrrhonian Skepticism* (2004) is an excellent collection of recent work.

Chapter 2 of Laurence BonJour, *The Structure of Empirical Knowledge* (1985) contains an influential presentation of the infinite regress argument and a challenge to the foundationalist's reply. Wilfred Sellars, *Science, Perception and Reality* (1963) and Roderick Chisholm's *Philosophy* (1964) contain earlier critiques of foundationalism. Andrew Cling's recent essay, "The Epistemic Regress Problem" (2008) rejects all extant responses.

Non-inferential knowledge is defended by a number of theorists, the most famous being Descartes, whose *Meditations on First Philosophy* and other important works can be found in his *Philosophical Writings* (1641/1993). Contemporary advocates of some form of foundationalism include John Pollock, *Knowledge and Justification* (1974); Chisholm, *Theory of Knowledge* (1966); William Alston, "Two Types of Foundationalism" (1976); James Van Cleve, "Foundationalism, Epistemic Principles and the Cartesian Circle" (1979); and Jim Pryor, "The Sceptic and the Dogmatist" (2000).

Locke limits his objections to non-inferential moral knowledge in his *Essay Concerning Human Understanding* (1690/1991), one of the most important works in the history of philosophy. Nicholas Sturgeon, "Ethical Intuitionism and Ethical Naturalism" (2002) notes how a theorist might be driven to moral intuitionism by the inability to see how knowledge of moral conclusions could be inferred from knowledge of wholly value-neutral premises.

W. D. Ross, *The Right and the Good* (1930) remains the most influential rationalist form of moral intuitionism. Sidgwick's discussion of intuitionist theses in *The Methods of Ethics* (1874/1981) is a common point of reference, as is Rawls' treatment in *A Theory of Justice* (1971). In *The Good in the Right* (2004) Robert Audi offers what is perhaps the most well-developed contemporary defense of the position. Other important recent attempts include Russ Shafer-Landau, *Moral Realism: A Defense* (2003) and Michael Heumer, *Ethical Intuitionism* (2005). The contributors to Phillip Stratton-Lake (ed.), *Ethical Intuitionism: Re-evaluations* (2002c) discuss epistemic intuitionism along with a number of metaphysical theses that are commonly associated with the view.

Jonathan Dancy defends particularism in his *Moral Reasons* (1993). Sean McKeever and Michael Ridge advocate a generalist alternative in *Principled Ethics* (2006). Brad Hooker and Margaret Little (eds.), *Moral Particularism* (2000) collects important contributions to the debate.

Moral knowledge is compared to sophisticated forms of perceptual knowledge by David McNaughton, *Moral Vision* (1988); Hubert Dreyfus and Stuart Dreyfus, "What is Morality?" (1990); and Michael Watkins and Kelly Dean Jolley, "Pollyanna Realism" (2002), while Hume describes how a moral sense generates judgments of virtue and vice in his masterpiece, *A Treatise of Human Nature* (1739–40/2000). Contemporary theories inspired by Hume's account include Shaun Nichols, *Sentimental Rules* (2004) and Jonathan Haidt and Craig Joseph, "The Moral Mind" (2007).

5

DEDUCTIVE MORAL KNOWLEDGE

5.1 On deducing "ought" from "is"

We have done our best to assess the intuitionist's claim to non-inferential moral knowledge. And we have seen that certain forms of intuitionism remain live theoretical options. But we will suppose going forward that the intuitionist is mistaken, and non-inferential moral knowledge is not to be had. Assuming that intuitionism is false will help us focus our attention on other approaches.

If Locke is right, and there are no non-inferentially justified moral beliefs, four possibilities remain. If (i) coherentism, (ii) infinitism, and (iii) skepticism are unacceptable, then (iv) we must be able to infer moral propositions from a body of non-moral evidence, where this body of evidence includes facts that are known to us in a non-inferential manner by perception and reflection. Locke's rejection of intuitionism, when conjoined with a foundationalist response to the Pyrrhonian problematic, forces us to allow the inference of an "ought" from an "is."

The question before us, then, is whether we can gain moral knowledge – or well-grounded moral beliefs – through arguments or inferences with wholly value-neutral premises, where our answer to this question must interact, in ways both subtle and brute, with our views on a more basic matter. Under what conditions will exposure to any good argument, or the execution of any good inference, provide someone with knowledge of – or a justified belief in – its conclusion? Though addressing this question will take us some distance beyond the investigation of moral knowledge to examine more general epistemological issues, this is unavoidable. For it is my sense that unwarranted assumptions about the nature of inference have led many to dogmatically assume that "ought" cannot be inferred from "is." I hope, in this section, to cast significant doubt upon that dogma.

We might begin our inquiry by listing those inferences that strike the vast majority of us as sources of knowledge. If we adopt this approach, and find ourselves including on our list certain arguments from "is" to "ought," we will have to answer our more general question with these arguments in mind. If, contrary to the common beliefs we have recorded, the skeptic advances a criterion from which it follows that all inferences from "is" to "ought" are incapable of producing knowledge, his criterion will be found wanting on these grounds alone. Thus, if he does not reject this first methodology outright, the skeptic must gamble on our failing to find an intuitively cogent argument from "is" to "ought." And it is highly unlikely that this gamble will pay off.

But the standard method of levels presents the skeptic with a second option. We first describe the various forms of inference to which we are prone; we then observe the sometimes customary, sometimes divergent ways in which we criticize and approve of these arguments; but we then try to evaluate the more common forms of criticism, revising them where we think necessary or warranted. If he assents to this approach, the skeptic can allow the zero-level observation that we commonly do infer "ought" from "is"; and he can allow the first-level observation that a certain number of these inferences are commonly thought to provide us with moral knowledge. But he must then point to some incoherence or deficiency in these epistemic practices – an error grave enough to warrant their revision or abandonment. The method of levels therefore offers the skeptic a tough row to hoe, but its chances for success are not to be dismissed out of hand.

But there is a third option. What if we begin by restricting our view to inferences that have nothing to do with morality? A survey, of, say, mathematical and scientific arguments might be thought weighty enough to provide us with the resources we need to establish a fully general epistemological criterion – a set of conditions that we think must be met by any argument purporting to establish knowledge of its conclusion. If we follow this approach, the fact that certain inferences from "is" to "ought" are universally accepted − or even universally thought to establish knowledge of their moral conclusions − need not supply us with any sort of evidence at all regarding their value. For if our criterion fails to mention universal acceptability, the fact that, before adopting that criterion, we would have agreed on a moral argument's epistemological merits will be neither here nor there.

The search for an "independent" account of an argument's value would therefore seem to provide the moral skeptic with his best chance at success. If he cannot succeed with this approach, it is highly unlikely that he will find success with the alternatives.

We can start with some common taxonomic maneuvers. As is generally acknowledged, good arguments come in both *deductive* and *non-deductive* (inductive, abductive, and probabilistic) varieties. The premises of a good deductive argument *entail* its conclusion; the conclusion of such an argument *must* be true so long as the premises are true; good deductive arguments are *valid*. In contrast, the premises of a good non-deductive argument do not entail its conclusion, and yet knowledge of − or justified belief in − the premises of such an argument can, in favorable circumstances, still provide a person with knowledge of − or justified belief in − its conclusion.

Valid arguments can be further distinguished into those that are *formally valid* and those that are only *informally* so. In what does formal validity consist? Readers who have taken a course in formal logic are probably familiar with a definition developed by Alfred Tarski (1901−83) along with its equally influential model-theoretic variants.[1] Are there formally valid inferences of "ought" from "is" given one or more of these differing accounts of formal validity?

Though a great deal of the literature on inferring "ought" from "is" focuses on precisely this question, its epistemological importance is minimal. If there is no possible world in which a moral argument's value-neutral premises are true and its morally loaded conclusion false, that argument will have at least one epistemologically desirable property: our knowing its value-neutral premises will preclude the possibility of our holding a false or mistaken belief in its morally laden conclusion. And this desirable characteristic is shared by formally and informally valid arguments alike. As we will see, knowledge of the premises of an informally valid argument won't in general be enough to supply us with *knowledge* of its true conclusion, so possessing an informally valid argument from "is" to "ought" won't necessarily give us everything we need to answer the moral skeptic. But, then, insisting on the formal validity of the argument wouldn't really help. For you can know the premises of a formally valid argument and directly infer its conclusion from them, and yet fail to know that conclusion so long as the connection between the argument's premises and its conclusion is not suitably obvious. Informal and formal validity are on a par in this regard. Both forms of argument can be used to extend our knowledge in some but not all cases.

For these reasons among others, we will concern ourselves here with the possibility of constructing good informally valid arguments with value-neutral premises and conclusions of direct moral significance. We will then take up non-deductive moral inference in the chapter to follow. Formal validity and model-theoretic proofs of validity are further addressed in the final chapter.

As we have noted, it is important to distinguish the (formal or informal) validity of an inference from its *epistemic value*. Of the greatest significance, given our current focus, is the ease with which we can construct valid moral arguments with wholly value-neutral premises so long as we are not concerned with using those arguments to acquire moral knowledge or arrive at justified moral beliefs (Prior, 1960a; Jackson, 1974; Nelson, 1995; Sinnott-Armstrong, 2006). A case in point:

1   Everything that the pope says is true.
2   The pope says that homosexuality is immoral.
Therefore,
3   Homosexuality is immoral.

Any plausible syntax and semantics for "says that" and "true" will allow us to prove the validity of this argument from the soundness of the inference rules to which it conforms. So the argument is probably not only valid, but also (in some sense) formally valid.[2] Moreover, when taken in isolation from one another, the argument's premises are each logically compatible with nihilism. Premise (1) is compatible with the pope's saying nothing about moral matters; and (2) is compatible with his asserting nothing but falsehoods. Thus, neither premise advances a truly moral claim. So have we here inferred an "ought" (or "ought not") from an "is"?

Clearly, what we have uncovered is just one of many cases in which validity – indeed, even formal validity – is of limited epistemic significance. The obvious fallibility of the pope means that it is impossible to come to know (3) on the basis of (1). And there are few instances in which someone could come to justifiably believe in the immorality of homosexuality through exposure to this argument. After all, it is hard to see how anyone – or anyone reading this – could justifiably believe that everything the pope says is true, as a belief in papal infallibility in this day and age is a sign of either imbecility or an overly poetic sensibility. In sum, what we care about as epistemologists and earnest thinkers is not the existence of a merely valid argument from "is" to "ought," but a valid argument that might help us gain knowledge of – or a reasonably held belief in – its conclusion. We can call an inference meeting this further condition an *epistemologically valuable* valid argument.

Admittedly, the argument from "My parents say that pulling my sister's hair is wrong" to "Pulling my sister's hair is wrong" looks to possess the decidedly epistemological virtues for which we are looking. But it is not deductively valid. And there are good reasons to think that the kind of moral knowledge it provides cannot end the story. For at some point, testimonial knowledge must yield to knowledge of some other kind. Alice knows from Margie, who knows from Nancy, who knows from Helen, who knows from Kim that she and Hugo are going steady. But this is only possible because Kim heard Hugo ask her out and accepted his "pin" in full awareness of its significance. Similarly, I know from my parents, who, perhaps, know from their own, that it is wrong to pull one's sister's hair. But someone, at some point, must have arrived at this knowledge in some other way.

Hume, who is famous for having questioned the inference from "is" to "ought," almost certainly had an epistemological thesis in mind. The passage in which he discusses the matter is one of the most famous in all of philosophy.

> In every system of morality, which I have hitherto met with, I have always remark'd, that the author proceeds for some time in the ordinary way of reasoning, and establishes the being of a God, or makes some observations concerning human affairs; when of a sudden I am supriz'd to find, that instead of the usual copulations of propositions, *is*, and *is not*, I meet with no proposition that is not connected with an *ought*, or an *ought not*. This change is imperceptible; but is, however, of the last consequence. For as this *ought*, or *ought not*, expresses some new relation or affirmation, 'tis necessary that it shou'd be observ'd and explain'd; and at the same time that a reason should be given, for what seems altogether inconceivable, how this new relation can be a deduction from others, which are entirely different from it. (Hume, 1739–40/2000, 3.1.2.27 [SBN 470])

Hume frames his question in linguistic terms. He contrasts "copulative" propositions with those involving "ought," and he speaks of a "deduction" of certain relations from others. And yet, if Hume were really asking for an explanation of the validity of arguments with premises featuring "is" and a conclusion featuring "ought," he would be forced to think certain intra-moral inferences in need of supplementation or explication. Consider, for instance:

4   Stealing is vicious.
Therefore,
5   One ought not steal.

But Hume did not find this inference problematic in any way, nor did he think it in need of support. Instead, he thought it fully explained by a perfectly fine rule – or inferential custom – connecting our use of "vicious" with our use of "obligatory."

> When any action, or quality of the mind pleases us *after a certain manner*, we say it is virtuous; and when that neglect, or non-performance of it, displeases us *after a like manner*, we say that we lie under an obligation to perform it. (Hume, 1739–40/2000, 3.2.5.4 [SBN 517])

From the grammatical point of view, premise (4) is surely an "is" proposition; it says that stealing is vicious. And yet, as far as Hume was concerned, it is to be treated as advancing a claim of "ought."[3]

In point of fact, Hume thought judgments of virtue and vice the most basic "ought" judgments of which we are capable. And the explanation for which Hume was asking in the now famous passage we have excerpted above is some reasonably coherent account of how we come to believe in the viciousness of an action from an entirely value-neutral appraisal of its motives and consequences. Notoriously, Hume's own answer to this question rejected wholly a priori reflection on the ideas involved in the premises and conclusion. (The transition is therefore, on Hume's lights, no "demonstration" of its conclusion.) Instead, he invoked special impressions of reflection: feelings of approbation and disapprobation without which, he argued, distinctively moral judgments cannot be executed (1739–40/2000, 3.1.1.26 [SBN 468–69]).

Importantly, on Hume's account, once grammatically descriptive judgments of virtue and vice are in place, an inference from them to grammatically normative propositions asserting our moral obligations proves easily explicable. It is easy to see, Hume claimed, that we judge ourselves obligated not to steal simply because we judge stealing vicious. What is hard to make out is the more basic inference that leads us to judge that stealing is a vice. Does it involve sympathy with the victims of theft and those who find themselves in the company of thieves? How might sympathy affect the transition? It must of course be admitted that contemporary philosophers have not followed Hume along this path, and have indeed puzzled over the relationship between judgments of vice and judgments of obligation. But we all agree with Hume in looking elsewhere for the more basic transition from "is" to "ought."

Our concern, then, is not merely semantic, nor wholly epistemic, but partly semantic and partly epistemic in nature. We draw a logical, semantic, or metaphysical distinction when insisting that the argument for which we are looking has value-neutral premises that *entail* its value-laden conclusion; but we impose an epistemic condition when asking whether the inference we have described might yield moral *knowledge* or *rationalize* our moral beliefs.

5.2 In search of an epistemologically valuable moral deduction

If you are to gain deductively grounded moral knowledge of some conclusion that you have drawn from a set of value-neutral premises, your premises must entail your conclusion. But what beyond this must be in place?

Let us first suppose that you actually know the premises from which your reasoning proceeds. (This immediately precludes inferring any moral knowledge from the supposed infallibility of the Torah, Bible, or Koran. The testimony of gurus and false prophets is ruled out as well.) You might then attempt to infer knowledge of an "ought" from a true "is" with the aid of a *deontic logic* specifying which value-neutral statements entail which statements of morality.[4]

Consider, for instance, our deontic concepts of *obligation* and *permission*, which resemble the modal concepts of *necessity* and *possibility* in certain important respects. We can always infer, without error, from the obligatory nature of an act to the impermissibility of its avoidance, just as we can always infer from the necessity of an event to the impossibility of its failing to occur. Can we find among these four concepts a valid inference from "is" to "ought"? Might knowledge of the inference's value-neutral premises supply us with knowledge of its moral conclusion?

We can start with a Kantian proposal: simply augment standard deontic logic with an additional axiom stating the possibility of our conjointly fulfilling all of our obligations. (The axiom rules out "moral tragedies" where an actor cannot help doing what he is morally obligated to avoid.) This Kantian maneuver will have the following two arguments come out valid:

6   It is impossible for X to act from duty.
Therefore,
7   X's not acting from duty is permissible.

8   X's acting from duty is obligatory.
Therefore,
9   X's acting from duty is possible.

But have we here inferred an "ought" from an "is"? Premise (8) is itself an "ought," so the second inference won't get it done, and the first inference looks too weak to get us what we want. That is, "Everything is permissible" sounds too much like a statement of Ivan Karamazov's skeptical worries to establish the existence of substantive moral knowledge, and the truth of (7) is compatible with the truth of Dostoyevsky's existential moan. (Since its truth is compatible with nihilism, (7) does not advance a genuine moral claim.) Of course, an inference from non-moral premises to "Something is morally obligatory" would do the trick, but it's hard to see how this particular rabbit might be pulled from our collective hat. We have yet to agree on any simple way of inferring from the necessity or possibility of a neutrally described state of affairs to some non-trivial conclusion of moral obligation.[5]

In fact, Kant looked beyond the link between "obligatory" and "possible" to our concepts of *desert* and *esteem* to find a more substantive basis for his derivations of the moral law (1785/2002, 13–15 [Ak 4:397–99]). In particular, he claimed that the moral excellence of acting from a sense of duty is analytically or conceptually ensured, as we need only think of what is involved in someone's acting from obligation to know that the motive is "unconditionally" valuable. His now famous discussion of the matter concerns an honest shopkeeper who charges the fair price to a customer he knows he can cheat, where the shopkeeper acts fairly not out of self-interest, prudence, kindness, or fellow feeling, but because he knows it is his moral duty to do so.

10 X acted out of a sense of duty.
Therefore,
11 X deserves moral praise or respect.

But the problems with deriving an "ought" from an "is" in this way make themselves known to us as soon as we try to interpret "acting from a sense of duty." Suppose we take this to mean, as in Kant's example, acting from *knowledge* of one's duty. Then, as only truths can be known, (10) entails that X has a moral obligation to act as he knows he should act, and this entails that there are indeed moral facts. But it seems we cannot know that X *knows* that he has a moral duty unless we *already* – or at least *therein* – know that there *exists* such a duty. Thus, while the intra-moral transition from "X acted from his knowledge of his moral duty" to "X deserves esteem" is a matter of some importance to moral theorists, our knowledge of the first of these propositions is itself moral knowledge. If we think of the sense of duty as infallible, we here derive knowledge of an "ought" from knowledge of an "ought." We do not derive knowledge of an "ought" from knowledge of an "is."

Suppose, then, that we interpret "acting from a sense of duty" so that it encompasses cases in which we act from *false beliefs* regarding our obligations. Then our knowledge of our premise is indeed value-neutral, but the inference is arguably invalid. The Nazi soldier might have ignored the cries of those he hustled off to the gas chamber out of a misplaced sense of obligation, but it would be a mistake to characterize this person or his actions as morally excellent or praiseworthy.

But mightn't the Nazi's motives demand respect even if his behavior does not? Perhaps. But it does not take a moral skeptic to think otherwise. We need only maintain that charging your easily duped customers the regular price out of a sense of obligation is a morally good thing to do, whereas marching Jews to their deaths is properly regarded with unmitigated horror no matter what its motive.

A perhaps more promising strategy for the Kantian to pursue would be to augment "acting from a sense of duty" with Kant's positive descriptions of the moral law. For instance, we might consider substituting in the "formula of humanity" rendition of the categorical imperative discussed in chapter 4.

10' X did what he did because he thought doing otherwise would involve treating someone (or someone's "humanity") as a mere means to his own ends.

Therefore,

11 X deserves moral praise or respect.

Premise (10') is surely an "is" proposition, as the claim that someone acted from a particular belief needn't be moral in content even if that belief is itself moral in subject matter. (That one knows something entails its truth; that one believes something is compatible with its falsity.) And it is at any rate plausible that the concepts X entertains in formulating the categorical imperative are themselves value-neutral.[6] The problem here, though, is that acting from what one takes to be the substance of Kant's law is almost certainly not a guarantee of moral excellence; and, as a result, it is arguable that (10') does not entail (11).

To see this, consider that Kant himself grasped the various incarnations of the categorical imperative sufficiently well to give them their initial articulation. So the suggestion that he never really grasped the categorical imperative is somewhat implausible.[7] But Kant's having an adequate grasp of the concepts *means, ends, humanity,* and so on, did not prevent him from falsely inferring that the categorical imperative prohibits such things as masturbation and lying to prevent murder (1797/1996). So, with this in mind, consider:

10" Immanuel refrained from masturbating as an adult – despite experiencing an extreme degree of sexual frustration – because he thought proceeding otherwise would involve treating his own humanity as a mere means to his ends.

Therefore,

11 Immanuel deserves moral praise or respect.

Our conclusion (11) might be false even on the supposition of our premise (10"); so the argument from (10') to (11) is invalid. At the very least, we must allow that questioning its validity stops well short of moral skepticism. We need only maintain that observing a blanket prohibition on masturbation is almost always silly, no matter how seriously the prude takes traditional religious prohibitions on the practice. In sum, the Kantian proposals are controversial because many of us think that motives deserve moral praise or esteem only when they are aimed at the avoidance of *genuinely* immoral outcomes, or the production of what are *in fact* morally good or choiceworthy states of affairs.

The problems we have uncovered with the Kantian approach are no accident. An inference cannot be valid unless a general principle derivable from that inference is true without exception and necessarily so. For example, *modus ponens* arguments are those in which one infers a conclusion Q from premises P and If P then Q. And modus ponens arguments are valid only because "Necessarily, if P then Q, and P, then Q" is true for all values of

"P" and "Q" that admit of truth and falsity. *Disjunctive syllogism* arguments are those in which one infers Q from premises P or Q and not-P. And disjunctive syllogisms are valid only because "Necessarily, if P or Q and not-P, then Q" is similar in status. (See sections 8.3–4 for further discussion of these matters.) Thus, we can find a valid inference of a moral conclusion, Q, from a value-neutral premise, P, only if the moral principle "If P, then Q" is necessarily true without exception. Our two Kantian proposals came to naught because "If X acted from his (fallible) sense of duty, then X deserves esteem" and "If X acted from his belief in the categorical imperative, then X deserves respect" do seem to admit of exceptions.

In other words, our search for an epistemically valuable, deductively valid inference from "is" to "ought" depends for its success on the existence of a necessarily true moral principle. And, as we saw when evaluating intuitionism in chapter 4, there is some doubt as to whether there exist simple, non-disjunctive, exception-free moral principles. If a moral principle is to marry simplicity with truth, it must incorporate a "catch-all" hedge.

Clearly, arguments that contain hedged moral principles as premises cannot affect the needed inference from neutral observations to moral verdicts. So let us consider, instead, arguments with hedged moral conclusions. Judith Jarvis Thomson (1990) offers a number of examples, including:

12 If C rings D's doorbell he will thereby cause D pain.
Therefore,
13 Other things being equal, C ought not ring D's doorbell.

14 B promised to pay Smith five dollars.
Therefore,
15 Other things being equal, B ought to pay Smith five dollars.

Are these valid arguments from value-neutral premises to moral conclusions? Might knowledge of their neutral premises provide us with moral knowledge?

Well, like Ross' term "prima facie," Thomson's "other things being equal" admits of different interpretations. Indeed, Thomson herself distinguishes between its *epistemic* and *metaphysical* readings (1990, 14–15). On the epistemic reading, (13) says that there is some *evidence* that C ought not ring D's doorbell, and (15) says that there is some *reason to believe* that B ought to pay Smith five dollars. In the absence of contrary evidence, or substantive reasons to think otherwise, you, who accept the arguments' premises, ought to believe that C should refrain from doorbell ringing and that B ought to pay up.

Suppose, then, that we adopt the epistemic reading and render Thomson's arguments in explicitly epistemic terms. We can concentrate on an epistemic interpretation of the first member of the pair:

12' You know that if C rings D's doorbell he will thereby cause D pain. Therefore,
13' In the absence of contrary evidence, you are justified in believing that C ought not ring D's doorbell.

A skeptic might object that (13') is not a moral proposition, as you can be justified in believing that C ought not ring D's doorbell even if your belief is false and there are no moral truths to be known. But this response will not rescue all-out moral skepticism, as the validity of (12')–(13') is itself sufficient to refute the strongest theses to which moral skeptics have been attracted. That is, if the argument under review is sound, you can arrive at a justified belief in the immorality of C's ringing D's doorbell from your neutral knowledge of the pain it would produce – and you can accomplish this feat without the aid of "additional" moral premises. (Here, "additional premises" denotes all those that you could fail to either know or justifiably believe compatible with your having the knowledge mentioned in (12').) Though your justifiably believing that C would act immorally were he to ring the bell is compatible with your failing to know the proposition in question, genuinely justified (or rationally maintained) moral beliefs are more than many skeptics are willing to allow.

But is the argument valid? Though Thomson tells us that D is "wired up" to his doorbell, no further details are provided (1990, 13). Suppose, then, that this is all we know about the case. Are we then really justified in believing that C ought not ring the bell? Perhaps D has asked C to ring the bell whenever it looks as though D is going to do something immoral or imprudent. Or perhaps D is depressed, and C, his medical student friend, is using the doorbell ringing as an inexpensive alternative to electro-shock therapy. Perhaps C and D are engaged in some *avant garde* performance art. Who is to know?

Of course, Thomson might argue that these possible alternatives to the immorality of D's actions are too far-flung to undermine the justification with which you would infer the immorality of the doorbell ringing from your knowledge of the fact that it will cause D pain. After all, when we exclude rabid skeptics from the conversation, the mere possibility that you are dreaming or hallucinating is not thought sufficient to undermine the justification with which you believe that things are as they look. Instead, you now know that you are reading this book because that is how it looks. You would need some positive reason to think that you are in fact dreaming or hallucinating to really undermine the rationality with which you believe that things are as they look to be.[8]

But is the rationality of inferring that C ought not ring the bell from your bare knowledge of the pain this will cause comparable to the rationality with which you believe that you are reading a book because it looks that way? The case Thomson describes is bizarre in its own right, so it is hard to know what to say about the matter. In the absence of a careful first-level review I can report only my own "intuition." And I think that knowing that C has caused D pain in the manner envisioned would warrant the *suspicion* that C has done something wrong, but that confidence beyond suspicion would be unfair to C.

The odder the case, the less reliable the intuition. Perhaps, then, we would be better served by considering the more mundane argument:

12" You know that C caused D pain.
Therefore,
13" In the absence of contrary evidence, you are justified in believing that C
oughtn't to have done what he did.

But this inference is almost certainly invalid. For what does (12") tell you? C may have given D a much-needed – though quite painful – shot of medication. Or perhaps C is D's coach, and is forcing the athlete to exercise "through the pain" so as to achieve truly extraordinary results. Or mightn't D have requested and then enjoyed C's rough methods of lovemaking? The cases in which causing pain is in no way immoral are legion. In what percentage of cases is pain's infliction genuinely wrong? Is the percentage sufficiently high that we can reliably infer immorality from the causing of pain? If the connection is a reliable one, is the reliability sufficiently entrenched or sufficiently obvious to supply us with justified beliefs in the absence of knowledge of its reliability? Again, it does not take a skeptic to deny the validity of Thomson's inference. Many of us who think that there are moral facts, and that we justifiably believe many of these facts, would still deny that justification for our beliefs can be derived from the extraordinarily slender evidence that Thomson describes.

What then of the metaphysical reading? On this, the "stronger" interpretation that Thomson favors, "All things being equal, C ought not ring D's doorbell" should be understood as saying that C's ringing D's doorbell is a "wrong-making" feature of C's action (1990, 14–15). Similarly, "All things being equal, C ought not cause D pain," means that the infliction of pain will "make" C's act wrong unless something prevents it from doing so.

Now, though Thomson's metaphysical proposal is only as clear as the metaphysical picture on which it relies – a model on which certain neutral features will "create" or "generate" immorality unless blocked, swamped, undermined or overrun – we can try to avoid the associated causal imagery. A less metaphysically fraught claim would be that necessarily, inducing pain is in some *way* wrong. Whatever good, right, or moral features a pain-causing action might have, it must also have at least one bad, wrong, or immoral aspect.

12   If C rings D's doorbell he will thereby cause D pain.
Therefore,
13'''   C's ringing D's doorbell is wrong in some respect.

When we "hedge" our moral conclusion in this fashion, do we therein secure its validity?

The question retains some of the controversy that attended our epistemic interpretation of the argument. First, suppose that C is non-culpably ignorant of the fact that he is causing D pain. Then, though the event has bad consequences, and we would advise C not to ring the bell, we might be thought to go overboard in calling his act "wrong" or "immoral." To respond to this objection, Thomson must say that immoral intent is not necessary for immorality. And the "intuitions" supporting this reply seem somewhat parochial.

Second, the pain caused may be the necessary means to the achievement of lesser overall suffering (as in the delivering of medical treatments), or the achievement of something exceedingly valuable (as in the pursuit of athletic or artistic greatness). And D may have enlisted C to bring about one of these desirable results. It is far from clear that pain caused in such circumstances is in any way immoral. To respond to this objection, Thomson might revert to her preferred metaphysics. The infliction of pain would have "made" the act immoral if it hadn't been "prevented" from doing so by its being the mutually desired means to the reduction of suffering, or the achievement of excellence. Again, the value of this reply depends upon the coherence of Thomson's quasi-causal conception of the moral realm.

But third, and finally, there are those Kantian theorists who think that a guilty man's pain and suffering are actually good "in themselves" (Kant, 1785/2002, 9 [Ak 4:393]; Kant, 1797/1996; Dancy, 1993, 61). For instance, in Hegel's view:

> Punishment is the right of the criminal. It is an act of his own will. The violation of right has been proclaimed by the criminal as his own right. His crime is the negation of right. Punishment is the negation of this negation, and consequently an affirmation of right, solicited and forced upon the criminal by himself. (Hegel, *Elements of the Philosophy of Right* (1821), quoted in Murphy, 1973)

According to the *strict Hegelian*, causing a criminal pain is obligatory rather than impermissible, good rather than bad, right rather than wrong. If this is right, the action C performs when intentionally causing D pain may have no wrong-making aspects whatsoever. Admittedly, the Hegelian view is somewhat harsh (cf. Ross, 1930, 63). But it stops well short of moral skepticism. And it presents a substantive obstacle to any modification of Thomson's premise (12) that would secure the uncontroversial validity of her argument.[9]

It seems, in summary, that "hedging" our moral conclusion in the two ways that Thomson suggests doesn't get the job done. To avoid controversy in deducing "ought" from "is" we should complicate the *premises* of our argument rather than (or in addition to) hedging its conclusion.[10]

And there is no need to resort to science fiction. As we saw above when discussing Madoff's Ponzi scheme, when we are willing to call someone's act "immoral" without qualification, the more thoughtful among us ordinarily have a rather sophisticated set of reasons for doing so. Consider, for example, the evidence of Saddam Hussein's villainy that is most commonly cited when arguing that his ousting was itself a "good thing" however horrible the violent means through which it was affected and the anarchic consequences that soon followed.

16 By deploying chemical weapons against the Kurds, Saddam was driven by his paranoia to knowingly kill and injure many civilians, while neither saving the life nor substantially mitigating the suffering of anyone.

Therefore,

17 Saddam acted immorally.

Of course, a dedicated Ba'athist might argue that premise (16) is false, as the suffering of Iraqi soldiers at the hands of the Iranians was forestalled when Saddam gassed the purportedly traitorous Kurds. But we can suppose – as is surely right – that the Ba'athist is just mistaken about the facts of the case. As (16) is a value-neutral premise, the assumption that it is not only true, but that its truth is known to you, begs none of the questions we are trying to answer.

We must, then, inquire into the argument's validity. Is it possible for (16) to be true and (17) not?[11] Our premise depicts a dictator motivated by his paranoid fear of insurrection; who destroys the lives of many civilians; in a manner prejudicial to the members of a particular ethnic group; while adding substantially to the store of human suffering; without any compensating gain in either happiness or the preservation of human life. It therefore describes the kind of act considered immoral by Kantians, utilitarians, virtue theorists, and lay-people the world over. So it is difficult to see how the validity of our argument could be denied without recourse to nihilism. If anyone ever does act immorally, then it would seem that Saddam actually did act immorally, so long as the events transpired in the way we have described.[12]

Since we are discussing epistemic skepticism rather than nihilism, we can continue to assume that nihilism is false. And when it is wedded to the conclusion that we have just drawn, this allows us to assume, again for the sake of discussion, that (16) and (17) are both true. And yet these assumptions are still not enough to focus our attention on wholly epistemic forms of moral skepticism, as complications arise from the *necessity* that marks genuine entailments.

The nihilist we encountered in chapter 3 would insist that our moral conclusion – (17) – is *actually* false: Saddam didn't act immorally, because *no one* acts immorally. But a sophisticated skeptic might reject the validity of our argument by restricting his claim to the *possibility* of (16)'s being true and (17) false. Even if Saddam did act immorally, if there are possible worlds in which Saddam fails to act immorally when gassing the Kurds in the manner we have described, our premise does not really entail its conclusion. And if our premise does not entail our conclusion, we cannot deduce knowledge of the latter from our knowledge of the former.

Again, if the skeptic just says that there is a world where (16) is true and (17) is false, this will do nothing to shake our conviction in the argument's validity. Instead, the skeptic must describe this world in enough detail to diminish our confidence in its impossibility. We have already addressed the arguments for actual world nihilism that a skeptic might deploy for this purpose. Are these arguments strengthened when their conclusion is weakened in the way we have imagined?

Suppose the skeptic admits, for the sake of argument, that our world contains a god who legislates and enforces moral sanctions, while insisting that there are at least possible worlds in which a being of this kind either does not exist or fails to flex his power. Or suppose the skeptic pursues a similar tactic with regard to motives and reasons internalism. If Saddam's immorality relies on the truth of these doctrines, and they are only contingently true – holding in some but not all worlds in which Saddam massacres the Kurds – our argument's premise will not entail its conclusion.

There are three ways of answering the more subtle skeptical arguments that result when the skeptic "goes modal" in this way. First, we might argue that divine sanctions and the truth of strong forms of motives and reasons internalism are not necessary for the existence of moral facts. If this is right, worlds without a divine moral enforcer, and worlds without internally motivating or reason-providing moral judgments, are not yet worlds where Saddam fails to act immorally. The skeptic would have to do more to describe a world in which (16) is true and (17) not.

Second, we might argue that motives and reasons internalism are necessary truths, and that god (qua moral enforcer) exists necessarily. If there are no worlds without the requisite features, the skeptic has yet to describe a possible world in which our conclusion is false and our premise true.

Third, we might admit that our argument is invalid, while pointing to the truth of its premise. Given its truth, we might argue, our conclusion could fail to obtain only were the world vastly different from what it actually is. If there are worlds without divine sanctions, and worlds where moral judgments fail to rationalize and motivate, but these worlds are radically different from our own, their mere existence need not undermine the rationality of confidently inferring (17) from (16). Our premise might provide us with excellent evidence of Saddam's immorality, even while failing to entail our conclusion. If this is right, knowledge of the neutral facts of the case might warrant a level of confidence sufficient for knowledge of Saddam's immorality, even if this confidence falls short of certainty. We might know that Saddam did the wrong thing in gassing the Kurds even if we are less sure of this than we are that $2 + 2 = 4$.

Note that the controversy we have been describing is entirely metaphysical in nature, concerning, as it does, the existence of god and the modal status of propositions linking our knowledge of our moral obligations to our motives and reasons for action. It therefore lies to the side of our current focus on wholly epistemic arguments. So let us suppose, if only for the sake of discussion, that chapter 3 has convinced us that moral obligations needn't be intrinsically motivating, reason-providing, or supported by divine sanctions. If we reject nihilism on these grounds, we can then suppose that (16)–(17) is in fact a *valid* argument. But does that mean you have deduced an "ought" from an "is"? In reasoning to Saddam's immorality from an accurate journalistic account of his actions against the Kurds, have you found your way to moral knowledge?

5.3 Assessing the epistemological value of our deduction

You know what transpired between Saddam and the Kurds. Or, at least, you know the value-neutral facts of the case. And we are supposing that you have inferred from these facts a conclusion they entail: Saddam acted immorally. Can't we then conclude that you know that Saddam acted immorally? Adapting a label of Paul Boghossian's (2000, 2001, 2003), we might call the view that would license this conclusion "simple inferential externalism" (SIE).

> *Simple inferential externalism*: if S knows P and directly infers from it some conclusion C that it entails, then S knows C.

If SIE is true, the suppositions we have made allow us to conclude that you have deduced moral knowledge from your knowledge of wholly value-neutral premises. You have inferred "ought" from "is."

The problem here is that SIE is not true, as simple inferential externalism faces a host of compelling counter-examples.

To see why SIE will not do, picture a classroom in some backwoods locale where the general population does not yet know that water is H_2O. The students are told that the test tubes before them contain water, and it is their job to measure the liquid's viscosity to determine whether water is H_2O or the superficially similar but significantly denser substance D_2O (heavy water). One student, Rush, does not perform the required experiments, but infers that the liquid before him is H_2O directly upon hearing that it is water.

Water Leap
18 There is water in the test tube.
Therefore,
19 There is H_2O in the test tube.

Now, though Rush is prone to describing his belief as an "intuition" of the essence of the liquid before him, he does not in fact have some novel method – or occult faculty – that enables him to determine the facts of chemistry without performing the requisite experiments. Indeed, if he continues answering the teacher's questions in this vein, his grade for the course will be a failing 50 percent. So does Rush know that the liquid before him is H_2O?

A first-level claim: most of us would say that Rush neither knows nor justifiably believes that his test tube contains H_2O, and this is so even though we know that the truth of what he believes is entailed by the premise from which he infers it. Next, a second-level claim: we are right to regard the matter in this way as Rush is appropriately criticized for having leaped to judgment. His belief is true, and his inference valid, but he is justly impugned for running ahead of the evidence. Though he has the level of conviction necessary for knowledge, Rush has just guessed the correct answer. And knowledge is no guess.

Of course, our knowledge that water is H_2O is a posteriori, not a priori, as it is grounded in the testimony of chemists, whose knowledge of chemical theory in turn rests on observation of the natural world. In consequence, the validity of Water Leap cannot be known a priori. (For instance, no one can know via reflection alone that if (18) is true, (19) must be true as well.) Might this fact explain why Rush must actually perform the requisite experiment to truly know that there is H_2O in the test tube? Might the a posteriori character of the connection between (18) and (19) provide us with a fully general explanation of the hastiness involved in his executing Water Leap?

With this thought in mind, we might amend simple externalism as follows:

> *Augmented inferential externalism*: if S knows P, directly infers from it some C that it entails, and the validity of this inference can be known through reflection alone, then S knows C.

If our revised principle were true, you could gain knowledge of the immorality of Saddam's treatment of the Kurds from your value-neutral knowledge of what transpired, so long as it can be known a priori that (16) entails (17).

So, we must ask: can we know in a wholly a priori fashion that there is no possible world in which Saddam fails to do something immoral when knowingly slaughtering civilians and neither saving a life nor substantially mitigating anyone's suffering? Again, it is hard to imagine such a world. But must experience enter into our justification for believing it impossible? Perhaps it need not; for the rationalists encountered in chapter 4 may be right in thinking that the most diligent efforts to conceive of such a world must come to nothing precisely because of our shared conception of the link between immorality and the intentional infliction of death and mayhem. And our conceiving of the relationship between suffering and immorality in this way might be thought to provide us with wholly a priori knowledge of our argument's validity.

On the other hand, there are modal claims known through observation. You know that the glass must fall if it is dropped because you have observed the work of gravity firsthand. So mightn't observations play some role in your knowing that Saddam's actions must be immoral so long as they meet the description advanced by our premise (Williamson, 2007)? Mightn't experience of pain and suffering, or a pained awareness of humiliation, fear, and despair play an essential role in your knowledge of the immorality that necessarily attends their intentional infliction? It is, to say the least, extraordinarily difficult to pry apart the respective roles of experience, emotion, and reflection in generating your belief in the immorality of Saddam's crimes. So, while the moral rationalist thinks that experience justifies belief in (16) but need play no role in the inference of (17) from (16), nor any role in justifying your belief in the inference's validity, the truth of moral rationalism remains controversial.[13]

If the validity of any argument can be proved to the skeptic's satisfaction, then you can prove your argument's validity by recasting it as a modus ponens inference.

16 By deploying chemical weapons against the Kurds, Saddam was driven by his paranoia to knowingly kill and injure many civilians, while neither saving the life nor substantially mitigating the suffering of anyone.
*   If Saddam was driven by his paranoia to knowingly kill and injure civilians while neither saving a life nor substantially mitigating the suffering of anyone, then he acted immorally.
Therefore,
17 Saddam acted immorally.

But if we add (*) to the premises on which you rely for your knowledge of the immorality of Saddam's actions, we can no longer say that you have deduced an "ought" from an "is," as (*) advances a substantive moral claim. The dialectic will then play itself out in predictable fashion, with the skeptic insisting that you do not know that Saddam acted immorally because you do not know (*), the moral principle on which your belief is premised. (Recall, that the skeptic joins Locke in arguing that you could not know (*) non-inferentially, as there can be no non-inferential moral knowledge; but the skeptic also insists, against Locke, that any inference to (*) must also involve a moral premise: a premise that you could not know without a supporting inference. The regress that then ensues provides the skeptic with his grounds for skepticism.) So, while recasting your argument in this way would ease the proof of its validity, the victory would be "Pyrrhic" in more than one sense of the word. In winning the battle against the skeptic, you would have lost the war. We would once again be forced to choose between skepticism and intuitionism.

Still, if, as a matter of descriptive psychological fact, everyone who actually has inferred (17) from (16) has assumed (*) in the process, then we should add this premise to our model to achieve a greater level of accuracy. Indeed, if we are psychologically *incapable* of moving directly from our value-neutral knowledge of what Saddam has done to a belief in its immorality, then we *must* alter our model in the manner suggested. If this means acquiescing in skepticism, or positing non-inferential moral knowledge, or embracing a coherentist conception of the justification enjoyed by our moral beliefs, we must follow our reasoning to one of these destinations, however unpalatable that might initially seem.

But how could (*) be thought psychologically necessary? Surely, we do not always infer in accordance with modus ponens, disjunctive syllogism, and the other rules of natural deduction that license the proofs of first-order logic. Nor do we always conform to either these rules or the rules that make for good inductions, abductions, or probabilistic inferences. For, at the very least, we sometimes make *mistakes* in our thinking. We assume the antecedent, generalize from a single case, commit the gambler's fallacy, and so on. Thus, while the Cartesian might say that in inferring (17) directly from (16), you commit some *fallacy* – a mistake you could only correct by incorporating (*) as a premise – he cannot reasonably argue that the commission of this fallacy is *impossible*. Indeed, whether directly inferring Saddam's immorality from a value-neutral description of what happened is fallacious – and so open to criticism – is precisely what is at issue when we argue over the possibility of arriving at moral knowledge from wholly value-neutral premises. That we should not reason in this way – but should instead limit ourselves to rules like modus ponens – cannot be assumed.

We are then justified in sticking to our original reconstruction of your reasoning as (16)–(17). Readers who are introspectively certain that they used (*) to reach (17) should treat the rest of this discussion as an investigation of someone else's thinking — the reasoning of some possible thinker who directly infers "ought" from "is" in the manner described.

But sticking with our original model does not allow us to entirely dodge worries about our knowledge of (*). For we are now confronting a question that is importantly comparable to the issue left standing at the close of our last chapter: do you know that your simple argument for Saddam's immorality is valid? Do you know this a priori? If you do reason in a valid manner when directly inferring the immorality of Saddam's actions from your neutral assessment of what happened in the case, the fact that your reasoning is valid is itself a moral proposition. "Necessarily, if it is true that Saddam acted thus and so, then it is true that he acted immorally," advances a moral claim. So if, as we have been assuming for the sake of discussion, Locke is right in denying the existence of non-inferential moral knowledge, you cannot know a priori that your argument is valid without inferring its validity from some other propositions that you know in a wholly a priori manner.

Can you accomplish this feat here? If you are anything like me, you do not have access to anything like a formal proof. You don't, for instance, have a proof on hand comparable to a logician's demonstration of the validity of all modus ponens arguments. (See chapter 8 for a description of this kind of demonstration.) Indeed, it's probable that all you have in the case on hand is one or both of the non-inferential "justifications" we described in chapter 4 when discussing intuitionism: (a) your failure to describe or imagine worlds in which Saddam does what we've said he has done and yet does not act immorally (and your observation that no one you know has yet articulated such a possibility); and (b) the anger, indignation, and sadness you experience when you do your best to think of the paranoid massacre of civilians from the perspectives of those involved.

We saw in chapter 4 that controversy besets the claim that these are reliable ways to form and renew our beliefs in moral principles. And similar questions will bedevil the claim that they provide us with non-inferential knowledge of our moral argument's validity. But we can put these worries to the side. For we have assumed for the sake of inquiry that intuitionism is false. And this implies that you cannot have non-inferential knowledge of your argument's validity. Neither empathy nor your imagination will do.

Can you convert your intuitive justification into an inference with which you can verify, in a wholly a priori manner, that your argument is valid? The prospects seem rather dim. For consider, as an example, the inference we might construct from your failure of imagination:

20 I cannot imagine how Saddam could have massacred the Kurds in the
    way described without therein acting immorally.
Therefore,
21 Saddam could not have massacred the Kurds in the way described
    without therein acting immorally.

The skeptic will allow that you have the introspective knowledge reported
by (20). But he will insist that it is a posteriori. Moreover, (20)–(21) is not
valid. And even if the truth of (20) provides you with good evidence for the
truth of (21), your knowledge that this is so must be a posteriori as well.

So let us suppose, if only for the sake of argument, that whatever non-
inferential justification you might be thought to have for believing in your
argument's validity cannot be successfully converted into an a priori inferential justification for the same conclusion. In consequence, you cannot
prove that your argument is valid in a wholly a priori manner. Still, mightn't
there exist someone, somewhere who has thought about your argument
long enough to deduce its validity from premises that *she* knows in a wholly
a priori fashion? If our augmented form of inferential externalism proves
correct, and some clever moral theorist – either now or in the future – could
prove your argument's validity without appealing to facts known via experience or observation, you will have used this argument to derive knowledge
of Saddam's immorality from your knowledge of a value-neutral premise
describing his gassing of the Kurds. The fact that the relevant soundness
proof currently evades your grasp need be of no direct concern.

On the other hand, if the proof cannot be had at all; and such a proof
really is necessary for a priori knowledge of the argument's validity; and
a priori knowledge of the argument's validity must indeed be possible if
the argument is to provide you with knowledge of its conclusion; then
the skeptic will have won the day. Admittedly, there are a lot of "ifs" conditioning this claim. But the suppositions we have made at least allow the
terms of the debate to be more precisely specified.

Note, however, that proofs of the soundness of inference rules like modus
ponens are, historically speaking, of quite recent vintage. And the reasoning
we employ when executing these proofs often involves the use of the very
rules whose soundness is being proved. (For an example, see chapter 8,
where we reason in accord with modus ponens when proving the soundness
of modus ponens.) Thus, whether soundness proofs play an important role
in providing us with a priori knowledge of the validity of modus ponens
arguments is open to debate (cf. Dummett, 1978b; Boghossian, 2000).

Indeed, we can press this point. For the Lockean skeptic does not reject all knowledge. He allows, for instance, that we have non-inferential knowledge of basic mathematical truths, and he allows that we can extend our knowledge beyond these facts by reasoning in accord with modus ponens and other rules of inference. But now suppose that Locke was wrong in thinking that we have non-inferential knowledge of logical truths. Suppose that is, that there is no such thing as logical intuition. And suppose, too, that the Lockean cannot prove that modus ponens arguments are sound without using modus ponens. Surely, what is good for the goose is good for the gander. So will the Lockean skeptic then allow you to use an inference rule that permits the derivation of (17) from (16) in your proof of your argument's validity? The rule in question is the rather unwieldy:

"Immoral"-Intro # 1
X was driven by his paranoia to knowingly kill and injure many Ys, while neither
    saving the life nor substantially mitigating the suffering of anyone.
X acted immorally.

How does reasoning in accord with "Immoral"-Intro # 1 when proving its soundness differ from the execution of a modus ponens inference in a proof of the soundness of modus ponens?

In sum, it is far from obvious what kind of proof we would need to have in hand to establish the validity of your argument in a wholly a priori manner. And if we do need a proof that is in some respects comparable to the logician's proof of the soundness of modus ponens, the possibility remains that moral theorists working on the analysis of the crucial terms involved in your argument – that is, "killed," "injured," "paranoid," "immoral," and so forth– will eventually settle on such a proof. In this eventuality, the truth of augmented externalism would allow us to prove the moral skeptic wrong. Whether we can refute a skeptic of this stripe would depend on what theorists must do to establish a priori knowledge of your argument's validity, and, if proofs are needed to accomplish this task, what kinds of proof might be developed.

But, unfortunately for us, though augmented externalism is less problematic than its simpler variant, it is similarly vulnerable to counter-example. For consider, in this light, the Pythagorean theorem, which tells us that the length of the hypotenuse of a right triangle is the square-root of the sum of the squares of the lengths of its two other sides. More economically: $a^2 + b^2 = c^2$. Now abstract away from the sides of right triangles to consider the equation we have just used to represent their interrelation. Does an equation of this sort hold among integers when our exponent is increased to something greater than 2? *Fermat's last theorem* conjectures that it does not. In the seventeenth century, Pierre de Fermat (1601/7–65) proved the special case where the exponent is 4, but its generalization remained a conjecture until Andrew Wiles' celebrated proof emerged in 1995 – a proof that utilized advanced mathematical techniques that Fermat could not have anticipated. Now, with all this in mind, consider Swifty, a rather incautious student of math, who, in complete ignorance of Wiles' results, infers the fully general conjecture from Fermat's proof of the special case.

Swifty's Leap

22   There are no positive integers x, y, and z such that $x^4 + y^4 = z^4$.

Therefore,

23   For all integers n>2: there are no positive integers x, y, and z such that $x^n + y^n = z^n$.

Since Swifty's conclusion is, presumably, a necessary truth, and since its necessity is a priori knowable, it is a priori knowable that necessarily, if Swifty's premise is true, then his conclusion is true as well. The validity of Swifty's Leap can therefore be established using wholly a priori methods. (Though, admittedly, when establishing the validity of the argument in this manner, a philosophically minded mathematician would not follow Swifty in inferring Fermat's last theorem from a single instance.) And yet, if common thought is to be trusted, Swifty is surely guilty of rushing to judgment. Swifty's Leap is no less of a leap than is Rush's, and Swifty's spurious claims to mathematical insight notwithstanding, he no more knows the conclusion of his inference than does Rush. In the absence of adequate testimony, Wiles' proof is essential to knowledge of Fermat's last theorem, and few people have the mathematical sophistication needed to so much as grasp its content. Thus, it seems that a valid argument can fail to provide you with knowledge of its conclusion even when you know its premises and its validity is itself a priori knowable (cf. Boghossian, 2001, 2003). In consequence, even if it is a priori knowable that the immorality of Saddam's actions is entailed by their destructive nature, if you do not yet know that your argument is valid, you may fail to acquire the knowledge that Saddam acted immorally by directly inferring as much from the suffering he spread amongst the Kurds.

We must, therefore, raise the bar on the epistemic value of a valid argument, where the obvious fix would swap modal talk of a priori *knowability* with a requirement of actual a priori *knowledge*. Might it be that the validity of your argument must not only be a priori knowable, but, in fact, a priori known to you, if you are to derive knowledge of its conclusion from your knowledge of its premises? Again adapting Boghossian's terminology, we can call the resulting view "simple inferential internalism."

> *Simple inferential internalism*: if S knows P and directly infers from it some C that it entails, S knows C only if she also knows that her inference is valid.

The suggested strengthening is surely strong enough to impugn the inferences of Rush and Swifty described above. Indeed, it may be sufficiently strong to undermine the ordinary citizen's knowledge of Saddam's immorality. (Again, whether it does undermine that knowledge depends, in part, on the prospects for intuitionism, and on whether our inability to describe or imagine worlds in which (16) is true and (17) is not provides us with knowledge of our argument's validity.)[14] But we can leave this matter to the side for the moment, as the requirement is almost certainly too strong. You can gain knowledge of the conclusion of a valid argument from your knowledge of its premises even if you neither consciously know nor explicitly represent its validity.

To see this, we need only consider Lily, a fifth-grader who performs her first chemistry experiment long before being exposed to a proof of the soundness of modus ponens. After being told by her teacher that the solution before her is acidic if it turns her blue litmus paper red, she performs the requisite test and reasons her way to the correct conclusion.

24 If a solution turns my blue litmus paper red, then it is acidic.
25 This solution turns my blue litmus paper red.
Therefore,
26 This solution is acidic.

Surely, all but the most skeptical among us will allow that Lily comes to know (26) by directly inferring it from her knowledge of (24) and (25). But though Lily has *executed* the inference from (24) and (25) to (26), she may not have *reflected upon* that inference at all. And if she has not reflected upon it, she is no position to consider whether it is valid, invalid, good, bad, or indifferent. Clearly, her acquiring rudimentary knowledge of chemistry in the way we have described is compatible with her failing to know that she accomplishes this feat by executing a modus ponens argument; just as it is compatible with her knowing nothing at all of the truth tables, Venn diagrams, or anything else that a theorist might use to prove the soundness of modus ponens and therein her argument's validity. Indeed, if she has not considered whether her argument is valid she cannot figure out that it is valid by trying and failing to imagine cases in which (24)–(25) is true and (26) false. Nor can she employ a purported faculty of logical insight wherein she "sees" the argument's validity in an intellectual manner comparable to the sensory manner in which the sighted among us can see the colors and shapes of the objects around us (Bealer 1998; Heumer, 2005; cf. Wright, 2001).

It seems then, that if Lily does know that her argument is a valid one, her knowledge of this fact is deeply tacit (Peacocke, 1998, 2000). Moreover, even if we are persuaded – on decidedly theoretical grounds – of the need to attribute to Lily some tacit *representation* of the validity of her argument, we will be left wondering whether this representation constitutes *knowledge* of the fact it represents. What distinguishes Lily's supposedly tacit representation of the validity of her reasoning from Rush's or Swifty's lucky guess at the validity of his?

Suppose, though, that we are persuaded that Lily must have some tacit representation of her argument's validity, and that we are further persuaded that this representation constitutes knowledge. Is the knowledge in question supposed to be grounded in an inference? We might suppose that it is, by supposing not only that Lily tacitly knows that her argument is valid, but that she has tacitly argued her way to this conclusion from her tacit knowledge of language and logic, including, we might hypothesize, her knowledge of such facts as that indicative conditionals with true antecedents and false consequents are all false. (This form of argument is specified in detail in chapter 8.) If this is right, then when we take our first logic class and prove the soundness of modus ponens in the way that we do, we are merely making explicit Socratic knowledge that we possessed all along.

Has Lily really performed a tacit inference of this kind? Surely, a well-grounded answer to this question would have to incorporate the best that the empirical study of psycho-semantics has to offer. More to the point here is the internalist's normative claim that Lily *must* have this tacit inferential knowledge of her argument's validity if she is to really *know*, via the explicit inference that we have described, that her solution is acidic. If the best psychological accounts reveal that simple modus ponens inferences are performed prior to tacit proof of their validity, must we conclude that these initial inferences fail to generate knowledge?

Note too the threat of epistemic regress. For if the internalist claims, on principled grounds, that Lily must tacitly know the validity of the explicit argument she executes when verifying the acidity of the solution before her, that same theorist would seem compelled to insist that Lily know the validity of this tacit argument itself. (She must tacitly know that the premises of her tacit proof of the soundness of modus ponens entail its conclusion.) But then her tacit knowledge of the validity of this tacit proof must either be non-inferentially grounded or supported by a distinct argument, the validity of which she also tacitly knows. It seems, then, that on pain of full-blown skepticism, coherentism, or infinite regress, the inferential internalist must allow people wholly non-inferential knowledge of the validity of at least some of their arguments, whether these arguments be tacit or explicit (cf. BonJour, 1980, 1985). Do we then contain innate representations of the validity of modus ponens arguments? Why think of these representations as knowledge? There are those theorists – Boghossian among them – who find these conjectures implausible, and the associated attempt to rescue simple inferential internalism not only desperate, but unpalatably obscure.

In sum, our externalist principles are too weak; and, on its most straightforward interpretations, our internalist principle is too strong. When you know an argument's premises, and infer from them some conclusion that they entail, your belief in that conclusion will be true. But reflection on cases reveals that these conditions are not sufficient to grant you knowledge of that conclusion, nor sufficient to justify your belief in its truth. If you also know that your premises entail your conclusion, then, in the absence of truly extraordinary circumstances, you will know your conclusion as well.[15] But though this provides us with the materials we need to construct a sufficient condition for the epistemic value of a valid argument, conditions that are both necessary and sufficient are not yet within reach.

Boghossian's own rather controversial response to this situation is to embrace an *inferential role* account of our possession of certain concepts (cf. Peacocke, 1992).[16] Even though Lily does not know that her modus ponens inference is valid, her execution of that inference provides her with knowledge of its conclusion. Why? Because, Boghossian argues, it is an inference she must perform and accept if she is to so much as grasp the concept associated with the indicative conditional. Since we must reason in accord with modus ponens to understand the word "if," Lily's inference is (to use Boghossian's words) "epistemically blameless." She can only be appropriately criticized for executing this inference if she can be blamed for so much as using indicative conditionals and employing the logical concept that they seemingly express.[17] In contrast, Swifty's Leap is not mandated by possession of the mathematical concepts of *integer*, *sum*, and *exponent* that we must grasp if we are to entertain its premise and conclusion, so Swifty needs additional premises and further bits of reasoning if he is to reach his result in an acceptable manner. If Boghossian is right, each of these more careful steps will be blameless so long as its performance is necessary for grasp of one or more of the concepts involved.

> *The inferential role account*: if S knows P and directly infers from it some C that it entails, then S knows C if and only if she either: (a) knows that her inference is valid, or (b) must infer as she does to grasp P or C.[18]

Now Boghossian's proposal is controversial even when it is restricted in scope to modus ponens, where the controversies stem, in part, from the very existence of philosophers who think the inference rule unsound. The most infamous renegade is Vann McGee (1985), whose assault began with a discussion of the 1980 US presidential election won by Ronald Reagan. A Democrat, Jimmy Carter, received the second-most votes, where Carter was followed in the polls by John Anderson, a Republican senator. With these facts in place, McGee describes an anxious voter supplying a counter-example to modus ponens in the days before the election:

27 If a Republican wins the election, then if it's not Reagan who wins, it will be Anderson.

28 A Republican will win the election.

Therefore,

29 If it's not Reagan who wins, it will be Anderson.

Are (27) and (28) true in the case, while (29) is false? The issues involved are subtle, as they seem to depend on McGee's rejection of certain – admittedly controversial – aspects of the classical semantics for indicative conditionals. (According to the classical account, (29) is made "vacuously" true by Reagan's victory.) But we need not concern ourselves with these matters here, for it is relatively uncontroversial that, as a *psychological* matter, McGee refuses to infer (29) from his knowledge of (27) and (28). So does McGee, an accomplished logician, fail to understand "if"?

Williamson (2003) argues that the inferential role account has this implication and that it must be rejected on these grounds. The attribution of concepts is a *holistic* matter. Thus, given a suitable background, we can properly attribute a logical concept to a person like McGee even when we know that he refuses to perform one or more of those inferences we might otherwise think necessary for the concept's possession. Indeed, Williamson's case against the inferential role account is only strengthened when we move from indicative conditionals and modus ponens to consider other less central concepts and forms of inference. The intuitionist denies that mathematical knowledge can be reached through the unaided application of double negation-elimination. (Establishing that the negation of some mathematical claim does not obtain falls short of establishing the claim itself; some more constructive demonstration of its truth is needed.) Does this mean, as Quine once suggested (1970/1983; cf. Dummett, 1978a), that the intuitionist and classical logician associate different concepts with "not"? Or must we agree with the intuitionist when he scolds, as overly hasty, those mathematicians who employ double negation-elimination in the unreflective manner in which Lily uses modus ponens? Nathan Salmon (1989) has argued for things that are impossible but possibly possible. (The possibly possible impossibility he claims to describe concerns a table's being made of wood substantially different from the wood of which it is actually composed.) To embrace Salmon's thesis is to reject an axiom of S4 modal logic. Does Salmon not grasp the S4 logician's concept of *possibility*? Or do we jump to conclusions when inferring in accord with the relevant rule of S4?

Mightn't a *disposition* to execute these inferences prove necessary for possession of the relevant concepts even if their *actual* execution is not?[19] Mightn't we say, for example, that McGee understands "if" because he is *inclined* to infer in accord with modus ponens, even though he resists this inclination in certain cases? (Alternatively, we might say that McGee understands "if" because he *regularly* infers in accord with modus ponens, even if he does not always do so.) But though this maneuver might save something like the inferential role account from counter-example, the claim it advances is too weak to insulate the relevant slate of inferences from all forms of epistemic criticism. Suppose, for example, that only McGee is in the right, and we should resist our inclination to infer in accord with modus ponens in certain cases such as (27)–(29) (cf. Williamson, 2003). Are we left with any principled reason for insisting that Lily should not also throw off the yoke of the inference rule? If there is a reason for thinking that Lily's *particular* instancing of modus ponens is kosher – as, indeed, there must be – the explanation must outstrip the mere fact that she must either make or be disposed to make *some* inferences of the modus ponens form if she is to grasp "if" and reason with the concept it expresses.

Nevertheless, despite these criticisms, it would seem that a defense of some form of the inferential role account would provide the skeptic with his best chance at success. For suppose that philosophical reflection has hit an immovable wall at this point in the dialectic. Suppose, that is, that there is no fully general criterion for the epistemic value of a valid argument that can be derived from an evaluation of the kinds of mathematical and scientific reasoning we have surveyed. Then we will be left, as theorists, with the standard method of levels and the ordinary beliefs that it records and evaluates. At the zero level we observe that your "is"–"ought" inference from (16) to (17) is fairly unexceptional. At the first level we note that only unrepentant Ba'athists deny you knowledge of your premise, and only nihilists are wont to deny your argument's validity. Is there, then, anyone out there who would admit that the argument is valid, but think it in need of supplementation? When we discover that you have inferred (17) directly from (16), will we accuse you of having leaped to judgment? Surely not. The skeptic's only hope, then, if we adopt the method of levels, is a second-level indictment of the critical practices that we have identified. But when we allow that you have reasoned justly in the case at hand, are we under-estimating the need for inferential caution? Do we court epistemic disaster when agreeing that you do in fact learn that Saddam acted immorally by directly deducing as much from the best journalistic accounts of the event? Since it is hard to see how considerations of coherence could be used to impugn our pre-theoretical approval of your argument, the skeptic really does need some criterion extracted from outside the moral sphere.

Let us then assume, on the skeptic's behalf, that there is some sense in which Lily's understanding of "if" *forces* her to infer her conclusion from her knowledge of her premises. And let us inquire, again on the skeptic's behalf, into whether your possession of moral concepts similarly *mandates* your infer-ring the immorality of Saddam's actions from your value-neutral knowledge of what occurred. We have seen that the nihilist manages to resist the infer-ence that you have made. But the force in question needn't be irresistible; the inferential mandate can include exceptions. Are nihilistic reactions to your argument different in kind from McGee's reaction to modus ponens? Were McGee to reject all, or even most modus ponens inferences, and were he to never reason in accord with modus ponens, even when using "if" in his least reflective moments, we would probably conclude that he does not mean what we mean by "if." Mightn't we argue, in a similar fashion, that skeptics who reject all, or even most moral inferences and never reason from neutral premises to moral conclusions, even when using moral terminology in their least reflective moments, mustn't use moral terms with their customary meanings? Of course, nihilism is far more common among philosophers than are objections to modus ponens. But, as far as I know, when he left his study, Mackie was a fine moral judge, who inferred from "is" to "ought" with great regularity. If he hadn't, could we still allow him an understanding of moral language? The matter is anything but clear.

5.4 Chapter summary

The skeptic's infinite regress argument forces us to explain how we know that certain actions are immoral and others not. And if we join the skeptic in rejecting intuitionism, we must describe the kinds of inference with which our moral knowledge is established. The skeptic might allow that we know various neutral facts about the actions we observe and yet deny that we can infer from these facts to knowledge of a moral conclusion. One way to refute the skeptic would be to show that we can deduce an "ought" from an "is."

Hume called for an explanation of how "ought" could be deduced from "is." The task is both metaphysical and epistemological. The premises of the inference must entail its conclusion. That's the metaphysical part. But we must also know the premises and use them to earn knowledge of the conclusion. That's an epistemological achievement.

Kant thought we could deduce that the motive of duty always deserves respect. But those who think that genocidal behavior is wholly bad, and that what motivates it cannot demand esteem, would deny this. According to Thomson, we can deduce that an action was in some way wrong from our knowledge of the pain it caused or the fact that it involved the breaking of a promise. But Thomson's claims also seem to admit of non-skeptical challenges. Still, if we include enough information in our premises, we can arrive at fairly uncontroversial, fairly compelling inferences from "is" to "ought" – inferences whose validity could be denied only by embracing the actual or possible truth of nihilism. The typical reader's inference to the immorality of Saddam Hussein's gassing of Kurdish Iraqis was supplied as a representative example.

One can know a premise and directly infer from it some conclusion that it entails and yet fail to know that conclusion. Indeed, even if it can be known a priori that your premises entail your conclusion, your knowledge of the premises needn't yield knowledge of your conclusion. The examples of Rush and Swifty described above show why this is true. So the skeptic can allow that we know our "is" premise; and allow that it entails the "ought" conclusion we draw with its aid; indeed, he can even allow that someone, somewhere, can prove our argument's validity in an a priori manner; and yet compatible with all this is his refusing to acknowledge that we know our moral conclusion.

On the other hand, if we currently know that our argument for the immorality of Saddam's actions is valid, our knowledge of our argument's premise does indeed give us knowledge of its conclusion. And yet it is hard to see how we can know that our argument is valid, unless some form of intuitionism is true. It seems the best most of us can do is to try, without success, to imagine or describe a case in which our premise is true and our conclusion false. If a more rigorous proof of the argument's validity is required, most (if not all) of us must be said to lack the knowledge we claim for ourselves.

Still, there are cases in which we come to know a conclusion by executing an inference that we don't know to be valid. Lily's simple modus ponens argument provides us with an illustrative example. So the skeptic cannot insist that we can know that Saddam acted immorally only if we know that our argument for this conclusion is valid. The skeptic might embrace the inferential role account, and claim that our argument cannot give us knowledge of its moral conclusion unless we either know that it is valid, or we are compelled – by our understanding of the concepts involved – to draw the inference. But the strongest interpretations of the conceptual role account are implausible, and if the claim is weakened to admit arguments that are compelling but not mandatory, it arguably allows us knowledge of our moral conclusion. It is arguable that we must be disposed to reason from "is" to "ought" – or at least sometimes reason in this way – if we are to truly grasp moral concepts.

5.5 Further reading

Interesting interpretations of Hume on "is" and "ought" include W. K. Frankena, "The Naturalistic Fallacy" (1939); Alasdair MacIntyre, "Hume on 'Is' and 'Ought'" (1959); chapter 9 of Don Garrett's *Cognition and Commitment in Hume's Philosophy* (1997); and Nicholas Sturgeon, "Moral Skepticism and Moral Naturalism in Hume's Treatise" (2001).

Important studies of Kant on the motive of duty include Onora O'Neill, *Acting on Principle* (1975); Barbara Herman, "On the Value of Acting from the Motive of Duty" (1981) and "The Practice of Moral Judgment" (1985); Henry Allison, *Kant's Theory of Freedom* (1990) and *Idealism and Freedom* (1996);

David Wiggins, "Categorical Requirements: Kant and Hume on the Idea of Duty" (1995); Paul Guyer, *Kant and the Experience of Freedom* (1993) and *Knowledge, Reason and Taste* (2008); Lara Denis, "Kant's Conception of Virtue" (2006); Christine Korsgaard, *Creating the Kingdom of Ends* (1996a); and John Rawls, *Lectures on the History of Moral Philosophy* (2000). Mark Timmons (ed.), *Kant's Metaphysics of Morals* (2002) contains a number of valuable essays on the topic.

Judith Jarvis Thomson defends the inference of an other-things-being-equal "ought" claim from an "is" claim in the first chapter of her excellent book, *The Realm of Rights* (1990).

The debate between "internalist" and "externalist" accounts of knowledge, justification, evidence, and inference runs deep, as the wealth of literature on the subject attests. Some recent highlights are collected in Hilary Kornblith (ed.), *Epistemology: Internalism and Externalism* (2001); and Laurence BonJour and Ernest Sosa (eds.), *Epistemic Justification* (2003). The distinction drawn in this chapter between internalist and externalist accounts of inferential knowledge owes a great deal to Paul Boghossian, "How Are Objective Epistemic Reasons Possible?" (2001).

Boghossian argues that we must perform certain inferences to possess certain concepts and that these inferences are therefore justified because blameless in his "Blind Reasoning" (2003). Timothy Williamson's objections appear in a companion piece, "Understanding and Inference" (2003).

A variety of inferentialist views have been explained and defended. These include Wilfrid Sellars, "Inference and Meaning" (1953); Hartry Field, "Logic, Meaning and Conceptual Role" (1977); Gilbert Harman, "The Meaning of the Logical Constants" (1986) and *Reasoning, Meaning, and Mind* (1999a); Christopher Peacocke, *A Study of Concepts* (1992); Robert Brandom, *Making It Explicit* (1994) and *Articulating Reasons* (2000); and Paul Horwich, *Meaning* (1998). Inferentialist accounts of specifically normative concepts are given by Philippa Foot, "Moral Arguments" (1958); and Ralph Wedgwood, "Conceptual Role Semantics for Moral Terms" (2001) and *The Nature of Normativity* (2007).

6

ABDUCTIVE MORAL KNOWLEDGE

6.1 Moral inference to the best explanation

Though the position is not immune to assault, we have seen at least some reason to think that we can derive moral knowledge from deductive arguments with entirely value-neutral premises. Suppose, though, that we are wrong about this: you do not know that your customary inferences from "is" to "ought" are valid, and there are no conceptually mandatory inferences of this kind. We can here note that even suppositions as controversial as these would be insufficient to force us to choose between intuitionism and full-throttle skepticism. As, for one thing, it is wrong to simply insist that all good arguments must be valid. To fully examine the possibility of inferring "ought" from "is" we need to expand our view.

Gilbert Harman (1977, 1984) and Nicholas Sturgeon (1984, 1986, 1995) have engaged in a sophisticated discussion of the matter. Though a vocal advocate for the utility and epistemic value of non-deductive argumentation, Harman expresses skepticism regarding its use in justifying moral belief. In contrast, Sturgeon has claimed that non-demonstrative reasoning can and does provide us with moral knowledge. We begin our assessment of the issue with Harman's (1973) description of the relevant mode of inference: *abduction* or *inference to the best explanation*.

Harman's theory of inference is supposed to describe our knowledge of all those facts that we cannot directly observe, remember, introspect, intuit, or deductively infer from such. Facts that are not known in these ways must be established by determining that their truth is essential to the *best explanation* of what we can observe, remember, and introspect.

> *The ubiquity of inference to the best explanation*: in order for S to gain non-deductive inferential knowledge of a proposition q, S must infer its truth from: (a) some propositions p_1 ... p_n that she can observe, remember, or introspect, and (b) the proposition that q is essential to providing a *better explanation* of p_1 ... p_n than is provided by any competing proposal.[1]

Suppose, for example, that I know by looking that the ground is wet. And suppose I also know that its having rained last night is the best explanation of the ground's wetness. I can then conclude, without further ado, that it rained last night.

1   The ground is wet.
2   Its having rained last night is the best explanation of the ground's being wet.
Therefore,
3   It rained last night.

Though the premises of my argument do not entail the conclusion I draw from them, they surely provide me with good enough reason to believe it. Moreover, says Harman (1973), so long as the conclusion and the premises from which I have derived it are all true – and I truly believe that there is no available conflicting or "defeating" evidence – I will have arrived at inferential knowledge of my conclusion.

Now we might wonder how I come to know premise (2). Do I know through a priori intuition or understanding that the rain provides the best explanation of the water I can see? Can I directly observe, introspect, or remember as much? If not, I must have some argument to support this belief, and, if Harman is right, it will also take the form of an inference to the best explanation.

So suppose (to enrich our example) that the only competing account of the ground's wetness is provided by the hypothesis that a neighboring stream overflowed last night. Then Harman (1999) will say that I know

(2) because I know both: (a) that its having rained last night provides a simpler, more elegant, more conservative explanation of the water on the ground than its competitor, and (b) simpler, more elegant, more conservative hypotheses better explain our observations than do theories that exemplify these virtues to a lesser extent.

But what gives me knowledge of (b)? If I cannot directly introspect, remember, observe, or intuit its truth, I must support my belief in it with a good abductive argument of its own – an argument whose premises I am also justified in believing. And if my grounds are not themselves infinite in extent, my knowledge of (2) will have to re-enter my reasoning at some point. My belief in the epistemic superiority of simpler, more conservative explanations will be supported by a large, interconnected body of convictions and assumptions – but a small part of this doxastic mass will include my belief that the hypothesis that it rained last night better explains the water I can see than does the hypothesis that a stream overflowed, where the first hypothesis is simpler and more conservative than the latter.

Thus, it can be seen that Harman rejects the skeptic's take on the epistemic regress argument by accepting a certain amount of "coherentism" in his accounts of non-deductive inferential knowledge and justification. On Harman's account, my knowledge of premise (2) can play a role in justifying my beliefs in the epistemic values of simplicity and other theoretical virtues that are in turn instrumental in justifying my belief in premise (2) itself. According to Harman, this rather indirect form of circularity is okay.

Still, though Harman eschews the more general Pyrrhonian route to moral skepticism we have been discussing, he insists that abduction cannot be used to acquire distinctively *moral* knowledge or justified belief. Why? Well on a fairly uncharitable reading, he would seem to draw this conclusion from the modest claim that it is always *possible* to explain our non-moral observations without citing moral facts. I say that this is an uncharitable reading – and that it cannot really be what Harman has in mind – because underdetermination is a feature of every abductive inference. For instance, its having rained last night is not logically, conceptually, or even physically necessary to explain the water on the street that I observe today; the alternative hypothesis we have considered is a possibility in almost every sense of "possibility" that might be offered. On Harman's own view of the matter, to rationally infer that it rained last night I needn't establish that rain is the *only* explanation of what I can now observe – I need only establish that it is the *best* explanation. So it seems, in the end, that Harman must reject the possibility of abductively justified moral belief because he thinks moral hypotheses are never necessary or indispensable components of the best explanations of those non-moral facts we know through observation (Sturgeon, 1984).

In his recent defense of moral skepticism, Walter Sinnott-Armstrong (2006) endorses Harman's argument on this construal of it. According to Sinnott-Armstrong, there are some observations that will be better explained by one moral theory rather than another, and this can provide us with justification for being more convinced of the first moral theory than the second. But for every observation that we can explain with a *positive* moral hypothesis – that is, a hypothesis according to which some people, acts, or institutions are moral and others immoral – there will be an alternative, entirely nihilistic explanation that does just as good a job. There are, therefore, no good abductive grounds that might supply our moral beliefs with the justification they would need to constitute "non-contrastive" moral knowledge.[2]

Sturgeon's (1984) now famous counter-example to this thesis is taken from Bernard DeVoto's (1942/2000) account of the Donner party, emigrants to California who were trapped high in the snowy Sierra Mountains. According to DeVoto, Midshipman Woodworth lobbied to be put in charge of the rescue effort, only to squander opportunities that almost certainly would have saved many of those who were trapped. Why did Woodworth spend his time and energy arranging his own conveniences rather than organizing an effective search? Because, DeVoto writes, he "was just no damn good" (442). Woodworth's morally reprehensible actions were the products of his vanity and cowardice – vices that constitute a morally contemptible character.

We can quite easily represent DeVoto's reasoning as an inference to the best explanation.

4   Woodworth failed to act rapidly to save the Donner party.
5   The fact that Woodworth was vain and cowardly better explains his failure to act than does any competing hypothesis.
Therefore,
6   Woodworth was vain and cowardly.

But has DeVoto here abductively inferred an "ought" from an "is"? That depends on whether (6) is itself a moral fact. Once DeVoto has inferred Woodworth's vanity and cowardice from his abandonment of the Donner party, does he need a further inference to conclude that Woodworth was no damn good? He certainly does, as to suppose that vain and cowardly people are never any good would be to implausibly assume that a pair of vices precludes substantive virtue of any kind.

Of course, it may be that "vanity" and "cowardice" are themselves terms of criticism; surely, DeVoto intends to use them as such. But need his criticism be construed as *moral* in character? Suppose a vain and cowardly man works around his deficiencies by avoiding situations in which they might lead him into substantive immorality. Might he then be vain and cowardly, but still wholly moral?

Perhaps this is impossible, as vanity and cowardice are (in Thomson's words) "wrong-making" features of a personality. And surely, the possibility that a vain and cowardly man might work hard to do no harm is compatible with vanity and cowardice contributing to the immorality of those who indulge these vices. At any rate, one might think that a grasp of the concepts *vanity* and *cowardice* provides all the justification DeVoto needs to know premise (7).

7   Vanity and cowardice are morally objectionable traits of character.

And this additional premise would allow him to deduce the explicitly moral proposition:

8   Woodworth had some morally objectionable traits of character.

Of course, this is not yet DeVoto's conclusion that Woodworth was a morally depraved man, but it is a straightforwardly moral conclusion nonetheless.

As Woodworth's inaction can be assumed for the sake of argument – and both parties to this dispute accept the epistemological credentials of inference to the best explanation – we are left to consider Woodworth's supposed vanity and cowardice along with the claim that these are moral vices. Are vanity and cowardice the *best* explanations of Woodworth's inaction? The *Hobbesian response* to Sturgeon's challenge is to answer this question in the negative and therein deny premise (5). According to the Hobbesian, an equally good explanation of Woodworth's failures can be given in critically neutral terms.

But even if we suppose that the Hobbesian response fails – and that sufficiently neutral, equally valuable explanations of Woodworth's behavior cannot be formulated – we will be left to consider whether the viciousness of vanity and cowardice can be known through a priori reflection. The *Humean strategy* is to deny that this is so by insisting that someone can grasp the concepts of *cowardice* and *vanity* (at least in a minimal way) without having the justification she needs to rationally conclude that they are vices. Thus, the Humean insists that DeVoto must have an *a posteriori* justified belief in the morally loaded premise (7) if he is to acquire knowledge of Woodworth's immorality from his knowledge of Woodworth's vanity and cowardice. If the Humean is right, (7) is a moral claim that cannot be inferred from wholly non-moral premises. As a consequence, DeVoto concludes that Woodworth's character has immoral aspects by inferring an "ought" from an "ought," not an "ought" from an "is."

We begin with the Hobbesian project. As Sturgeon notes, we ordinarily invoke the virtues and vices to explain and predict behavior. "John is lazy, so he won't make it out tonight." "Bill refused to wear his glasses because he's so vain."[3] But the virtues and vices are also cited to distinguish the sort of people we think we should emulate (the kind and righteous) from the (mean and unjust) people we think we should not. Now, as we've said, Hobbes' strategy is to pry these functions apart by providing critically unbiased descriptions of our character traits that have the same explanatory properties as our ordinary terms for the virtues and vices.[4] So, for example, DeVoto might predict Woodworth's failure to aid the Donner party not by citing Woodworth's vanity and cowardice, but by instead writing of Woodworth's *general tendency to see to his own comforts before attending to other matters* and Woodworth's *disposition to avoid danger to his person at all costs*. Now if a Hobbesian can always provide these neutral characterizations, he will be able to refute premise (5) and its kin. For instance, the Hobbesian might maintain that the fact that Woodworth has a general tendency to see to his own comforts before attending to other matters, when taken alongside Woodworth's disposition to avoid danger at all costs, explains his failure to act rapidly on behalf of the Donner party just as well as does the hypothesis that Woodworth was vain and cowardly.

But can the Hobbesian successfully prosecute this strategy? Well, the "neutral" explanation of Woodworth's behavior that we've provided on Hobbes' behalf probably isn't equivalent to DeVoto's. A person can be cowardly without being disposed to avoid danger at all costs, and someone can act from vanity even though she regularly sees to the comforts of others before her own. (For instance, Harriett's refusal to hide an escaped slave in her basement may be attributable to moral cowardice even if she regularly kills the snakes that threaten her children and livestock; and Liberace's constantly grooming and preening in the powder room can be chalked up to vanity even if he always sees to his guests first.) If this is right, the morally neutral Hobbesian hypothesis we have provided will diverge from DeVoto's morally loaded one in its predictions of Woodworth's future behavior, where DeVoto's explanation might very well provide the more plausible account (McDowell, 1979, 1985). Of course, it is possible that a scientific psychology will eventually realize Hobbes' ambitions by supplying us with more highly predictive and explanatory accounts of human behavior than can be formulated in the virtue-theoretic terms employed by common thought. Or the most predictive, explanatory account of our behavior may eschew character traits altogether (Doris, 1998, 2002; Harman, 1999b, 2000b). But the current state of inquiry does not provide us with compelling reasons to think that this is what the future will hold (Flanagan, 1993; Sreenivasan, 2002; cf. Kamtekar, 2004 for alternative criticisms). Predicting the future shape that scientific psychology will assume is a fool's game.[5]

Admittedly, it is fairly clear that facts of virtue and vice *supervene* on critically neutral facts (Kim, 1984, 1992), as there can be no change in a person's characteristics without some change in the underlying physical state of the universe in general and her nervous system in particular. But then economics also supervenes on physics in this sense, as there can be no change in the economy without some alteration in the locations and characteristics of the universe's fundamental particles, fields, and forces. But does this at all suggest that a misconceived laissez-faire regulatory policy will never provide the best explanation of an economic bust? Can we always better explain an economic downturn by adverting to the concepts of fundamental physics? Surely not. The debate between Sturgeon on the one hand and the Hobbesian on the other, concerns the role that our concepts of virtue and vice will play in the best, most predictive form of distinctively *psychological* explanation. And there is no a priori guarantee that the Hobbesian will be able to adequately explain human behavior at the right level of generality without the help of critically biased notions.[6]

What then of the Humean response to Sturgeon's argument? Hume rejects Hobbes' ambitious attempt to replace virtue-theoretic terms with a set of neutral surrogates. But he still claims that we cannot derive an "ought" from an "is" in the way that Sturgeon suggests. Why? Well, let us suppose that we are genuinely curious as to why Woodworth failed to rescue the Donner party. If true, DeVoto's hypothesis that Woodworth was no damn good provides us with some sort of explanation. (For instance, it allows us to rule out the hypothesis that Woodworth mounted a sincere effort on the Donners' behalf only to be thwarted by the weather or another rescuer's incompetence.) But the added specificity and explanatory power of DeVoto's more detailed claim that Woodworth was vain and cowardly helps it to *better* explain Woodworth's inaction. Woodworth's vanity "retrodicts" (Dennett, 1987) the inordinate amount of time he spent basking in self-regard, and his cowardice explains why he never considered leading a charge into the dangerous mountain pass on his own. If Woodworth had instead rescued the Donner party only to rob and torture them, his actions would still be (partially) explained by his being no damn good, but then greed and cruelty would be central components of the best hypothesis rather than vanity and cowardice. What this means for Sturgeon, however, is that we cannot directly ground our belief in Woodworth's *immorality* or *badness* in an inference to the best explanation. A better explanation can be had if we eschew fairly abstract, relatively uninformative, or *thin* hypotheses like "Woodworth was bad" for more concrete, more informative, *thicker* hypotheses like "Woodworth was selfish." Thin moral concepts are explanatorily inferior to thick ones.[7]

But is this always the case? Sturgeon suggests otherwise (1984, 64) when he cites a historian's claim that intense moral opposition to slavery arose in the eighteenth and nineteenth centuries in North America simply because slavery was then much worse than it was before, and worse there than it was in South America (cf. Miller, 1985). But wouldn't a better explanation of the rising abolitionist movement sacrifice some of this generality by describing the *ways* in which slavery was more oppressive in these regions and times?

So let us suppose that DeVoto could not have come to know that Woodworth was immoral by directly inferring it as the best explanation of Woodworth's inaction. How then does DeVoto come to know the "thin" moral fact in question? According to the typical rationalist view of the matter, the immorality of selfishness, cowardice, and vanity is knowable via "cool" understanding alone, as our knowledge of the immorality of these characteristics and the actions that manifest them is an instance of non-inferential a priori moral knowledge. But by Hume's empiricist lights, this is a mistake. We justifiably believe that selfishness is a vice because we experience disapprobation when we consider how selfish actions affect a selfish person and his circle of friends, associates, and compatriots. If we did not have these experiences, our belief in the viciousness of selfishness would either be entirely unjustified or derivatively grounded in the testimony of others.

Indeed, this is precisely the position we are in with regard to the so-called "monkish" virtues. Certain people in Hume's milieu thought the virtuousness of self-denial and the viciousness of pride thoroughly self-evident. In contrast, Hume argued, the proposition that pride is a vice is not even true, much less known via understanding alone (1739–40/2000). In fact, Hume claimed, because the puritan's belief in the virtue of self-abnegation does not have the requisite experiential pedigree, it lacks the kind of basic empirical justification we have for regarding kindness and courage in the same light. We don't feel good around ascetics; nor does extreme self-denial bring joy to those who practice it. We need an alternative explanation of why this trait has been thought a virtue. And Hume was willing to bet that the correct explanation would be of the debunking variety. When the puritan learns why he thinks it is wrong to dance, sing, and feast with abandon, he will lose this conviction.

In sum, DeVoto will not have inferred an "ought" from an "is" until he moves from "Woodworth was vain" to "Woodworth was in some way vicious," where "Vanity is a vice" is neither true by definition nor known to him a priori. But then he won't be able to acquire the distinctively moral knowledge that Woodworth was morally flawed via inference to the best explanation unless he has a distinct, justified belief in the moral viciousness of Woodworth's vanity and cowardice. Now Sturgeon might claim that DeVoto's justification for believing in the immorality of these traits will take the form of another inference to the best explanation.[8] But this is psychologically implausible. Of course, we, as moral theorists, may examine the nature of such things as vanity, selfishness, cruelty, disobedience, and lust. And we may decide that vanity really is a vice because injustice and cruelty are vicious, and vanity more closely resembles these core moral vices in relevant respects than it does the spurious "vices" of disobedience and lust. (Put to the side, for the moment, the question of how we know that cruelty and injustice are themselves vicious.) But this is surely not DeVoto's route to his conclusion. If DeVoto does not simply accept the viciousness of vanity and cowardice on the basis of testimony alone, and Hume is right in thinking that pure a priori reflection is not up to the task, DeVoto must here rely on his experience with those affected by the possession and expression of these traits. In sum, while the coherentist response to the regress argument may help account for the reflective or theoretical moral knowledge possessed by philosophers and psychologists, it does not provide a plausible account of the kind of basic knowledge DeVoto expresses when writing about the Donner tragedy.

6.2 Chapter summary

According to Sturgeon, we can infer the existence of cowardice, vanity, and other vices as the best explanations of vicious behavior. In response, Harman argues, with Hobbes, that the best explanations of human behavior would eschew character traits altogether or utilize value-neutral surrogates for our ordinary concepts of virtue and vice. The outcome of this debate will be settled by the trajectory of scientific psychology.

The Humean allows that our ordinary concepts of vanity, cowardice, courage, and benevolence will continue to find their ways into the best explanations of our actions. But he insists that an inference from premises framed with these thick evaluative concepts to a relatively thin verdict regarding the virtuousness or viciousness of an action must always be a posteriori in nature. Without an appropriate emotional reaction to the suffering of those who are affected by vanity and cowardice, belief in their viciousness would be either groundless or based in testimony alone. Without augmentation, abduction cannot yield genuinely moral knowledge.

6.3 Further reading

Harman describes and defends inference to the best explanation in a number of books and essays including *Thought* (1973) and *Reasoning, Meaning, and Mind* (1999a). He argues that neither moral knowledge nor justified moral beliefs can be acquired in this manner in *The Nature of Morality* (1977). Jonathan Vogel, "Cartesian Skepticism and Inference to the Best Explanation" (1990) situates the abductionist view of inference with respect to the skeptical worries raised in 4.1.

Sturgeon's famous defense of abductive moral knowledge can be found in his "Moral Explanations" (1984), "Harman on Moral Explanations of Natural Facts" (1986), and "Evil and Explanation" (1995). Harman reiterates his skepticism in "Is There a Single True Morality?" (1984). Walter Sinnott-Armstrong, *Moral Skepticisms* (2006) endorses Harman's argument in a modified form.

Hobbes defines terms for the virtues and vices with both a neutral core and a sentiment felt by the person using the term in *Human Nature or the Fundamental Elements of Polity* (1650). So called "expressivists" often follow a similar strategy. Perhaps the most influential such analyses were offered by Charles L. Stevenson, *Ethics and Language* (1944) and *Facts and Values* (1963); R. M. Hare, *Freedom and Reason* (1963); Simon Blackburn, *Spreading the Word* (1984); and Allan Gibbard, *Wise Choices, Apt Feelings* (1990). John McDowell argues against the project in *Mind, Value, and Reality* (1998).

A number of theorists have argued for and against the existence of character traits. Attacks include John Doris, "Persons, Situations and Virtue Ethics" (1998) and *Lack of Character* (2002); and Harman, "Moral Philosophy Meets Social Psychology" (1999b). Defenses include Nafsika Athanassoulis, "A Response to Harman: Virtue Ethics and Character Traits" (2000); Gopal Sreenivasan, "Errors about Errors" (2002); and Rachana Kamtekar, "Situationism and Virtue Ethics on the Content of Character" (2004). Owen Flanagan's *Varieties of Moral Personality* (1993) initiated the debate.

7

THE RELIABILITY OF OUR MORAL JUDGMENTS

7.1 Acquiring moral concepts and exercising objectivity

When your moral beliefs are supported by reasoning, you can often use your premises to defend your conclusion in the face of challenges. If someone claims that Creakle did nothing immoral, Copperfield can point to the suffering of the man's chubby pupils, the ineffectiveness of the lashings, the humiliation wrought. If someone challenges your belief in the immorality of Saddam's actions, you can similarly respond with the facts of the case. The Kurds posed no real threat; chemical weapons are verboten by international treaty; the death and destruction were avoidable; and so on.

Sometimes, genuinely non-inferential knowledge can be defended in the same way. You know, simply by introspecting, that you are in pain. But if someone challenges your belief, you might point to an MRI or X-ray image as proof of the damage that is its cause. ("Look," you say, "the crack in my spine is there to be seen; my nerve is pinched; my pain is real.") What, though, can be done when objective proof of this kind is not forthcoming? Someone accuses you of hypochondria, and all you can do is flat-footedly assert that you really are in pain. Dialogue gives way to distrust and dogmatism.

The skeptic argues that you do not know that Saddam acted immorally when gassing the Kurds; that Creakle acted immorally when lashing his pupils; that Madoff acted immorally when defrauding his investors; that Spitzer acted immorally when cheating on his wife with a prostitute; and so on. In response, the intuitionist invokes what he claims is a non-inferentially justified belief: if not a belief in the immorality of the particular acts here described, then belief in complex but fairly general moral principles from which their immorality can be deduced.

If the intuitionist's moral beliefs are non-inferentially justified, but he can nevertheless defend them with arguments, he can invoke the premises of these arguments in response to a skeptical challenge. (We might compare this to his supplying an X-ray or MRI image to prove to someone that he is not just bitching and moaning without cause.) But what should we say when the arguments in question are either absent or evade articulation? Simply insisting that one really does know the moral claim under consideration – and that one knows it via "reflection" or "intuition" – is decidedly unsatisfying.

There look, in fact, to be at least two ways to avoid the charges of dogmatism that arise in the conditions we have described. These roughly correspond to what Jim Pryor (2000) calls the "modest" and "ambitious" anti-skeptical projects. The ambitious project would culminate in our proving to the skeptic's satisfaction that there exists moral knowledge or adequately justified moral beliefs. If the skeptic will not accept any premises with moral content, and he rejects all inferences from "is" to "ought" as untenable, the prospects for an ambitious anti-skeptical crusade look to be rather weak.

But this still leaves us with Pryor's modest anti-skeptical project: to defend our moral knowledge from skeptical challenge in a rational or reasonable way so as to justifiably retain our moral convictions. And the first thing to note when assessing the prospects of this more modest pursuit, is that despite the skeptic's wishes to the contrary, the modest project cannot be reduced to the ambitious project in any straightforward way. It should go without saying that every argument has premises, and every argument utilizes or conforms to rules of inference of one sort or another. So it should come as no surprise that a good-faith effort to debate a skeptic who rejects all normative or evaluative premises and all inference from neutral premises to moral conclusions must culminate in either dogmatic assertion or silence. But where is it written that we must convince such a skeptic if we are to rationally retain our belief in the moral knowledge that he doubts or denies? Why is it not rational to retain our conviction in moral knowledge in the absence of an effective argument against its existence? Why, that is, doesn't the burden of argument rest squarely on the skeptic's shoulders rather than our own (Williams, 2001, 2004)?

Note that in locating the burden of argument in this position we needn't suggest that the skeptic is justified in doubting or denying the existence of moral knowledge only if he can convince us that there is none. It need only leave us justified in retaining our belief in the existence of moral knowledge in the absence of a novel skeptical argument against that belief's truth or justification. We can leave it open, that is, whether both parties to the dispute might be justified, at least initially, in their respective beliefs and doubts. (Though we might doubt that the skeptic can rationally resist adopting moral beliefs once he has been exposed to (what we take to be) our effective rebuttals.) Indeed, this is the strategy we pursued in the preceding chapters when discussing nihilism and epistemic skepticism – views we found to be under-motivated if nevertheless coherent. Strong internalisms regarding moral judgment are not features of common thought, whereas weak internalisms seem compatible with the facts. There are unexceptional inferences from "is" to "ought" that are epistemologically on a par with recognizably sound forms of inference. Common thought admits a category of non-inferentially justified belief, and there are no obvious reasons why certain beliefs in moral generalities should be denied membership in this class. At this stage in our inquiry, our belief in moral knowledge looks to be defensible if not demonstrable.

But can we justly shift the burden of proof onto the skeptic in this way? Can we rationally execute the modest anti-skeptical project without its more ambitious cousin? We might consider, in this regard, a romantic poet who believes in invisible pixies and dares us to demonstrate their absence. Even supposing that she could effectively undermine our attempted demonstrations, wouldn't her belief still be aptly criticized as irrational? What distinguishes our moral beliefs from her childish fantasies? Doesn't justification and much else that we think important in belief require *positive* support?

It is at precisely this point that a discussion of the origins of our moral concepts and most basic moral beliefs comes into its own (Goldman, 1988b), as the needed positive support needn't consist in backing from belief in distinct propositions that might provide us with a non-circular argument for the initial proposition believed. How has our imagined subject come to acquire and retain her belief in pixies? Is there any coherent conception of their existence that would sustain a theorist's confidence in the reliability or truth of beliefs generated in this way? If not, then, though the belief may result from a blameless love of myth, we (as theorists) will be justified in concluding that it lacks many of the positive characteristics we look for when evaluating someone's frame of mind. We can quite easily see that no one knows that fairies exist. And a belief in fairies will almost always lack both argumentative backing and a secure or reliable cognitive source.

Thus, to fully defend our most basic moral beliefs from skeptical assault we would seem to need some causal or descriptive account of our moral judgments. How do we come to possess those moral beliefs in which we are most confident? If the process does not always provide us with premises with which we might defend our beliefs from criticism, might it nevertheless provide us with a *reliable* way of judging certain actions right and others wrong? Though the psychology of moral development is an immense field, we can take some steps toward answering these questions by sketching the barest of accounts.

As we've maintained from the outset, there are several different kinds of moral judgment we might try to examine. These include beliefs about which people, institutions, and actions are morally good and which bad, which virtuous and which vicious, and which morally right and which wrong. We will focus our account on the evaluation of actions that affect the happiness or well-being of others, not because evaluative concepts are more important than other moral concepts, but because concern with the suffering of others seems to predate by almost a year concern for deontic phenomena such as fairness and equality (Davidson, Turiel, and Black, 1983).[1]

Let us then begin by assuming that the child we are investigating has learned to discriminate, in a partial and somewhat inaccurate way, between what is good for him and what is not. (The etiology of prudential thought would require another book entirely.) What more does he need if he is to form distinctively *moral* beliefs? Well, what is judged bad for me needn't be judged in the least morally bad or immoral. For one thing, what I think detracts from my well-being in a fairly minor way I may know to be morally required because so much better for the rest of those affected than is any other available course of action. Think here of the selfish person – described in 1.3 above – who fails to act as he knows he morally ought when his desire to preserve his shoes leads him to ignore a child drowning in shallow water. Perhaps his well-being would not be diminished by the rescue, but he certainly *thinks* that it would. For this reason (among others) wholly egocentric thought and judgment is not yet moral thought and judgment. To think in moral terms, a child must be capable of thinking about what is good for other people or what serves their ends and projects – ends and projects that will sometimes conflict with her own.[2]

The most basic form of other-directed prudential cognition is typically in place at an early age, as normal two-year-old children react in roughly appropriate ways to the suffering of other people and animals (Simner,

1971; Zahn-Waxler and Radke-Yarrow, 1982). Indeed, it has long been known that newborn infants cry when they hear other infants cry, mimic the sad or happy faces that are shown to them, and display similar forms of emotional sensitivity long before their second year (Meltzoff and Gopnik, 1993; Gordon, 1995; Hauser, 2006).

In fact, several forms of emotional expression seem to be unlearned or innately specified. As the sociologist James Q. Wilson notes:

> Infants born blind will smile though they have never seen a smile; infants born deaf and blind will laugh during play, though they have never heard laughter, and frown when angry, though they have never seen a frown. (1993, 7; quoted and discussed in Filonowicz, 2008, 207)

But to affirm the spontaneity of other-regarding emotion is not to deny its malleability. "Social referencing" begins immediately, as children look to the smiles and grimaces of their caregivers when deciding which activities and novel objects to pursue and which to avoid (Klinnert *et al.*, 1987; Walker-Andrews, 1998). A responsible parent who sees her child growing sad at the perceived distress of another can reinforce the reaction with a sad face of her own. And a homicidal parent set on quashing her child's sympathy might instead smile when her child acts aggressively and look disgusted at each display of kindness. From the very beginning, then, it will be extraordinarily difficult to neatly deconstruct a child's emotional dispositions into their innate and learned components.

During this same early period children can be observed trying to help and console each other. For example, Martin Hoffman (2000) describes a ten-month-old child looking sad and burying his face in his mother's lap at the sight of another child in distress, and a one-year-old child leading his own mother by the hand to help soothe an infant crying in the room. (Hoffman is interested in exactly when and how a youngster will come to the realization that the other child's own mother is more likely to provide the succor that child desires.) Of course, a child can conceive of the suffering or flourishing of others in a cold or merely intellectual manner, or can instead go on to imagine the harm or benefit from the inside. For instance, she might infer, in an affectively barren way, that the shrieking cat on whose tail she is standing is experiencing pain. Or she may go on to imagine what things are like for the cat and feel bad at the pain she is causing. Again, in the absence of a Humean argument to the contrary, we can allow that bare knowledge of the cat's suffering might be enough to move our child into action, while allowing that the probability of an evasive measure will greatly increase if the child vicariously experiences the cat's displeasure.

Still, there is a second respect in which prudential thought stops short of moral concern. Tornados, plagues, and weather-induced famine are not just bad for me, they are bad for almost all of us. But, as philosophers have long noted, natural disasters are neither morally bad nor wrong. Witness Hume:

> Tis a will or choice, that determines a man to kill his parent; and they are the laws of matter and motion, that determine a sapling to destroy the oak, from which it sprung. Here then the same relations have different causes; but still the relations are the same: And as their discovery is not in both cases attended with a notion of immorality, it follows, that that notion does not arrive from such a discovery ... Tis evident, that when we praise any actions, we regard only the motives that produc'd them, and consider the actions as signs or indications of certain principles in the mind and temper. (1739–40/2000, 3.1.1.24–3.2.1.1 [SBN 466–77])

If a child says that the sapling is "ungrateful," "despicable," or "immoral" because it has killed its parent oak, she is just confused. And we might say something similar if she calls the hurricane-force winds shaking her home "morally bankrupt," "malicious," or "cruel." But in what would the child's confusion consist? The destruction of her home is certainly detrimental to her. Indeed it may be bad for all those affected. So why can't it be properly thought of as immoral? The answer is obvious: an action or event can only be immoral if it is the product of an *intentional agent* (Nichols, 2004; Hauser, 2006).

But how does a child come to distinguish the intentional actions of people and animals from the non-intentional behavior of inanimate systems? Testimony surely plays a central role. But the literature on the issue contains two additional sorts of proposals. First, a child might proceed in an entirely discursive way, as a young scientist might, by figuring out whether the operations of a mind provide the best explanation of the events or patterns of behavior that she has observed. In the case at hand, she might use abduction to figure out that the shaking house is not the activity of a minded agent by uncovering a better, purely mechanical explanation for the phenomenon. Second, our child might use her imagination in a rationally constrained, productive way to reach the same conclusion. In effect, she might figure out that the cause of her home's destruction is something wholly non-conscious by trying and failing to imagine how things would seem to someone destroying her home in the precise manner in which the weather is taking it to pieces. Though it risks describing the process in an overly rationalistic way, we might think of the child as asking herself, "What is it like to be or directly enact hurricane-force winds?" and when she finds no positive answer, concluding that the storm neither has nor results from intelligence. Of course, if we conclude, with certain anthropologists and intellectual historians, that "primitive" people have a fully romantic, anthropomorphized view of nature, we will have to grant a larger role to the help and testimony of adult heirs to modernity. Perhaps most children would think of storms as intentional agents if left to their own devices.

There are many different extant accounts of how discursive inference and imaginative simulation might be employed to gain knowledge of the minds of others, and some are more plausible than others. But as things currently stand, exactly how we gain knowledge of other minds is still a matter of some dispute, with *theory theorists* emphasizing the role of discursive inference, and *simulation theorists* focusing in on the role of imaginative projection (Davies and Stone, 1995; Carruthers and Smith, 1996; Malle, Moses, and Baldwin, 2001).[3] We can just note here that *both* simulation and purely discursive inference are fairly regularly employed in gathering knowledge of (or belief in) the existence and character of the minds of others, where the imaginative processes hypothesized by simulation theorists may be more directly linked to other-regarding action than the wholly intellectual exercises described by theory theorists.

Now a minimalist view of evaluative moral concepts would require nothing more rigorous for moral thought than sensitivity to mindedness as the source of some harm or benefit, a sensitivity apparently present – in a crude or undeveloped form – in many infants. For example, researchers showed toddlers a computer display of certain geometrical shapes aiding completion of a task (e.g. helping a character climb an incline) and other geometrical shapes inhibiting its completion (e.g. blocking ascension). And the children showed a marked preference for the helpful characters by choosing similarly shaped objects over their unhelpful counterparts (Hamlin, Wynn, and Bloom, 2007).

But there are several possible sources of dissatisfaction with the kind of minimalist view that would attribute moral thought to all those who limit immorality to the actions of intentional agents. For one thing, most of us think that non-human animals (or non-primates) cannot be appropriately criticized in moral terms even when they intentionally harm others.[4] If a child witnesses a tiger mauling its handler and reacts by calling the tiger or its act "mean" and therefore "immoral" does she therein evidence her failure to adequately grasp moral means of evaluation? At exactly which station should we urge that she disembark as her train of thought travels from the tiger's "viciousness" to its "meanness" to its "cruelty" to its "immorality"?

Most of the adults I have surveyed initially find it obvious that non-human animals cannot be meaningfully assessed in moral terms, though some restrict the claim to anything less intelligent than a dolphin, and many will describe so-called "lower" animals in those virtue-theoretic terms we use to categorize the hazy boundary between the moral and the non-moral. Surely, the common man insists, there are lazy dogs and gluttonous cats. But can a domesticated feline really be cruel? And if so, what distinguishes the sort of cruelty it displays in toying with its prey from the truly immoral variety?

Philosophers who try to explain why non-human animals cannot be evaluated in moral terms – by addressing what Michael Zimmerman (1988) calls the conditions that must be met for *moral appraisability* – typically cite two sorts of considerations relevant to the distinction, the first of which is supposed to supply an *epistemic condition* on moral assessment (Feinberg, 1986, 269–315; Haji, 1998, 172–74) and the second a *motivational condition* (Frankfurt, 1971; Watson; 1975; Wolf, 1990; Fischer and Ravizza, 1998; and Yaffe, 1999). We impose an epistemic condition on moral evaluation when we claim that non-human animals are incapable of immorality because they lack any *awareness* of right and wrong; we impose a motivational condition on the same when we remove animals from the scope of moral evaluation because they lack the kind of *self-control* they would need to regulate their behavior in accordance with such awareness. Without moral concepts and/or self-control (it is claimed) an agent is incapable of immorality.

Let us suppose, then, that our child restricts her use of "moral" and "immoral" to the intentional actions of animals that have some awareness of right and wrong and the self-control necessary to act on that knowledge. And let us suppose too that her moral judgments are linked, in a substantial way, to her beliefs about the harm and benefit we generate through such actions.[5] Still, if she calls "immoral" all those acts that thwart her ends, and thinks that everything she wants is morally acceptable, she will almost certainly arrive at many false moral beliefs. And the bare knowledge that what is in her self-interest needn't be morally good probably won't be enough to instill the requisite reliability, as *partiality* may prevent this knowledge from guiding her beliefs when morality and self-interest conflict. The reliability of our moral judgments therefore awaits a kind of *neutrality* that most healthy adults manage to achieve – to at least some extent – in our core moral judgments; though the precise manner in which objectivity is most commonly secured remains a matter of some debate.

Dickens' description of Creakle's immorality provides us with some interesting hints, as it quite clearly shows Copperfield's sensitivity to the distorting influence his own interests might be playing in the case. Like many children, Copperfield is tempted to use the language of morality for any action he finds unpleasant or unwelcome. There have been times when he falsely judged his mother mean for forcing him to take his medicine and his nanny cruel for making him go to bed at an early hour. And there were occasions on which he wrongly accused a playmate of cheating because he couldn't bear the frustration of losing a fair contest. But Copperfield satisfies himself that partiality is not distorting his present judgment of Creakle when he correctly surmises that he would feel truly "disinterested indignation" and retain his conviction in Creakle's immorality if he had "known all about him without having ever been in his power." Thus, Copperfield doesn't merely judge Creakle immoral because he feels indignant over what he perceives to be the man's mistreatment of him. Instead, he correctly judges that he would still feel this way were he merely observing from afar Creakle's similar treatment of boys wholly unrelated to him.

In point of fact, this is precisely the sort of counterfactual reasoning Hume invoked to explain how we maintain consistency in our moral judgments across temporal and spatial distances.

> We blame equally a bad action, which we read of in history, with one perform'd in our neighbourhood the other day: The meaning of which is, that we know from reflection, that the former action wou'd excite as strong sentiments of disapprobation as the latter, were it plac'd in the same position. (1739–40/2000, 3.3.1.18 [SBN 584])

Of course, we often continue to feel something like indignation or disapprobation toward someone who has frustrated our interests even after we realize that we wouldn't feel this way were we observing the scenario as a disinterested party. In such cases, Hume points out, our moral beliefs and assertions properly align themselves with our counterfactual judgments as to what we would feel rather than the negative sentiments we actually do feel.

> The passions do not always follow our corrections; but these corrections serve sufficiently to regulate our abstract notions; and are alone regarded when we pronounce in general concerning the degrees of vice and virtue. (1739–40/2000, 3.3.1.21 [SBN 585])[6]

Now it is worth remarking that the neutrality a person needs if she is to execute a sufficiently reliable set of moral judgments is most difficult to secure when her own present actions are under review. Thus, we would stack the deck in the moral skeptic's favor if we were to follow many moral theorists in concentrating all our attention on a subject's first-person, present-tense moral beliefs. Consider, for instance, Creakle's opinion that he is doing nothing immoral in striking the boys when they falter during their examinations. What would it take for the headmaster to think of his own actions as a disinterested third party might? What would it take for him to admit that he enjoys the beatings, that he is prejudiced against the fat children, and that he has little if any evidence that the lashings he delivers sufficiently improve the performance of his pupils to compensate for the pain and misery they must feel? It is hard to see how the man could be made to think of his actions in this light without the intervention of third-party criticism.

But mightn't Creakle judge the case aright in a "cool hour" when recollecting the day's activities alone in his study? Our evaluations of our own past actions constitute an intermediate case, where neutrality, though difficult to attain, is not quite so hard to achieve as it is when we are judging our current behavior. For instance, looking back on his career as an educator, Creakle might experience remorse; or he might even judge, in an entirely dispassionate way, that his sadistic tendencies poorly suited him for his chosen vocation. But even here the crucial judgment will more often than not result from a comparison to other cases in which Creakle was not himself the perpetrator but instead suffered or observed cruelty on the part of another person.

Suppose, for instance, that reflecting on his own childhood, Creakle comes to recall with indignation the lashings his own father gave to him. Noting no relevant difference between the beatings he received and his mistreatment of his pupils, Creakle might then feel compelled to achieve consistency by either excusing his father's behavior or condemning his own. That is, after comparing his own actions to his father's relevantly similar behavior, Creakle might think, "What a little brat I was; thank God the man had the strength of will to sort me out," or he might instead retain his anger at his father and direct some of it toward his own past behavior. And if he did adopt the later course, he would be in an excellent position to acknowledge his own cruel and immoral behavior, behavior he had until then denied.

Now, as we have already noted, a third party might try to spur the relevant reasoning "on the spot" by stopping Creakle, strap in hand, and asking him to consider how he would feel were he the chubby boy about to receive the blow. And this might buy neutrality in a manner quite different from that described by Dickens. That is, Dickens has Copperfield basing his judgment of Creakle on the determination that he would feel indignation were he a *neutral observer* who had never experienced mistreatment at Creakle's hand. But we have here forced Creakle to occupy the *second-person perspective* of Copperfield and the other chubby boys affected (cf. Darwall, 2006). Indeed, Thomas Nagel's description of how objectivity is achieved provides us with a third option by replacing judgments about what you would *feel* were you a neutral observer, or what you would *experience* were you one of the affected parties, with judgments regarding the *reasons* to refrain that you would attribute to the immoral act's perpetrator were you one of his victims:

> "How would you like it if someone did that to you?" It is an argument to which we are all in some degree susceptible ... The essential fact is that you would not only dislike it if someone else treated you in that way; you would resent it. That is, you would think that your plight gave the other person a reason to terminate or modify his contribution to it, and that in failing to do so he was acting contrary to reasons which were plainly available to him. (1970, 82–83)

Nagel is of course right. Only a pathologically egotistical agent – a *practical solipsist* as we might call him – would both admit that he would justly resent the lashings were he to receive them and at the same time insist that there is no reason at all for him to refrain from delivering the blows to others. The kings of old, who thought they ruled by divine right, had a justification of some sort for thinking their subjects bound to respect them even though they had no reason at all to respect their subjects. But they were surely mistaken in adopting this attitude, and without a false metaphysical back-story of this kind, the first-person belief that I am an exception to otherwise universally valid moral norms is not just false, but genuinely delusional. "You shouldn't beat me, but I can justly beat you. And this is just because I am *me* and you are *you*." While not logically inconsistent in any obvious way, the reasoning in question is baldly *incoherent* in the sense given in 1.3 above. It draws a distinction in moral status between two prospective actions while acknowledging that there is no conceivably "relevant" difference between them that might justify the distinction drawn.[7]

Nevertheless, as noted above, there are two distinct ways for Creakle to retain the kind of coherence that only the extraordinarily solipsistic among us lack: he can condemn his treatment of his students as cruel and worthy of resentment, or he can instead insist that he would not justly resent them were he their target. (We here put to the side a third fairly common way of resolving the tension: inventing a transparently spurious ground of difference between his treatment of his students and his father's mistreatment of him.) And it seems more than likely that the heat of the moment would have the headmaster ignoring or rationalizing the abuse he suffered at his own father's hand rather than reasoning from its immorality to the immorality of his current behavior. "How would I like it if someone beat me for similar behavior?" Creakle might ask. "I should like to say that I'd welcome the attempts at my improvement; and if I didn't, my failure would be further testament to my needing the correction."

In sum, self-censure is extraordinarily uncomfortable. When it does accompany an immoral action it usually does so in a largely tacit form, as it is only once the deed is completed that the sentiment creeps back into consciousness as guilt or remorse. (It is instructive to think again here of Spitzer's adultery.) Nor is the passage of time any guarantee of accuracy. Some of us "beat ourselves up" by wallowing in shame and embarrassment at every past indiscretion. Others buy inner peace by rationalizing their transgressions and lingering over reminiscence of triumphs long gone. It is exceedingly difficult to evaluate one's own actions, whether present or past, in neither too harsh nor too lenient a light.

Indeed, neutrality is even difficult to achieve when we are evaluating some range of those alternatives open to us in the course of deciding what to do. One needn't endorse Singer's incredibly demanding conception of morality to note our tendency to wed moral permissibility more closely to self-interest than is truly warranted. In our more reflective moments, many of us would admit that we wouldn't have thought that using plastic bags – or constantly running the air conditioner, or eating gavage-generated foie gras – was a morally acceptable course of action, if we hadn't stood to gain in pleasure or convenience from the adoption of the attitude. Surely, if it is immoral to eat the deliciously bloated liver of a force-fed goose, it must be likewise immoral to eat chickens raised in cramped, feces-ridden captivity (Caro, 2009). Many carnivores, worried that the force of consistency might lead them to vegetarianism, take the coward's way out and avoid the issue altogether. Just as the most reliable legal judge lacks any vested interest in the case brought before her, the most reliable moral judge of someone's actual or prospective actions is another person with sufficient critical distance to distinguish her own particular quirks and interests from the interests of the parties that are or will be affected.

Admittedly, a rational agent's primary or most fundamental concern is not with judging other people, or even with evaluating her own actions in retrospect, but with figuring out what to do here and now. (Many students turn to ethicists for *guidance*.) And if we were wholly incapable of exercising critical reflection while deciding what to do, we could never reliably distinguish the morally permissible courses of action open to us at any given time from their impermissible alternatives. Since agents incapable of counterfactual reasoning will have a hard time judging their own possibilities for action as a neutral party would judge them, they are unlikely to know what they morally ought and ought not do here and now with any great regularity. It seems, for instance, that until a child is sufficiently advanced to admit upon reflection that he would condemn the pulling of his sister's hair were he to judge the activity as a third party would judge it, he is unlikely to conclude that his now pulling his sister's hair would be immoral because cruel. And until a child can judge that an action of this kind would be cruel were he to perform it at present, and that cruel behavior is morally verboten, he will lack the motive to virtue that these judgments typically (if not invariably) bring in tow. In contrast, a child's moral evaluations of other people may be justly held (or even constitutive of knowledge) at a significantly earlier stage than this. He will know when his sister is being cruel to a sibling long before he knows when he is being cruel to the same party. Light dawns slowly over the whole.

In any event, while looking at Copperfield's retrospective judgments of another man's actions has the non-skeptical moral epistemologist focusing in on something close to the epistemologically best-case scenario, this needn't be construed as an act of theoretical desperation. For the best case for moral judgment is not the only good one we might survey. We have every reason to believe that those adolescents capable of moderately demanding forms of counterfactual reasoning can obtain moral knowledge in the less favorable conditions prevalent when they begin to exercise moral judgment in the course of deciding what to do. And we have already remarked in considerable detail upon the conditions that must be in place if they are to then do what they know they morally ought.

We have not yet considered the most "advanced" moral judgments of which we are capable. Though we have allowed our child to think of the (actual or prospective) actions that he is judging from a variety of different perspectives, we have not followed him to the classroom, the church, or the university. So we have not had him consider the sophisticated moral views he is bound to encounter in these locales. Will his moral knowledge grow or wilt in the face of extra-familial instruction? Are moral theories and religious ideologies – once digested and applied – likely to render his moral judgments more or less reliable?

We cannot answer these questions in a responsible manner here, as their resolution depends on the content of the theories or dogmas taught, the abilities of the student exposed to them, and the sense of right and wrong he brings to his studies. The case histories we would need to canvas are therefore too many and too varied to assess. For instance, it is likely that some people have been improved by their encounters with academic ethics, and some have not.

So let's instead focus on the fairly unsophisticated moral judgments of a young man like Copperfield (no Kant he): judgments that nevertheless incorporate an assessment of motives and consequences; stem from an empathetic and sympathetic understanding of those directly affected; and arrive upon the kinds of counterfactual reasoning necessary to instill a certain degree of neutrality or objectivity. Are these judgments comparable to a romantic's belief in fairies? Or are the processes responsible for them sufficiently reliable to support moral knowledge?

To answer these questions, I would like to return to the case on hand: Copperfield's condemnation of Creakle. My preferred reconstruction of Copperfield's reasoning would integrate features of several epistemological models we have already seen. First, Copperfield observes Creakle's comportment and the pattern of lashings. Next, he infers from these observations that Creakle took pleasure in delivering the beatings and singled out the chubby boys for special attention. (The penalties were neither dispassionately enforced nor appropriately linked to academic demerit.) With this assessment in hand, Copperfield deduces, straightaway, that the acts were mean and unfair, where his beliefs in these matters are awash in emotion, reflecting the shame he has felt when beaten in front of the class, his indignation at the injustice he has identified, and his hatred for (and fear of) the sadist who is its cause. It is in this frame of mind that Copperfield judges the act immoral, a conclusion he has drawn from his thick evaluation.

1   Creakle enjoyed causing the boys to suffer, singling out the chubby boys for special attention.

Therefore,

2   Creakle acted in a mean and unfair way.

Therefore,

3   Creakle acted immorally.

Now, in the course of ordinary events, no one outside the academy will question this form of reasoning. For example, to defend himself against Copperfield's charges, Creakle will challenge the value-neutral premise from which the reasoning precedes; he won't admit to his sadism and the lopsided nature of the beatings, and instead challenge the cruelty, injustice, or immorality of acting in this way. And it is in part because of this that Copperfield won't have yet had occasion to judge that if (1) is true, then (2) must be true, or that if (2) is true, then (3) must also be. So Copperfield won't yet have considered whether his argument is valid. And if Copperfield hasn't considered whether his argument is valid, he cannot be said to know its validity. And yet, if ordinary thought is to be trusted, this won't prevent the boy from knowing (3) on the basis of (2) and knowing (2) on the basis of (1). Common sense allows the unaided inference of "ought" from "is."

But let us suppose that a skeptic does challenge Copperfield's inference. Then, though he may not be able to articulate the argument we have used to model his thinking, Copperfield will have sufficient cognizance of its content and structure to formulate the moderately complex moral principles he needs to insulate his inference from cogent critique – principles whose antecedents are his argument's premises and whose consequents are his conclusions. In other words, the boy will say to himself in this or equivalent language, "If I'm right that Creakle enjoyed causing us boys to suffer, and I'm right that he singled out the chubby boys for special attention, well then *of course* he acted in a mean, unfair, and hence immoral fashion. This much is obvious." The structure then in place will constitute a straightforward argument via modus ponens.

1   Creakle enjoyed causing the boys to suffer, singling out the chubby boys for special attention.
4   If Creakle enjoyed causing the boys to suffer, singling out the chubby boys for special attention, then he acted in a mean and unfair way.
Therefore,
2   Creakle acted in a mean and unfair way.
5   If Creakle acted meanly and unfairly, then he acted immorally.
Therefore,
3   Creakle acted immorally.

Because he does not yet have access to a moral theory, Copperfield won't be able to defend his belief in (4) and his belief in (5) with much in the way of argument. Instead, his beliefs in these moderately complex moral principles will have the affective and cognitive backing of empathetic objectivity: the frame of mind responsible for most of his core moral convictions. Moreover, though I haven't formally evaluated our opinions on the matter with a first-level epistemological investigation, I suspect that this is enough for the common man to side with the boy against the skeptic. Empathetic neutrality is commonly thought sufficient for moral knowledge.

But is common thought *right* to award Copperfield non-inferential moral knowledge of the principles we have articulated? Though our answers to this second-level epistemological question will surely improve with further advances in our understanding of ethical action and ethical judgment, I think we can be forgiven an optimistic appraisal of the facts currently known. For one thing, empathetic, neutral judgment is incredibly different from the feelings of disgust, unthinking reliance on religious texts, and the blind acceptance of customary taboos on which skeptics train their focus. The latter three methods of belief formation wear their unreliability on their sleeves. But empathetic neutrality at least looks – to me, at any rate – to be a fairly good guide to moral truth.

Of course, when I make this determination I am already assuming a fairly determinate set of moral facts. For when I suggest that the method of empathy is reliable, I therein suggest that it issues in many more true than false beliefs. And in suggesting that the method issues in true beliefs, I am assuming that there are moral truths to be believed. Is this assumption problematic at this stage of inquiry?

There are two things to note on this score. The first has been a constant refrain since our chapter 3 came to an end: we are not now addressing nihilism. The claim that there are no moral facts is an entirely metaphysical matter – a matter we addressed in detail in chapters 2–3. Nihilism must be assessed on its own merits, by directly confronting the arguments that have been advanced in its favor.

But when we turn our attention to wholly epistemological skepticism, it is often fair to assume, if only for the sake of argument, that there are moral facts. We do this to determine whether we might know moral facts, if – as we have independently argued – there are moral facts to be known. So we can ask: if there are moral facts – or, given that there are moral facts – mightn't they be the kinds of things that can be more or less reliably detected with empathetic neutrality? Wouldn't denying Copperfield moral knowledge force us into the kind of nihilism we have already rejected?

Second, the fact that we must use moral thinking to verify the reliability of our moral thinking – if, indeed, it is a fact – does not distinguish moral thinking from other forms of thought. For instance, it seems we must use our perceptual faculties to both verify their reliability and identify those cases in which they lead us into error. And it seems we must think in accordance with our logic when establishing the infallibility of its principles and the mistakes we often make in their application. Morality would seem to be no worse off in this regard than logic and observation.

But let's not pretend that we accomplished more than we have. We set out to assess the reliability of our moral judgments, and in the end were forced to use our moral faculties to complete the task. Surely, this robs our investigation of value, doesn't it?

Though these matters continue to elicit a fair amount of debate, it is my sense that our demonstration was not empty.[8] We could have discovered that our core moral judgments were sustained by nothing better than disgust. Or our ethical judgments might have turned out to be entirely supported by the testimony of erroneous religious texts and false prophets. But things have not turned out this way. Instead, we have uncovered a different – seemingly more credible – source for our core moral convictions. Our conclusion is Hume's:

> It requires but very little knowledge of human affairs to perceive, that a sense of morals is a principle inherent in the soul, and one of the most powerful that enters into the composition. But this sense must certainly acquire new force, when reflecting upon itself, it approves of those principles, from which it is deriv'd, and finds nothing but what is great and good in its origin. (1739–40/2000, 3.3.6.3 [SBN 619])

The moral faculty approves of itself.

Admittedly, some philosophers would insist that we agree on a metaphysical account of moral facts *before* we attempt to gauge the reliability of our moral judgments. If an "ideal observer" account of morality is correct, and what it is for x to be immoral is for x to be judged immoral by a sympathetic, neutral observer, then the method of empathetic neutrality will prove reliable. But if x is immoral just in case it fails to maximize utility; or if x is immoral just in case it would be legislated against by dispassionate members of an idealized deliberative body; or if x is immoral just in case it violates the tenets of Judaism, Christianity, or Islam; then the reliability of Copperfield's method must come into doubt.

But this would be akin to insisting that we agree on a metaphysical account of the colors before assessing the reliability of our visual judgments, or a metaphysical account of time before assessing the reliability of our memories. If a physician can gauge the health of a man's color vision and memory without the aid of philosophers of mind, then we should be able to assess the health of the moral faculty without recourse to metaphysics. The inquiry is immanent, but enlightening nevertheless.

We are first and foremost epistemologists. And if we insist that epistemology is "first philosophy," we will insist that an accurate moral metaphysics would have to vindicate the core moral judgments that we have uncovered in the course of our inquiry. Perhaps moral metaphysicians – who, as we have seen, typically construct their theories by applying the method of reflective equilibrium – will find themselves rejecting at least some of the core moral convictions we have exposed. But this will prove reasonable only if they have compelling theoretical reasons for the revision. The fact that a strong theoretical rationale must be given to justify the maneuver attests to the independent evidential weight that moral theorists must initially assign to the products of objective, empathetic judgment.

Metaphysics may be first in the order of being, but it is last in the order of knowledge. We must begin our metaphysical inquiries with what we know. Or, if we do not yet have moral knowledge, we must start with those moral beliefs that have withstood skeptical critique.

7.2 Chapter summary

We have defended ourselves from the skeptic's arguments against moral knowledge and justified moral beliefs. But are these defensive maneuvers enough to show that we actually have moral knowledge and justified moral beliefs? This question is particularly urgent when aimed at moral judgments that are supposed to be wholly non-inferential in their justification. If we cannot support these beliefs with arguments, what distinguishes them from a romantic's groundless belief in fairies or ghosts?

We can answer this question to our satisfaction – if not the most unyielding skeptic's – by describing the developmental history of our moral concepts and beliefs. Those who grasp moral concepts must limit their moral judgments to an evaluation of actions and institutions shaped by intentional agents who have some understanding of morality and the self-control necessary to act in accord with that understanding. But reliable moral judgment requires, in addition, the kind of neutrality that results from thinking of actions from many different perspectives: the agent's point of view, the point of view of those people affected by the action, and, perhaps, the point of view of a neutral party who has nothing at stake. When a sympathetic person forms moral judgments in this manner, we can reasonably claim that her beliefs will be much more often true than false, and that they will attain some degree of reliability even if she has no arguments to offer in their support.

It is hard to see how we can avoid using our powers of moral judgment when assessing whether empathetic neutrality is a reliable way to reach moral verdicts. But this form of circularity does not distinguish our assessment of core instances of moral judgment from assessments of the reliability of our perceptual and wholly logical beliefs. One might turn to metaphysics for an independent account of moral truth against which we might assess the method of empathetic neutrality. But metaphysicians must await the results of our study for constraints on their theories. When it comes to philosophical knowledge of morality, moral epistemology comes first.

7.3 Further reading

Developmental psychologists have been writing about moral thought for some time, but the literature has blossomed as of late. Three important collections of essays are Usha Goswami (ed.), *Blackwell Handbook of Childhood Cognitive Development* (2002); Melanie Killen and Judith Smetana (eds.), *Handbook of Moral Development* (2006); and Willem Koops *et al.*, *The Development and Structure of Conscience* (2009).

Adapted from the work of Jean Piaget (1896–1980), Lawrence Kohlberg's hypothesized stages of moral development were the focus of a great deal of discussion in the 1970s; see his "From Is to Ought" (1971) and "The Claim to Moral Adequacy of the Highest Stage of Moral Judgment" (1973). The pre-eminent moral philosophy journal *Ethics* devoted the April 1982 issue to an assessment of Kohlberg's views. Criticisms came from a number of different directions including Carolyn Edwards, "Societal Complexity and Moral Development" (1975); Carol Gilligan, *In a Different Voice* (1982); and Elliot Turiel, *The Development of Social Knowledge* (1983).

Martin Hoffman's *Empathy and Moral Development* (2000) presents a broadly Humean alternative to Kohlberg's stages. Daniel Batson's experiments, which are described and interpreted in *The Altruism Question* (1991), are supposed by their author to show that empathy motivates altruistic action. Karsten Stueber's *Rediscovering Empathy* (2006) traces the history of the concept and the significance of empathy for debates regarding the nature of psychological explanation.

R. M. Hare, *The Language of Morals* (1952) and Thomas Nagel, *The Possibility of Altrusim* (1970) are important philosophical treatments of perspective-taking. Both are broadly Kantian in inspiration. John Deigh, "Empathy and Universalizability" (1995) nicely marries the Kantian and Humean approaches to the phenomenon.

A great deal has been written on our understanding of the thoughts, feelings, and intentions of other people. The theory theory was endorsed by David Lewis, "Psychophysical and Theoretical Identifications" (1972) as a way of understanding the relation between the (folk) psychological and neurological realms. Daniel Dennett's *The Intentional Stance* (1987) is an accessible discussion of this approach. Alison Gopnik and Henry Wellman, "Why the Child's Theory of Mind Really Is a Theory" (1992) and Gopnik and Andrew Meltzoff, *Words, Thoughts, and Theories* (1997) are fairly recent defenses.

Robert Gordon defends a simulation theory in "Folk Psychology as Simulation" (1986) and discusses its relation to ethical judgment in "Sympathy, Simulation and the Impartial Spectator" (1995). Collections of essays on the debate between theory theorists and simulation theorists include Martin Davies and Tony Stone (eds.), *Mental Simulation* (1995) and Peter Carruthers and Peter Smith (eds.), *Theories of Theories of Mind* (1996). The essays in Bertram Malle, Louis Moses, and Dare Baldwin (eds.), *Intentions and Intentionality* (2001) address a broad range of issues relating to the development of psychological understanding.

Michael Zimmerman, *An Essay on Moral Responsibility* (1988) and John Martin Fischer and Mark Ravizza, *Responsibility and Control* (1998) discuss the conditions creatures must meet to be properly assessed in moral terms. Fischer's "Recent Work on Moral Responsibility" (1999) is a useful summary of the issues and guide to further reading.

Philosophers have long debated whether it is acceptable to use a faculty (or putative source of knowledge) to establish that faculty's reliability. Recent discussions include William Alston, "Epistemic Circularity" (1986); Jonathan Vogel, "Reliabilism Leveled" (2000); Stewart Cohen "Basic Knowledge and the Problem of Easy Knowledge" (2002); and James Van Cleve, "Is Knowledge Easy – or Impossible?" (2003).

8

EPILOGUE: CHALLENGES TO MORAL EPISTEMOLOGY

8.1 Frege, Moore, and the definition of "immorality"

Recall the representation of Copperfield's inference to Creakle's cruelty presented in 1.4 above:

1   Creakle enjoyed causing others to suffer.
2   Someone acts cruelly just in case she takes enjoyment in causing others to suffer.
Therefore,
3   Creakle acted cruelly.

We assume that Copperfield knows (1) via observations of Creakle's behavior. And we continue to assume that the *OED* is to be trusted in its assertion that (2) is true. But these assumptions would seem to leave unanswered the distinctively epistemological questions we have addressed in this book: does Copperfield know (2)? And if so, how?

And yet, though these look like difficult philosophical matters that demand epistemological investigation, adopting a *Fregean view of moral concepts* would force us to conclude otherwise. For according to the Fregean view, in describing how Copperfield comes to know the suffering of his school-mates and the delight his headmaster takes in its infliction we have *already* described how Copperfield comes to believe in Creakle's cruelty. That is, on the Fregean account, Copperfield needn't infer that Creakle is cruel from a relatively neutral assessment of the man's motives and his Socratic knowledge of the defining essence of cruelty. Instead, in the very act of judging that Creakle enjoys making others suffer, Copperfield *therein* judges Creakle cruel.

If we think of moral epistemology as a distinctive branch of epistemology devoted to the study of moral thought, the Fregean view of moral concepts presents a challenge to the very coherence of our enterprise. Why? Because the Fregean view equates moral thought with psychological thought and value-neutral cognition of other kinds. The Fregean claims that there are no irreducibly moral concepts and beliefs. And if there are no irreducibly moral beliefs, there can be no irreducibly moral knowledge.

The account is called "Fregean" because it builds upon a view, advanced by the father of analytic philosophy, Gottlob Frege (1848–1925), that epithets are equivalent in meaning to certain non-derogatory expressions. For example, "dog" and "cur" are on Frege's reckoning *synonymous*; they agree in both reference and sense; they pick out the same range of animals by expressing the very same concept. The two expressions differ only in that "cur" evokes certain negative images and feelings that "dog" does not.

> If we compare the sentences "This dog howled the whole night" and "This cur howled the whole night," we find that the thought is the same. The first sentence tells us neither more nor less than does the second. But whilst the word "dog" is neutral as between having pleasant or unpleasant associations, the word "cur" certainly has unpleasant rather than pleasant associations and puts us rather in mind of a dog with an unkempt appearance. Even if it is grossly unfair to the dog to think of it in this way, we cannot say that this makes the second sentence false. (1897/1997, 240–41)[1]

Extrapolating now to the morally relevant case of "cruelty," the Fregean might say that "Creakle acted cruelly" is used to assert nothing beyond "Creakle took pleasure in harming another." (As Frege might himself say,

"The first sentence tells us neither more nor less than does the second.") Note, then, that according to the Fregean proposal, in advancing his conclusion (3), Copperfield asserts nothing more than he does when asserting his first premise (1). That is, when Copperfield concludes that Creakle acted cruelly in hitting the boys, he believes nothing beyond what he affirms when remarking that Creakle took great pleasure in delivering his beatings. Thus, so long as she is not prepared to attribute to Copperfield two different beliefs in one and the same proposition, the Fregean must say that Copperfield's belief in Creakle's cruelty *just is* Copperfield's belief that Creakle enjoyed causing suffering.[2] And if the Fregean is right in thinking that these beliefs are truly identical, there can be no difference in their – that is, *its* – epistemological properties. In sum, if the Fregean analysis of "cruelty" is correct, only a general skepticism about other minds could prevent Copperfield from knowing that Creakle is cruel. We must say that Copperfield's apparent moral knowledge is entirely grounded in – or based on – his observations of his friends and teacher. The questions we have discussed regarding his knowledge of premise (2) simply disappear.

Now I am convinced that the Fregean treatment of "cruelty" must be mistaken in one way or another, and I aim to support this conclusion by the end of this chapter. But I first want to inquire into whether this way of treating value-laden terms like "cruelty" can be applied across the board. Might someone really argue that what looks like distinctively moral knowledge is really nothing over and above our knowledge of other minds?

Note, in this regard, that Copperfield needn't limit himself to judging Creakle's actions cruel; he might very well reason from their cruelty to their immorality.[3] We can ask, therefore: what, if anything, distinguishes knowing that an action is cruel from knowing that it is immoral? Are these distinct states of knowledge or really different descriptions of our knowledge of a single fact? And if they are distinct items of knowledge, when are we entitled to infer the immorality of an action from our knowledge of its cruelty? What role does our knowledge of a definition of "immorality" – or the fact it might be used to state – play in our knowledge that a given act of cruelty is immoral?

Recall that our initial characterization of Copperfield's reasoning made use of a fairly attractive definition of "cruelty," where the truth of that definition, when wedded to the accuracy of Copperfield's rather astute psychological observations, was seen to entail Creakle's cruelty. The difficulty, though, in extending this model to Copperfield's belief in Creakle's immorality, is the absence of any similarly attractive definition of that term. The OED's definition of "immoral" offers nothing more helpful than "not moral" and a string of equally value-laden supposed equivalents: "evil," "sinful," "vicious," "wicked," and "wrong."

Suppose, then, that in an ill-conceived first attempt, we define "immoral" just as we have defined "cruel."

1   Creakle enjoyed causing others to suffer.
4   Someone acts immorally just in case she takes enjoyment in causing others to suffer.
Therefore,
5   Creakle acted immorally.

It doesn't take a Gettier to see that premise (4) is patently false. A man acts immorally but not cruelly when he is motivated by greed to steal luxury goods from a miser's warehouse while regretting the act throughout its performance. If common thinking is any guide, cruelty is at best just one form of immorality.

But might the Fregean try to define "immoral" in value-neutral terms of a more general kind? Though the dictionaries cannot help us here, the two major kinds of normative moral theory that have been defended in the last two centuries might. Kantianism has as its first principle the categorical imperative, and utilitarianism has its principle of utility. And there are versions of utilitarianism and Kantianism that treat these first principles as definitional or analytic truths. Indeed, though Mill and Kant did not consistently treat their respective first principles as definitions of "immorality," they sometimes did think of them in this way.[4]

So let us first consider the following three claims:

i   Mill's generic utilitarian view that happiness is the only thing that is *intrinsically good*, and an action consequently *bad* just in case it detracts from the amount of happiness that would otherwise exist in the universe.
ii   Mill's associated claim that a certain kind of action – such as cheating, lying, snorkeling, or playing whist – is *right* to the degree that it promotes happiness and *wrong* to the degree to which it tends to promote suffering ("Actions are right in proportion as they tend to promote happiness, wrong as they tend to produce the reverse of happiness" [1861/1998, 55]).

iii   And, finally, the associated claim, also attributable to Mill, that individuals act *immorally* just in case they intentionally induce suffering or
rob someone of happiness.[5]

And let us bracket for the moment the issue of whether there are moral acts
that intentionally detract from happiness, or immoral acts that intentionally
add to the same. (Again, we will have ample opportunity to question this
assumption in what follows.) If an accurate, relatively simple definition of
"immorality" could be drawn from these utilitarian claims, and if the facts
they state really were known to Copperfield, we could model his knowledge
of Creakle's immorality as follows.

6   Creakle intentionally detracted from happiness.
7   Someone acts immorally just in case she intentionally detracts from
happiness.
Therefore,
4   Creakle acted immorally.

With these assumptions in place, we would only have to inquire into how
Copperfield manages to know premise (7).

But there is a way to argue that this question is spurious. For a *Fregean
utilitarian* would take Mill's identification of moral wrongness with willed
detraction from happiness one step further, and claim that "immoral"
and "intentionally detracts from happiness" express the very same
concept.

> ***Fregean utilitarianism***: the judgment that someone's act is immoral
> just is the judgment that, with its performance, she intentionally
> detracts from happiness.

That is, just as on Frege's account "dog" and "cur" agree in both sense and
reference and differ only in tone or coloring, so too, the Fregean utilitarian maintains, "acted immorally" and "intentionally detracted from
happiness" differ only in that the former expression is associated with feelings and images not brought to mind by its neutral correlate. Thus, if the
Fregean utilitarian is correct, Copperfield's belief in Creakle's immorality
just is Copperfield's belief that Creakle willfully stole from the common weal.
Premise (7) is an idle wheel. The Fregean utilitarian reduces moral epistemology to a study of the calculation of utilities.

Are there any Fregean utilitarians? Though Mill never swayed from the exceedingly general idea that happiness is the whole point of having moral rules and institutions in the first place, it is well known that his work gave substance to this proposal in a number of different, seemingly incompatible ways (Urmson, 1953; Lyons, 1965; Crisp, 1992). It should then come as no surprise that there are indeed passages in which Mill endorses something like the Fregean thesis.

> Desiring a thing and finding it pleasant, aversion to it and thinking of it as painful, are phenomena entirely inseparable, or rather two parts of the same phenomenon; in strictness of language, two different modes of naming the same psychological fact: *that to think of an object as desirable (unless for the sake of its consequences), and to think of it as pleasant, are one and the same thing.* (1861/1998, 85; emphasis added)

> What is the principle of utility, if it be not that "happiness" and "desirable" are synonymous terms? (1861/1998, 105n.)

Looking at these passages in isolation, one would expect Mill to simply equate Copperfield's judgment that Creakle's actions were bad or undesirable with Copperfield's belief in the unpleasantness of their consequences. To conclude that Creakle's actions were immoral, the boy would only then need to establish the immorality of someone's doing something bad or his intentionally doing such. If Mill were to then equate the judgment that an act is immoral with the judgment that its intended consequences were undesirable or bad, he would therein embrace the full-blooded Fregean position. Copperfield's knowing that Creakle's acts were immoral just *is* his knowing that they achieved their intended unpleasantness.[6]

Of course, we can only use Mill's Fregean proposals to accurately model the entirety of Copperfield's reasoning if the utilitarian analysis of "immoral" is correct. So we must drop the rather implausible assumptions we have been making and return to the truly fundamental question at hand: does "immoral" mean what the Fregean utilitarian claims it means? Is there perhaps some other, more plausible, and yet equally value-neutral description that might be thought to share the sense and reference of the term? Can we really define substantive moral epistemology out of existence?

The prospects for an affirmative answer to these questions were perhaps most famously assessed by G. E. Moore in his extraordinarily influential work *Principia Ethica*. At the outset of a truly "scientific" moral inquiry, Moore there argues, we must ask what distinguishes ethical or moral thought from cognition of all other kinds.

> In the vast majority of cases, where we make statements involving any of the terms "virtue," "vice," "duty," "right," "ought," "good," "bad," we are making ethical judgments ... What is it that is ... common and peculiar ... to all such judgments? (1903/1929, 1)

And as a first step in attempting to answer this question, Moore claims, we can correctly define the expression "ethical" in terms of the expression "good." This maneuver will allow us to conclude that, properly conceived, ethical theory is just the study of goodness and badness.

> That which is meant by "good" is, in fact, except its converse "bad", the only simple object of thought that is peculiar to Ethics. Its definition is therefore the most essential point in the definition of Ethics. (5)

> It is asked, "What is a man's duty under these circumstances?" or "Is it right to act in this way?" or "What ought we aim at securing?" But all these questions are capable of further analysis; a correct answer to any of them involves both judgments of what is good in itself and causal judgments. (24)[7]

So far, Moore's thinking is no different from that evinced by Mill in the passage quoted above. Moral actions generate goodness; immoral actions generate badness. But the two thinkers begin to part ways when Moore tries to say what goodness and badness *are*, a question Moore regularly conflates with *defining* "good" and "bad." ("What then is good? How is good to be defined?" [6]) And it is then soon made clear that the "definition" which Moore seeks needn't capture all the vagaries and subtleties endemic to our ordinary usage of "good," but need only unpack or analyze the "object or idea ... that the word is generally used to stand for," so as to "discover the nature of that object or idea" (6).

Can the clever Socratic analyst uncover the requisite definitions of "good" and "bad"? Can we formulate analyses that at once uncover the ideas associated with these terms and explicate the natures of the objects, properties, or phenomena they delimit? Moore famously concludes that we cannot, as "propositions about the good are all of them synthetic and never analytic" (7). All candidate accounts must be rejected, Moore claims, because:

> Whatever definition be offered, it may always be asked, with significance, of the complex so defined, whether it is itself good. (15)

For instance, Moore claims that "x is good" cannot be defined as "x is what we want to want" because we can ask, in a significant way, whether what we want to want is good. Similarly, "goodness" cannot be defined as "happiness" as we can always ask with significance whether those activities (and experiences) that bring (or constitute) happiness are also good. On what we might call *Moore's test* for successful definition, then, "x is F" can only be defined as "x is G," if there is a point at which we cannot meaningfully ask whether what is G is itself F. I think we can best interpret this as follows:

> *Moore's test*: if "Fness" is accurately defined as "Gness" then those who understand the proposal cannot reasonably wonder whether what is G is also F.

Moore's might be said to be a test for the *self-evidence* of a definition, in something like Locke's sense of "self-evidence."[8]

Now, we can fairly easily see that all value-neutral definitions of "goodness" fail the requisite test and so are not self-evident in Moore's sense. Most relevantly, given our current focus on utilitarianism, we, who understand the proposal, can indeed coherently wonder whether happiness is intrinsically good, and what brings us happiness good in consequence. Mightn't we find happiness in the wrong sorts of things? Mightn't undeserved happiness be bad "in itself"? Even if these questions deserve negative answers, they are not trivial to the point of incoherence. Thus, what has come to be called Moore's *open-question argument* casts serious doubt on the Fregean method for dealing with "immorality" and similar terms. Since, as Moore points out, we can coherently wonder whether what detracts from happiness is also wrong, thinking that something is wrong is not the same thing as thinking that it detracts from happiness.

It should also be clear that Moore's reasoning in *Principia* generalizes beyond just utilitarian forms of Fregeanism. Consider, for instance, Kant's universal law formulation of the categorical imperative, "I ought never to conduct myself except so that I could also will that my maxim become a universal law" (1785/2002, 18 [Ak 4:402]). A *Fregean Kantian* would take Kant's proposal one step further and equate our *knowing* that an action is immoral with our *knowing* that it is guided by partial maxims (i.e. maxims that cannot be willed as universal laws). But it seems we can apply Moore's test to show that "immoral" is not synonymous with "guided by maxims impugned by their partiality" and that knowledge of an act's immorality is something distinct from knowledge of the unfairness behind it. For, we might ask, mightn't it be perfectly moral, and yet unfair, to deny a man his due, when doing so would confer enormous benefits on the suffering masses? Perhaps the answer is "no," but is the question incoherent? The Kantian Fregean errs in equating the concept *immoral* with the concept *unfair*.[9]

Applying Moore's test to Copperfield's evaluation of Creakle is a relatively straightforward matter. Since "immoral" has no neutral synonym, the Fregean strategy cannot be carried through to the end of the boy's reasoning. That is, as the open-question argument shows, the proposition that Creakle acted immorally cannot be equated with the proposition that Creakle intentionally detracted from his pupils' happiness, nor can it be identified with the claim that Creakle's policy of corporal punishment was prejudiced against the chubby boys. The Fregean's case against moral epistemology is at best incomplete.

Indeed, the relatively weak implications we have assigned to the open-question argument might be thought strong enough to impugn the whole Fregean approach. For it is now time to put the thin concept of "immorality" to the side to ask whether a Fregean analysis of the thick concept of "cruelty" built upon the testimony of the *Oxford English Dictionary* really can pass Moore's test. Is it really *impossible* to coherently wonder whether an instance of taking pleasure in knowingly harming another person is an instance of cruelty? We might examine, in this light, the tentative suggestion, most recently advanced by Audi, that pleasure taken in the infliction of pain is not necessarily bad,

> in special circumstances, such as causing suffering in administering deserved punishment, as where the jailer – within limits – takes pleasure in causing the pain that an unrepentant violent criminal feels in being locked up. (2006, 88; cf. Portmann, 2000)

Suppose we follow Audi and entertain the possibility that the jailer's satisfaction isn't really bad. Might the relish he takes in inflicting suffering upon the criminal entrusted to his care then fail to be cruel? Perhaps this is an incorrect description of the case, but is its inaccuracy obvious? One begins to worry that a clever enough attorney might cast doubt on the cruelty of the interrogations at Guantánamo Bay.

Or consider an example somewhat less fraught with controversy: the pleasure a triumphant boxer typically takes in delivering the knockout blow. A pacifist might insist that this reaction is cruel. But he would surely depart from common thought in adopting this stance. At the very least, we must allow that an aficionado of the sweet science might coherently ask herself, in a moment of self-doubt, whether the sport in which she takes such pleasure really is rife with cruelty. If the question she poses is not trivial to the point of incoherence, the concept *being cruel* cannot be equated with the concept *taking pleasure in the infliction of suffering*. And if these concepts are not equivalent, the thought that Creakle took pleasure in beating his pupils is distinct from the thought that Creakle acted cruelly. The Fregean strategy never gets off the ground.

8.2 Common-sense objections to non-cognitivism

Fregean accounts of moral thought seek to undermine substantive moral epistemology by reducing our moral beliefs to psychological and sociological judgments that are value-neutral in content. We are now in a position to evaluate the next hurdle to establishing a meaningful moral epistemology: that presented by *strong non-cognitivists* – like Rudolf Carnap (1937) and A. J. Ayer (1946/1952) – who deny that we have moral beliefs that are fit for epistemic assessment.

According to strong non-cognitivism, we simply cannot use moral language to express moral beliefs or judgments, or if we can in some attenuated sense speak of "beliefs" with moral content, the states of mind in question must differ so radically from our non-evaluative beliefs and judgments as to preclude the very possibility of moral epistemology (Harman and Thomson, 1996). Whereas my belief that humans first evolved some 250,000 years ago can be assessed in epistemic terms, by, for example, asking whether it is supported by good evidence, the non-cognitivist argues that if we can even coherently speak of my "belief" that it is immoral to kill people for pleasure, we cannot make sense of someone's concluding that this belief is true, nor can we speak of its content as something I know or fail to know, or something for which I have good or bad evidence. Instead, when I say that the thug's acts of violence are immoral, I am simply expressing my regret or anger that he is acting in this way, or my desire that his behavior not be replicated.

> *Strong non-cognitivism*: either (a) there are no beliefs or judgments with moral content, or (b) if there are, they are so unlike our non-evaluative beliefs that they cannot be coherently assessed in epistemic terms.

Clearly, if strong non-cognitivism is right, moral epistemology is grounded in a fundamental misconception of morality, epistemology, and their intersection.

Thus, there is a sense in which those wishing to pursue the study of moral epistemology must first answer the strong non-cognitivist's challenge. The problem with this, though, is that the literature on non-cognitivism has become so extensive that diligent discussions of the issue have come to fill books on their own.[10] We must therefore limit ourselves here to a cursory review of some reasons for thinking that strong non-cognitivism, if not clearly untenable, is at least quite difficult to defend.

Our first observation is that moral discourse exhibits what Peter Railton (1996, 2003) calls "surface cognitivity" (cf. Horgan and Timmons, 2006a, 262–67). When we conduct our first-level moral inquiries we discover people speaking of one another's moral knowledge, beliefs, and assertions. "Colin knows that it was morally wrong of him to lie." "A year ago, Senator McCain, you asserted that abortion is morally permissible." "Henry believes that the torture at Abu Ghraib was immoral."

Indeed, a test for ambiguity supplied by verb-phrase ellipses suggests that "belief" and "assertion" do not have distinct moral and descriptive senses. Rather, we at least commonly conceive of the moral beliefs and assertions we attribute to one another as similar in kind to those with wholly non-moral content. Consider, for instance, "Schwarzenegger asserted that steroids have no adverse effects and that abortion is morally permissible," or "Singer believes that humans evolved from apes and that it is immoral to imprison any primate in a zoo." In each case a single occurrence of "belief" or "assertion" is used to denote the relation between an individual and two propositions – one moral in content and the other wholly non-moral or scientific. Does this not suggest that our ordinary concepts of belief and assertion are applied to moral and non-moral propositions alike? And if the non-cognitivist is using "belief" and "assertion" in some distinct, technical sense, why should moral epistemologists worry that the states and acts that the non-cognitivist is talking about are unfit for epistemic assessment?

Moreover, though many of the purportedly moral beliefs we attribute to one another are ingrained through conditioning and other forms of brute enculturation – and some may in large part owe their existence to neural structures that are to a substantial degree innate or genetically encoded – we sometimes call for and ask for arguments on behalf of the propositions so believed. "Okay, so you were raised by conservatives to think that homosexual marriage is immoral, but do you have any reason for thinking that this is really so?" "So, you were brought up by liberals to think that it is morally permissible for a woman to extract the fetus growing within her at any stage of pregnancy, but you agree that it is never morally permissible to allow one's newborn child to die from neglect. Can you give some reason for distinguishing the cases in this manner?" Of course, we rarely if ever require that people supply reasons for embracing their most fundamental moral beliefs – such as the belief that one should not harm others for selfish reasons – but the same goes for our basic perceptual and conceptual beliefs. We are not commonly required to defend the belief that $2 + 2 = 4$ or the claim that we are human.

Similarly, just as we fairly often write and speak of assertions and beliefs with moral content, we commonly describe the propositions so believed as true and false: "George said that homosexual sex is immoral, but that is just plain false." "There is no fact more obvious than that slavery is morally wrong." "The pope's beliefs on moral matters are all true." If common thought and usage are taken at face value, the non-cognitivist challenge must come to naught.

8.3 The Frege–Geach problems: semantics v. pragmatics

The kind of surface cognitivity identified above is intimately connected to the often-discussed *Frege–Geach problem* of how non-cognitivists can account for the distinctively "logical" or "formal" properties of sentences containing moral vocabulary (Geach, 1957–58, 1960, 1965; Searle, 1962; Hare, 1970; Hale, 1993; Price, 1994; Schueler, 1988; Stoljar, 1993; Unwin, 1999, 2001; and Ridge, 2006). A warning though: those uninterested in the logic of moral discourse should end their reading here. If you are not concerned with these matters, you are unlikely to find illumination in what remains of this chapter.

To see what is at issue, we need to consider the kind of moral argument that would seem to have little going for it except for some kind of formal goodness.

1   Lying is immoral.
2   If lying is immoral, then cruelty is immoral.
Therefore,
3   Cruelty is immoral.

The cognitivist admits, of course, that there are respects in which (1)–(3) is an odd piece of reasoning. Most notably, its second premise seems to assert a link between the immorality of lying and cruelty that is hard to make out. And yet the cognitivist is prone to insisting both that the argument is logically or formally valid and that its validity is no trivial matter. The argument's value consists in its conforming to a highly prized rule of inference: it is a modus ponens argument. And if a modus ponens argument has true premises, it must also have a true conclusion. Modus ponens is valued because it is a *sound* form of inference.

The classical cognitivist explanation of our argument's non-trivial validity rests on three claims:

i   "If lying is immoral, then cruelty is immoral" is an *indicative conditional* (though not necessarily a material conditional): that is, a conditional sentence in the indicative mood. Its antecedent is "Lying is immoral" and its consequent is "Cruelty is immoral."
ii   The antecedent of an indicative conditional is either true or false but not both; the same goes for its consequent.[11]
iii Every indicative conditional with a true antecedent and a false consequent is itself false.

The assumption of (i) allows us to classify (1)–(3) as a modus ponens argument, where this means thinking of it as conforming to a rule permitting a reasoner to infer a sentence Q from the assumption or derivation of sentences P and If P then Q. The rule in question is typically represented as follows:

Modus ponens
P
If P then Q
Q

And the assumption of (ii) and (iii) allows us to show that modus ponens is a *truth-preserving* rule of inference. We can utilize the relevant portion of one of Ludwig Wittgenstein's (1889–1951) *truth tables* to provide a graphic representation of the relevant claims.[12]

P (Lying is immoral)	Q (Cruelty is immoral)	If P then Q
True	False	False

We begin our proof by recalling our definition of "validity" from which it follows that our argument is invalid only if its premises – (1) and (2) – can be true and its conclusion – (3) – false. But the shaded row of our table indicates that when (1) is true and (3) is false, (2) is also false. So it seems that premise (2) cannot be true when (1) is true and (3) is false. Thus, if the argument under discussion really is a modus ponens argument, and our truth table really does capture all the possibilities that are in play when we are evaluating a modus ponens argument, the cognitivist can use this table to explain the "formal" goodness of (1)–(3). The argument's value consists in its conforming to modus ponens, where modus ponens is a necessarily truth-preserving rule for reasoning.

Note, though, that non-cognitivists cannot endorse this explication of our argument's validity. For the truth table above incorporates the assumption that each of the atomic sentences in our argument – "Lying is immoral" and "Cruelty is immoral" – admits of the two classic *truth values*: true and false. If we adopted the most straightforward non-cognitivist's proposal, we would reject assumption (ii) in our proof and fill all three boxes in the shaded row with "neither true nor false." A meaningful proof of the soundness of modus ponens – and the consequent validity of our argument – would then prove impossible. In sum, the non-cognitivist cannot adopt the classical explanation of the non-trivial validity of modus ponens arguments when these arguments are couched in evaluative vocabulary.[13]

Of course, nothing precludes the cognitivist from admitting that (1)–(3) is not only valid but also good along a second, substantially different dimension that consists in substantially different facts from the soundness of modus ponens. An otherwise rational agent who was fixed in her belief in the argument's premises, and who then considered the argument's conclusion, would find herself compelled to believe it. And we can say, as a fully general matter, that one ought either to believe the argument's conclusion in such a case, or abandon belief in at least one of its premises. Moreover, no one should assert the argument's premises while denying its conclusion, and no one should hope to remain solvent when betting heavily on the truth of its premises and the falsity of its conclusion. We call these kinds of coherence "psychological" and "pragmatic" because our characterization of them employs psychological and speech-theoretic notions like *belief* and *assertion* that play no obvious role in our account of the argument's non-trivial validity. In contrast, when we provided a cognitivist explanation of our argument's validity, we employed the semantic notions *truth* and *falsity*, and the syntactic notion *modus ponens* – notions that do not directly enter into our description of the argument's psychological or pragmatic coherence.[14]

Admittedly, the psychological coherence of (1)–(3) almost certainly does have something to do with "truth" and other semantic notions. It seems, for instance, that we judge someone irrational when she believes contradictory claims precisely because we think their conjoint falsehood a relatively obvious matter. By believing both a proposition and its negation a person ensures for herself that one of these two beliefs is false, and rational people avoid believing falsehoods when this can be reconciled with other important ends. But the link between the rationality of our beliefs and actions on the one hand and, on the other, the validity of the arguments we give and accept when defending our beliefs and actions is an exceedingly complex one to describe. At the very least, it seems our theorizing is best served by distinguishing in thought between the two. We will then treat the discovery of a precise coordination between, on the one hand, irrational actions of some kind and, on the other, a certain range of contradictory statements with the respect such a discovery deserves, as an achievement of remarkable philosophical insight.

But now, by way of contrast with (1)–(3), we have the imperatival cousin of our argument – the kind of non-declarative structure on which the non-cognitivist trains his focus.

1'   Don't lie.
2'   When refraining from lying, don't be cruel.
Therefore,
3'   Don't be cruel.

Argument (1')–(3') has something like (1)–(3)'s psychological coherence. A rational agent who commands its premises will find herself compelled to command its conclusion. We can say in full generality that one ought to command the argument's conclusion or cease commanding at least one of its premises. Someone set on obeying the argument's premises must obey the conclusion. And so on. But without making strides towards an imperatival syntax and model theory, we cannot say that (1')–(3') is valid or that it exhibits some non-cognitivist surrogate for classical validity. Thus, while the badness endemic to commanding or emoting the premises but not the conclusion of an imperatival argument like (1')–(3') is not altogether unlike the badness of believing or asserting the premises but not the conclusion of a classically valid argument, these distinctively psychological and pragmatic shortcomings are conceptually distinct from the more obviously logical fact that the conjoint truth of a valid argument's premises and the negation of its conclusion is provably impossible (cf. Schueler, 1988; van Roojen, 1996).

8.4 Non-cognitivist forms of validity

The non-cognitivist might simply reject the cognitivist's "intuition" that declarative argument (1)–(3) is good in some distinctively logical, non-psychological, non-pragmatic respect. But many non-cognitivists have avoided this stance and have instead tried to carve out a more formal or logical means for evaluating moral arguments. Recent years have seen some influential, much-discussed attempts from the likes of Simon Blackburn (1984, 1988), Allan Gibbard (1990, 1992a,b), and Mark Schroeder (2008), though none of these theorists is whole-hearted in his dissatisfaction with treating psychological or pragmatic incoherence as the end of the story so far as moral argumentation is concerned.

The non-cognitivist might inaugurate the project by challenging our characterization of the "badness" involved in: (a) commanding someone to both refrain from telling lies and to refrain from cruelty when refraining from lying, while (b) refusing to command her to simply refrain from cruelty. Surely, the non-cognitivist might argue, what is good about (1')–(3') has everything to do with the *meaning* of "when" just as the logical or formal value of (1)–(3) has everything to do with the *meaning* of "if" (Hare, 1952; Smart, 1984). So why can't we capture the formal or logical validity of our initial argument by comparing it to the presumably formal or logical goodness of its imperatival surrogate? In both cases, the incoherence is "logical" precisely because it is "semantic" or derived from the meanings of certain key expressions involved in the argument.

But what is the connection between, on the one hand, the meanings of paradigmatically logical expressions like "if", "or", "and", "not", "some", "all", and "many", and, on the other, the validity or formal goodness of the arguments in which these expressions figure? On the classical account, the meaning of a word like "or" determines a *truth-function*: a function from the truth values of the sentences to which the expression is applied to the truth value of the sentence that results from its application. Epistemologically speaking, knowing the meaning of, say, "or" centrally involves knowing how to compute the truth or falsity of a sentence "P or Q" from your knowledge of the truth or falsity of P and the truth or falsity of Q. And at the level of thought, grasping the concept *disjunction* – that is, the concept conventionally associated with the word "or" – involves knowing how to compute the truth or falsity of P or Q from one's knowledge of the truth value of P and the truth value of Q. In consequence, on the classical account, the meaning of "or" – or certain central aspects of its meaning – can be accurately represented with a full truth table – a completion of the kind of model we used above to represent the claim that indicative conditionals with true antecedents and false consequents are all false.

The classical table for "or" incorporates the claim that "P or Q" is false if P is false and Q is false, but that it is otherwise true. That table consists in the first three columns of the following representation:

P (*Lying is immoral*)	Q (*Cruelty is immoral*)	P or Q	Not P
True	True	True	False
True	False	True	False
False	True	True	True
False	False	False	True

Note, too, that our representation of the meaning of "or" is the very same representation we use when explaining why certain arguments employing "or" are formally good or valid. Consider, for instance, *disjunctive syllogism*, which employs both "or" and "not":

4   Lying is immoral or cruelty is immoral.
5   Lying is not immoral.
Therefore,
6   Cruelty is immoral.

The cognitivist can explain why this argument is non-trivially valid –
and in so doing demonstrate the soundness of disjunctive syllogism – by
reflecting on the shaded rows of truth values in the table given above, as the
impossibility of (6)'s being false when both (4) and (5) are true is there
represented.[15]

There is, therefore, a substantive challenge for the non-cognitivist who
would deny that the meanings of "or" and "if" determine the formal goodness of declarative moral arguments – like (1)–(3) and (4)–(6) – in the
classical way, while arguing, instead, that there is an alternative manner in
which these expressions fix the "validity" of the arguments in which they
figure. According to the non-cognitivist, the formal or logical goodness of
(1)–(3) is fixed by the meaning of "if" in that manner, *whatever it is*, in
which the meaning of "when" is supposed to determine the formal value
of the imperatival argument (1')–(3') above. But how does the meaning
of "when" serve to make (1')–(3') a formally good argument? Since
the non-cognitivist thinks that moral sentences can be neither true nor
false, she must answer this question without using central elements
of the classical cognitivist account of the validity of run-of-the-mill
inferences. When explaining what makes the imperatival argument
(1')–(3') formally good, she must replace truth-functions – along with
sub-sentential models of soundness and validity that employ relations
of *reference* and *satisfaction* – with structures and relations of a wholly
different kind.

There look to be two ways in which she might go about this task. First, the
non-cognitivist might modify or add to modus ponens, disjunctive syllogism, and similar rules of inference to arrive at rules explicitly defined over
commands, exclamations, or something else non-declarative in form. She
might, for instance, try to develop an *imperatival logic* with its own syntax and
semantics to provide a general account of what makes arguments like (1')–
(3') formally good (Vranas, 2008). And she might then attempt to provide
a *translation manual* that represents superficially declarative moral sentences
– like (1)–(3) – in imperatival form – as, for example, (1')–(3'). If this
were accomplished, the non-cognitivist could then try to "explain away"
the cognitivist's intuition that (1)–(3) really is non-trivially classically valid.

What our intuitions are really tracking in this case, she might argue, is the imperatival analogue of classical validity exemplified by our moral argument's imperatival translation.

But let us suppose that the first half of this project can be successfully completed, and the community of logicians converges on a well-understood imperatival logic with an accompanying characterization of "imperatival validity" couched not in terms of "truth" and "falsity" but in terms of the "satisfaction" and "violation" of the imperatives in question, or their "bindingness" and "non-bindingness" (Vranas, 2008, 531). Suppose, that is, that an imperatival argument is *i-valid* just in case it is impossible that its premises be binding and its conclusion non-binding, or impossible that its premises be satisfied and its conclusion violated. And let us suppose that (1')–(3') is i-valid in one or both of these ways. Why should we then follow the non-cognitivist in understanding the apparently classical (truth-defined) *validity* of declarative moral arguments in terms of the non-classical (satisfaction- or bindingness-defined) *i-validity* of their imperatival translations? Why isn't it more plausible to think that we can only understand imperatival validity by translating imperatival arguments into declarative form? Perhaps, that is, we are only led to characterize (1')–(3') as formally good because we tacitly convert it into the classically valid (1)–(3) (or something relevantly similar). Or perhaps, as seems the most plausible of the varying views on offer, neither form of argument is reducible to the other.[16]

Alternatively, the non-cognitivist might adopt a more straightforward, head-on approach, and allow for the non-trivial formal goodness of moral arguments by providing a non-classical semantics for *declarative* moral sentences themselves – a strategy explored in some detail by Mark Richard (2008) and Schroeder (2008). But if she is to minimize the radical implications of this approach, the non-cognitivist must argue that logical terms are actually ambiguous as between their moral and non-moral uses. Perhaps the truth tables accurately capture aspects of the meanings of "or" "not" and "if … then" when they are used in non-moral declarative sentences by representing the truth-functions they then denote, whereas the significance these terms accrue in moral sentences is best represented as something like a function from certain emotions, desires, or "pro-attitudes" – or the "commitments" shouldered in experiencing these emotions or adopting these pro-attitudes – onto others. Here the function assigned to the moral use of "if … then" must be carefully picked so as to establish the non-cognitive (truth-eschewing) analogue of validity for moral arguments like (1)–(3) that conform to modus ponens, and similar care must be exercised when providing a semantics for the other connectives and those inferences that conform to their introduction and elimination rules.[17]

One apparent difficulty with this approach, though, is that logical connectives can be coherently applied to moral and non-moral sentences in one fell swoop. Consider, for instance, conditionals with morally loaded antecedents and non-moral consequents, as in "Mother Theresa won't do it if it is morally impermissible," or "Private Muster always joins the charge when remaining behind would be immoral." Of course, the non-cognitivist might stipulate that the connectives in logically complex declarative sentences with moral constituents must always be given their non-classical interpretations, and reserve the classical semantics for value-neutral language. But this seems implausible. Suppose I hear someone say, "If George won't do it, then it must be really ... " as he moves out of earshot. Can it be plausibly maintained that I must ask for the end of the sentence to interpret the words I've already heard? Does my understanding of this use of "if ... then" depend on whether the speaker concluded her utterance with "expensive" or "immoral"? Surely not. Since I understand "if," I know that something false is here asserted so long as George won't do something that isn't ... ish in the least. I know this much without knowing what fills the gap – ... – in what was said.

Perhaps, then, the non-cognitivist should supply her deviant semantics for the logical connectives across the board, as Schroeder (2008) suggests (compare with Richard, 2008, 58–59). But this would undermine the application of classical logic to natural language en masse. It would, for instance, preclude us from using the first of the two truth tables presented above to explain the non-trivial validity of:

1''   Lying is common.
2''   If lying is common, then cruelty is often alleged.
Therefore,
3''   Cruelty is often alleged.

And if the non-cognitivist renounces the use of "truth" in explaining the goodness of

7   Honesty is obligatory.

Therefore,

8   It is not the case that honesty is not obligatory.

she loses an almost irresistible explanation of the verbal artistry displayed by the promoter Don King when building tension through logical equivalence.

7'   It is not the case that Tyson is not in the house.
8'   Tyson is in the house.

Surely, the moral non-cognitivist does not want to deny that King says something true when barking (7') to the crowd as the heavyweight's hands are being taped for the fight. And it is hard to see how the non-cognitivist can deny that (8') must also be true in such a case. But if the non-cognitivist is unwilling to posit an ambiguity in the meaning of "not," we must here have an explanation of our argument's (classical) soundness that is wholly unconnected to the meaning of "not." According to the non-cognitivist under consideration, "not" is univocal. And its one and only meaning is correctly represented with a function from emotions to emotions, commitments to commitments, or some such thing. But the natural, nearly irresistible, explanation of the soundness of King's argument would be couched entirely in terms of the truth of (7') and the classical, truth-defined soundness of *double-negation elimination*, the inference rule the promoter here follows. Is the case for moral non-cognitivism strong enough to warrant a wholesale revision in our understanding of the logic of ordinary discourse?

To answer this question, we must examine the case that has been presented on behalf of strong non-cognitivism. But we can here simply note that coherence is insufficient for truth. Even if strong non-cognitivism can eventually be formulated in a consistent, explanatorily adequate form, it may, for all that, still be quite mistaken.

Notice, however, that the Frege–Geach difficulties do not arise for *weak* forms of non-cognitivism – like the one suggested by Hare (1952) and endorsed by David Copp (2001, 2007) – according to which the primary or most basic function of moral language is the expression of emotion or desire rather than belief, but sentences with moral content are *also* used to assert various moral propositions and express various moral judgments.[18] Might it be that when I say that you were wrong to lie to me, what I first and foremost do is express my anger at your lying or my desire that you not continue to lie, but that the selfsame utterance also serves to express my belief that you were wrong to lie by asserting as much? Perhaps, though the priority of encouragement over description is more likely when I coo the syntactically declarative, "You're such a good boy," toward a young child's generous act. At any rate, even if it is correct, weak non-cognitivism of this kind poses no threat to the legitimacy of moral epistemology. So long as the expression of moral belief is one among the functions served by our use of moral vocabulary, and so long as the moral beliefs so expressed resemble our ordinary beliefs in being amenable to epistemic assessment, the line of inquiry with which we are here concerned is a legitimate one to pursue.

But mightn't a more reductive form of weak non-cognitivism claim that we use moral language to both express our emotions and assert a set of entirely *non-moral* propositions? Though a position of this kind would pose a threat to the coherence of moral epistemology, it would seem vulnerable to Moore's open-question argument. Indeed, it seems as though weak non-cognitivism of this stripe is just one version of the Fregean position we discussed above. For consider an arbitrary moral sentence: "Lying is immoral" will serve as an example. According to the position on offer, this sentence is used to both: (i) express an emotion and (ii) assert — as its semantic or logic-relevant content — a wholly value-neutral proposition. But which proposition? If Moore is right, the choice almost doesn't matter.[19] Let it be the proposition that lying is condemned by us all, the proposition that lying detracts from our happiness, or the proposition that maxims permitting lying could not serve as a universal guide to conduct. If one of these propositions were the conventional meaning of "Lying is immoral" and, therefore, the proposition one believes in believing that lying is immoral, those who assert, "Lying is immoral," could not then fail to assert that lying is globally condemned, that lying detracts from happiness, or that lying cannot be universalized. Nor would it be coherent to suppose that lying is immoral and then wonder whether it is also globally condemned (and so forth). But, Moore would argue, it seems that we, who understand "Lying is immoral," can coherently assert its truth while at the same time doubting that lying is globally condemned, detracts from happiness, or fails tests of universalization. Moral thought is both real and autonomous.

8.5 Chapter summary

Despite the difficulties involved, Fregean theorists have argued that moral terms can be defined, and that moral terms are actually synonymous with their value-neutral definitions. According to the Fregean, the two sorts of expression differ only in that value-laden language tends to invoke strong feelings and emotions. Fregeans therefore equate moral knowledge with knowledge of various psychological and sociological facts. But Moore's open-question argument refutes Fregean treatments of moral thought.

Moral epistemology cannot be pursued in standard ways if the non-cognitivist is right in thinking that there are no moral beliefs sufficiently like our non-moral beliefs to be assessed in epistemic terms. The non-cognitivist argues that there is no sense to be made of our ordinary practice of calling certain moral beliefs "true" and others "false," our asking for "evidence" in support of certain moral beliefs, and our labeling some moral judgments "hasty" or "unwarranted" and others "well-grounded" or constitutive of "knowledge." But the Frege–Geach problems present a strong case against this form of non-cognitivism. Non-cognitivism would require us to abandon the standard ways of sorting good from bad arguments along with the classical ways of explaining why certain inferences are logically good or formally valid. And though a revision of the requisite severity may prove to be coherent, it might for all that still be mistaken. Moral epistemologists can happily acknowledge that moral language has many functions. It can be used to praise, cajole, command, and recommend. So long as it can also be used to make assertions and to express distinctively moral beliefs that admit of truth, justification, and evidential support, moral epistemology – and its method of levels – remains a legitimate pursuit.

8.6 Further reading

Frege draws the distinction between sense and tone in the posthumously published essay "Logic," which is collected along with other works in Michael Beany, *The Frege Reader* (1997). Michael Dummett's *Frege: Philosophy of Language* (1973) helpfully discusses the distinction along with Frege's better-known contrast between the sense and reference of an expression. Mill advances Fregean utilitarianism alongside more plausible versions of the theory in his justly influential work *Utilitarianism* (1861/1998). Moore's famous critique of the position is advanced in the first chapter of *Principia Ethica* (1903/1929). The force and limitations of Moore's criticisms are highlighted in the many contributions to Terrence Horgan and Mark Timmons (eds.), *Metaethics after Moore* (2006b).

Non-cognitivism has its roots in the semantic views of the logical positivists. Examples include A. J. Ayer, *Language, Truth and Logic* (1946/1952); Rudolph Carnap, *Philosophy and Logical Syntax* (1937); and Charles L. Stevenson, *Ethics and Language* (1944) and *Facts and Values* (1963). Peter Geach argues that non-cognitivists have no coherent account of logically complex moral language in "Ascriptivism" (1960); "Assertion" (1965); and other essays. Peter Vranas develops concepts of validity suitable for imperatival arguments, and cites a great deal of the relevant literature, in his "New Foundations for Imperative Logic" (2008). Mark Schroeder, *Being For* (2008) and Mark Richard, *When Truth Gives Out* (2008) address the Frege–Geach problems by describing expressivist forms of validity.

GLOSSARY OF PHILOSOPHICAL TERMS

abduction a form of inference in which a conclusion *q* is drawn from a premise *p* and the additional premise that *q* provides the best explanation of *p*.

amoralist, motives a character who is supposed to know what he is morally obliged to do without being in any way motivated to respect his obligations.

amoralist, reasons a character who is supposed to know what he is morally obliged to do without having any reason to respect his obligations.

anti-skeptical project, ambitious proving to the skeptic's satisfaction that we have moral knowledge or justified moral beliefs.

anti-skeptical project, modest retaining our moral knowledge or the justification with which we hold our moral beliefs in the face of skeptical challenges.

a posteriori knowledge knowledge that is dependent on experience, experimentation, or observation in the way that our knowledge in the natural sciences at least seems to be.

appraisability, moral the conditions an animal must meet if it is to be properly evaluated in moral terms.

a priori knowledge knowledge that is independent from experience, experimentation, or observation in the way that mathematical knowledge at least seems to be.

augmented inferential externalism the claim that if a subject S knows a proposition P, directly infers from it some C that it entails, and the validity of this inference can be known through reflection alone, then S knows C.

authority of moral obligations   the claim that if you are morally obligated to refrain from some action, then you ought to refrain from it all things considered.

basic moral knowledge   our knowledge of the premises of those moral arguments we offer to one another in contrast with their conclusions.

besires   hybrids of belief and desire. Besires are supposed to be states of mind that – like beliefs – admit of truth and falsity but – like desires – are satisfied when the agent performs some action or achieves some goal.

canonical moral knowledge   moral knowledge reached in a central or paradigmatic way. For example, we acquire canonical knowledge of an object's color by seeing it. But if we cannot see it, we can acquire derivative or non-canonical knowledge of its color by asking someone who has seen it.

catch-all hedge   "all things being equal," "typically," "tends to be," or "except in special circumstances." A catch-all hedge is a way of modifying a principle to avoid counter-examples without specifying the exceptions in detail.

categorical imperative, formula of humanity   Kant's claim that we should never treat humanity, whether in ourselves or another, merely as a means, but always as an end. Kant uses "humanity" to denote our ability to set projects for ourselves, organize them into a coherent plan for our lives, and effectively pursue the goals we have set for ourselves.

categorical imperative, formula of universal law   Kant's claim that you should act on maxims and principles, but only those that you can at the same time will or legislate as universal laws. You should act on rules that meet a certain test   (a) you can coherently or rationally do what you propose to do when acting on them, while (b) at the very same time as you are rationally doing this, you are also making the principle part of a universal code of conduct.

categoricity of morality   the claim that if you are morally obligated to refrain from a given action in any case, your being so obligated cannot depend on your happening to have a desire (or desiderative structure) that you might lack.

cognitive disagreement   after some S has knowingly asserted P because she believes P, someone else S* asserts not-P because S* believes not-P and intends to deny the very proposition S* knows S has asserted.

coherentism, minimal   someone can be justified in believing a proposition p by accepting a series of distinct reasons $q_1 \neq p \ldots q_n \neq p$ for believing p, even though at least one of her reasons for believing one or more of $q_1 \ldots q_n$ is p itself.

confabulation   inventing reasons for a judgment or action after the fact.

constructive moral epistemology   attempted explanations of the moral knowledge that, by hypothesis, we do in fact have.

contextualism, moral   one or more moral expression is properly used to denote or express different things in different contexts of utterance. As a result, sentences containing that expression will be properly used to assert different things in different societal contexts.

debunking explanation   an explanation of the origin of a set of beliefs or concepts that puts into doubt the truth or reliability of those beliefs or the truth or reliability of beliefs involving those concepts.

deduction   inferring a conclusion from some premises that entail it. An inference conforming to this description is a deduction; the form of inference is deductive.

defensive moral epistemology   an attempt to show that we have moral knowledge.

deontic logic   a systematic account of inferences involving terms like "obligation" and "permission."

disagreement, the argument from moral   the claim that moral nihilism or moral skepticism is the best explanation of radical differences in our opinions on moral matters.

disjunctive syllogism   an argument with premises (1) P or Q and (2) not-P, and a conclusion (3) Q. Alternatively, "disjunctive syllogism" can denote a rule permitting someone constructing a proof to infer Q from premises P or Q and not-P.

doctrine of recollection   the claim that items of a priori knowledge are recalled from a previous existence in which we learned them.

empathetic basis   your knowledge of P is non-inferentially grounded in empathy (or held on an empathetic basis) just in case (i) you employ empathy in considering P, where (ii) your consequent emotional reaction leads you to believe P quite apart from any inference to P from distinct propositions that you know or believe.

empathy   the process by which you (a) think of an event, action or scenario from another person's perspective, and (b) respond in emotionally appropriate ways to (what you take to be) the situation's likely impact on her. Note that some theorists would restrict "empathy" to (a) and use "sympathy" to denote (b).

empiricism, moral   all moral knowledge is a posteriori as it depends on (emotional or affective) experience.

entailment p entails q just in case it is impossible for p to be true and q not true.

epistemic value   an argument is epistemically valuable just in case it can be used by someone to gain knowledge of its conclusion (or a justified belief in its conclusion) from her knowledge of its premises (or her justly held beliefs in its premises). If common sense is to be trusted, certain arguments are epistemically valuable even though the person executing them doesn't know that they are valuable (or valid), whereas other arguments are valuable only when we know that they are valuable (or valid).

epistemology   the study of knowledge and related phenomena.

externalist epistemology   (i) accounts of knowledge that allow knowledge that the knower doesn't know he has; (ii) accounts of knowledge that allow knowledge even when the knower does not have an accessible argument, inference, or body of evidence to support or defend his knowledge.

first-level epistemological inquiry   a description of the distinctively epistemological evaluations (e.g. criticism and praise) that people level at the beliefs and belief-forming practices of people and institutions.

first-level moral inquiry   a description of the distinctively moral evaluations (e.g. criticism and praise) that people level at the motives and behavior of people and institutions.

folk physics   the concepts we use and assumptions we make when, in the course of ordinary life, we explain and predict the behavior of inanimate objects.

folk psychology   the concepts we use and assumptions we make when, in the course of ordinary life, we explain and predict the behaviors, judgments, and decisions of other people.

foundationalism, minimal   we can and do believe things for reasons, where our reasons aren't distinct things that we believe. For example, the fact that $2 + 2 = 4$ or the fact that you are in pain might itself constitute a good reason for you to believe that $2 + 2 = 4$ or that you are in pain; or your having a suitable course of experience might itself provide you with a good reason to believe that there is something red in front of you.

generalists   theorists who think moral generalizations play an important epistemic or metaphysical role.

Gettier example   an example in which someone has a true, justified belief in some proposition without knowing that proposition.

Hegelian, strict   someone who thinks that pain and suffering are intrinsically or inherently good when they are deserved.

Hobbesian response   a challenge to the claim that virtues and vices help provide the best explanations of human behavior. The Hobbesian tries to argue that better explanations of our actions can always be formulated in value-neutral language.

how question   how do we know what we know?

Humean response   a challenge to the claim that virtuousness or viciousness can be directly inferred from observations of behavior. According to the Humean, thick traits like cowardice or bravery can be inferred from observations of behavior. But the Humean tries to argue that knowledge of the viciousness of cowardice and the virtuousness of bravery is substantive and a posteriori.

incoherent evaluative practices   the judgment that x is right (or that x is knowledge) and that y is wrong (or that y is ignorance) is incoherent if there is no relevant difference between x and y that might support the difference in evaluation.

induction, intuitive   an intuitive induction is the inference of a moral generality (e.g. that lying is wrong) from one's non-inferential knowledge of its instances (e.g. that z was a lie and it was wrong, that y was a lie and it was wrong, and so on).

inference to the best explanation   see "abduction."

inference to the best explanation, ubiquity of   Gilbert Harman's claim that in order for someone to gain non-deductive inferential knowledge of a proposition q, she must infer its truth from (a) some propositions $p_1 \dots p_n$ that she can observe, remember, or introspect, and (b) the proposition that q is essential to providing a better explanation of $p_1 \dots p_n$ than is provided by any competing proposal.

inferential role account (of epistemically valuable inference)   the claim that if a subject S knows a proposition P and directly infers from it some C that it entails, then S knows C if and only if she either: (a) knows that her inference is valid, or (b) must infer as she does to grasp P or C.

infinite regress argument   an argument for skepticism from three initial premises: (1) if S knows p, then S is justified in believing p; (2) if S is justified in believing p, then S must have some reason to believe p; (3) S's having a reason to believe p must consist in S's justifiably believing some $q \neq p$. The resulting Pyrrhonian problematic forces those who accept (1)–(3) to choose between circular justifications, infinite justifications, and skepticism.

infinitism   someone S can be justified in believing a proposition p by having some distinct reason $p_1 \neq p$ for believing p, where S is justified in believing p_1 because she has some distinct reason $p_2 \neq p_1$ for believing $p_1 \dots$ where S is justified in believing pn because she has some distinct reason $p_{n+1} \neq p_n$ for believing p_n for all $n>2$.

internal moral sanction   a motive to moral action that does not depend for its effectiveness on an agent's judgments about what rewards or punishments other people will bestow upon him.

intuition   there are several different senses of this term: a belief; a non-inferentially justified belief; an item of non-inferential knowledge; an act of reflection that provides someone with a non-inferentially justified belief or item of non-inferential knowledge; or the faculty with which we execute such acts of reflection.

intuitionism, moral   the claim that we have non-inferential moral knowledge or non-inferentially justified moral beliefs.

invariantism, moral   the rejection of moral contextualism. The invariantist claims that the sense and reference of moral terms do not vary in any relevant way with variations in the context in which these terms are uttered.

justified belief   a belief that is not properly subjected to certain forms of criticism.

m-how question   how do we know those moral facts we know?

M'Naghten Rules   rules that admit a defense of "not guilty by reason of insanity" for any defendant who did "not know the nature and quality of the act he was doing; or if he did know it ... did not know he was doing what was wrong."

modus ponens   an argument with premises: (1) P and (2) If P then Q, and a conclusion (3) Q. Alternatively, "modus ponens" can denote a rule that permits someone constructing a proof to infer Q from premises P and If P then Q.

moral epistemology   the study of our knowledge of right and wrong and related topics.

moral grammar   a purported body of innately known or believed moral principles that are akin to the principles of Chomsky's universal grammar in certain respects.

motives internalism   the claim that if a person consciously or explicitly knows that she is morally obligated to x, then she has a motive for x-ing, and therefore will x unless prevented by contrary motives or external impediments.

motives internalism, radical   anyone who can be credited with knowing that x is morally obligatory will always have an unimpeded motive to x so long as she retains this knowledge.

motives internalism, weak   dwelling on the moral impermissibility of a deed will provide (or even constitute) some motive against its performance.

m-what question   what moral facts do we know?

nativism, moral   we have a substantial body of innate moral beliefs.

nihilism, moral   the view that there are no moral truths.

open-question argument (Moore's)   the claim that "good" cannot be reductively defined or held synonymous with "utility," "happiness," or any similar predicate F, as we can always meaningfully ask whether what is F is also good.

particularists, radical   theorists who argue against the existence of true moral principles of any kind.

phenomenological   of or relating to what things are like for a subject at a given time; the intrinsic aspects of a subject's experience; thoughts, feelings, or events that occupy a subject's attention.

positive (epistemic) support   something substantial that justifies a person in believing the proposition for which it provides support. The clearest example of positive support would be some evidence that the believer can cite in defense of what she believes, though the reliability of the process that produces the belief might be allowed as well.

presupposition, non-negotiable   a feature commonly attributed to a purported phenomenon that the phenomenon must possess if it is to exist. For example, there are no material objects if nothing exists independently of our thoughts. Independence is a non-negotiable presupposition of the existence of material objects.

prima facie right   an action, event or institution is prima facie right (relative to a certain context) if it would seem right to a rational agent (in that context). For example, helping someone across the street is prima facie right, as it would seem right to a rational person who saw it happen.

pro tanto right   an action, event or institution is pro tanto right just in case it will (or would) be right so long as one of a number of exceptional circumstances fails to obtain. For example, keeping a promise is pro tanto right because promise-keeping is right so long as the promisor doesn't knowingly do a great deal of damage in keeping his promise, the promisor wasn't coerced into making the promise, and so on.

Pyrrhonian problematic   the problem we face once confronted with the infinite regress argument. We must join the foundationalist in denying one of its premises or choose between circular justifications, infinite justifications, and skepticism.

rationalism, moral   we have a substantive body of a priori moral knowledge.

reactive attitudes   emotional responses to morality and immorality.

reasons internalism   the claim that if a person consciously or explicitly knows that she is morally obligated to *x*, then she must have some reason for *x*-ing, so that in the absence of substantive reasons against *x*-ing, *x*-ing will be what she has most reason to do.

reasons qua brute causes   causes.

reasons qua rationalizers   the agent's state of mind when acting, a state of mind in light of which the performed action is made intelligible.

reasons qua relevant considerations   pros and cons; considerations in favor of (or against) the action, decision, or judgment to be made.

reflection   a way of establishing or deepening your understanding of a claim that is supposed to supply you with a non-inferentially justified belief in that claim or non-inferential knowledge of its truth.

reflective basis   your knowledge of some proposition P is non-inferentially grounded in reflection (or held on the basis of reflection) just in case   (i) you reason, in a wholly intellectual way, to a justified belief in P, where (ii) this thought process is internal to (or part of) your understanding of P.

reliability   a belief-forming process or method is reliable if it does produce – or would produce when operating or used properly – substantially more true than false beliefs.

second-level epistemological inquiry   an evaluation (critical review) of the distinctively epistemological evaluations uncovered by first-level episte-mological inquiry.

second-level moral inquiry   an evaluation (critical review) of the distinctively moral evaluations uncovered by first-level moral inquiry.

simple inferential externalism   the claim that if a subject S knows a proposi-tion P and directly infers from it some conclusion C that P entails, then S knows C.

simple inferential internalism   the claim that if a subject S knows a proposi-tion P and directly infers from it some C that it entails, S only knows C if she also knows that her inference is valid.

simulation theories   accounts of our understanding of the thoughts and feelings of other people that emphasize the role of imagination and perspective-taking.

skepticism, Lockean   we have no non-inferential moral knowledge nor any non-inferentially justified moral beliefs, though we have non-inferential knowledge of various non-moral facts.

skepticism, moderate moral   we have no moral knowledge.

skepticism, purely epistemic moral   whether or not there are moral truths, we (extreme) are not justified in believing any of them, or (moderate) at least do not know them.

skepticism, radical moral   none of our moral beliefs is justly or rationally held.

social referencing   looking to others when deciding which activities to pursue and which to avoid.

solipsism, practical   someone who thinks that others shouldn't act in certain ways towards him, whereas he can rightfully act in these ways toward others, simply because he is he and they are they.

soundness, proof of   proof that a form of inference has no invalid instance – that is, no instances with true premises and a false conclusion. To prove that an inference rule is sound is to prove that it never permits an invalid inference – that is, it never permits the inference of a false conclusion from true premises.

supremacy of instrumental rationality   the claim that if you ought not perform some action all things considered, there must be something that you want that you can get by refraining from performing the action, where you want this more than whatever you can get with its performance.

teleological scheme of individuation   categorizing psychological processes, modules, or faculties by their functions when constructing a theory of our minds and behavior.

theory theory   accounts of our understanding of the thoughts and feelings of other people that emphasize the application of the tenets of a shared, largely tacit folk psychological theory.

thick concepts or terms of evaluation   words or concepts like "vain," "cruel," "courageous," and "kind" that are fairly concrete and informative, as compared to thinner words or concepts like "good," "bad," "moral," and "immoral."

thin concepts or terms of evaluation   words or concepts like "good," "bad," "moral," and "immoral" that are fairly abstract and uninformative as compared to thicker words or concepts like "vain," "cruel," "courageous," and "kind."

validity   an argument is (informally) valid just in case it is impossible for its premises to be true and its conclusion not true.

verdictive   an all-things-considered or all-in judgment regarding the morality or immorality (rightness or wrongness) of a particular action, person, or institution.

"what" question   what do we know?

zero-level epistemological inquiry   a description of the beliefs and belief-forming (-maintaining, -revising) practices (processes, methods) of people and institutions.

zero-level moral inquiry   a description of the motives and behaviors of people and institutions.

NOTES

Chapter 1

1   "Verdictive" is reported to be Philippa Foot's expression for judgments of this kind; see Stratton-Lake (2000, 14) and Dancy (2006, 40). The term is also used by Cullity (2002) and Shafer-Landau (2003).

2   Indeed, it is likely that Socrates, the master ironist, is really just teasing his aristocratic interlocutors by derogating statecraft as mere true opinion.

3   Though Socrates does offer definitions in the *Meno*, "knowledge" is not one of the terms defined. In fact, he may think the expression ill-suited to definition, for though he defines "shape" first as the necessary concomitant of color and then as the limit of a solid (75b–76), when pressed to define "color" he repeats an empirical theory attributed to Empedocles and then derides the account as "theatrical" (76a–77b).

4   Another important factor was Ludwig Wittgenstein's (1953/1958) exploration of terms like "game" that, in his view, express "family resemblance concepts" not amenable to definition.

5   One might think that Kant's moral theory constitutes an influential counter-example to these generalizations about the methodology followed by moral theorists. After all, Kant thinks that we can know *a priori* – or by reflection alone – both that we ought to be motivated by a sense of duty, and that (because we ought to act in this way) we must be able to act from duty. But Kant's theoretical arguments for these conclusions begin with the premise that we, his audience, *believe* that we ought to act from duty – that respect for known obligations is a commonly shared ideal. And this is a first-level epistemological claim. There is no contradiction here. Empirical observations of our evaluative practices might help a theorist discover (in an a posteriori manner) that some of the people she is studying have wholly reflective (or a priori) knowledge of the value inherent in acting out of a sense of justice.

6   Norman Daniels (1996, chs. 1–8) argues that the inclusion of psychological and sociological theory helps distinguish Rawls' method of *wide reflective equilibrium* from the more common practice of moral theorists who focus entirely on the coherence of the general principles they posit with our "intuitions" about particular cases – a practice Daniels dubs *narrow reflective equilibrium*.

7   Lest the reader think the example wholly fictitious – or of wholly historical interest – note that teachers in the United States continue to spank their students and issue other corporal punishments, and these are disproportionately aimed at disabled students; see Dillon (2009).

8   On fairly intuitive glosses of "analytic" and "a priori," I have just noted, as many philosophers have, that a demonstration or explanation of a sentence's *analyticity* fails to provide a demonstration or explanation of the *a priority* with which one might come to know the fact it is used to state. We will discuss a priori knowledge further in what follows.

Chapter 2

1   For recent discussion see Hudson (1967, 58–60); Mackie (1977, 36–38); Miller (1985); Layman (1991, 179–80); Brandt (1996); Heumer (2005, ch. 6); Sinnott-Armstrong (2006); Tersman (2006); McGrath (2007); and Prinz (2007).

2   Aquinas tried to reconcile the Aristotelian virtue of magnanimity with the Christian virtue of humility in the *Secunda Secundae* (qq. 123–35). See Irwin (1997, 209–10) for discussion.

3   Relevant too are data that suggest that a greater percentage of men in the southern United States approve of violence in defense of honor than do men in the northern states; see Nisbett and Cohen (1996).

4   This is not to say that retributive violence is always an ideal (or even a necessarily just) reaction to the absence of effective, appropriately neutral state security. If the state is sufficiently powerful and uncorrupted that it would protect your family, clan, or group were you to mount a non-violent protest, and you can make this happen, civil disobedience is the morally preferable (if not required) course. I have in mind here the decisions many minority civil rights workers made in reaction to racist violence in the United States in the 1950s and 60s; see Garrow (1986).

5   These reflections do raise a philosophical (or semantic) puzzle. When a contemporary Westerner confidently says, "Infanticide is immoral," should we interpret her as (perhaps falsely) asserting that infanticide is always and everywhere immoral or as merely (truly) claiming that the practice is immoral in circumstances now normal in the Western world? If she has never contemplated whether infanticide might be the morally permissible "least of all evils" in extreme conditions, and if, were she to consider the issue, she would insist that she was never committed to the immorality of the practice in extreme cases of this kind, a charitable construal might restrict the scope of her intended assertion. Alternatively, we might interpret her as falsely asserting the always, everywhere immorality of infanticide – i.e. as expressing a belief she would abandon were she to consider various extreme cases. See 2.2 for some (rather tentative) discussion of the kind of context dependence that affects semantic interpretation.

6   Suppose you disagree with someone on a moral matter, where you *know* that her evidence is as good as yours and that your judgments on these matters tend to be equally reliable. (We might compare the case to one of David Christensen's [2007] scenarios in which you and an equally alert, equally able colleague come up with divergent answers when calculating each person's share of a group check.) Should you move your belief toward your friend's or instead retain the high level of conviction you had prior to learning of her divergent view? There is a growing literature on the general issue. See, e.g., Kelly (2005) and Elga (2007).

7   John Doris and Alexandra Plakias (2008) point out that Chinese and American subjects seem to disagree about the correct moral response to such scenarios. Indeed, because, contrary to what I am arguing here, Doris and Plakias consider our verdicts regarding this scenario a "core case" of moral judgment, they take the variance to support their rejection of "moral realism." I have done my best to exclude moral metaphysics from the scope of this inquiry, but if rejecting moral realism means rejecting all moral knowledge, Doris and Plakias move too fast in drawing so skeptical a conclusion from their study of a difficult case.

8   We also ignore here a misconceived utilitarian justification for denying the permissibility of homosexuality. That is, some might argue that if prejudice against homosexuality is sufficiently widespread: (a) the disgust of being made aware of homosexual practice will be greater in quantity than (b) the joy and pleasure that might be gained through open homosexual romance, even when (b) is conjoined with (c) the suffering homosexuals experience when forced to either end or conceal their relationships or endure social censure. (More precisely, the absolute value of (a) is greater than (b) plus the absolute value of (c).) In consequence, one might argue, our obligation to promote as much happiness as possible demands efforts to mitigate (or at least hide) homosexual practice. But since, we can assume, an acceptance of consenting, loving, homosexual relationships would lead to more happiness than suffering were non-utilitarian prejudices against homosexuality eliminated, the disutility in (a) depends for its existence on our failing to adopt the utilitarian perspective. Thus, the most plausible or defensible forms of utilitarianism would insist that we discount (if not ignore) these prejudices in our calculations of what would be best. See Smart and Williams (1973) among others for arguments of this kind.

9   The kind of confabulation is often predictable. Haidt and Hersh (2001) explore differences in the justifications liberals and conservatives provide when defending their beliefs in the immorality of seemingly victimless transgressions of "our" moral code – transgressions such as masturbation, homosexuality, and consensual adult incest. Wheatley and Haidt (2005) explore the effects of hypnotism on confabulation.

10   Though even here polygynous arrangements may be economically advantageous only because women are being denied employment outside the home from ignorance of their capabilities and/or institutionalized forms of fear and jealousy. For more on the issue see Grossbard-Schechtman (1984) and White and Burton (1988), cited and discussed in Prinz (2007). We must also note the substantial evidence that women in polygamous societies do not endorse the practice (Wikan, 1996) and in fact resent paternalistic social structures in general (Abu-Lughod, 1991; Wainryb and Turiel, 1994).

11   The question here is whether "immoral" and other English expressions
      exhibit context-sensitivity, and if so, what kinds. Similar issues arise when we
      wonder whether a given expression in Kilivilan (the language indigenous to the
      Trobriands) is aptly translated as "immoral." Since Trobriands who (seemingly)
      learn English may still dissent from the English sentence, "Sex with a first cousin
      is immoral," the suggestion that apparent disagreements as to the morality
      of incest are all entirely due to errors in translation is fairly implausible. For
      extensive discussion of these issues see Cook (1999); Cooper (1981); Gibbard
      (1992a,b); Moody-Adams (1997); and Snare (1980).

12   A critic might argue that relational moral knowledge isn't really *moral* knowledge
      at all, as genuinely moral knowledge cannot be wholly divorced from motivation
      in the way that relational moral knowledge looks to be. The criticism presents a
      serious obstacle for moral contextualism of the type we have considered.

Chapter 3

1   Compare with the characterizations of Pyrrhonic skepticism in Fogelin (1994)
     and Sinnott-Armstrong (2006).

2   Mill argues that though these are initially "external" sanctions, they will become
     instinctive or "internal" in their connection to the idea of the prohibited act once
     the child is successfully conditioned (1861/1998, ch. 3).

3   Locke writes here of god as both moral legislature and executive – as the writer,
     enacter, and enforcer of the moral law. But an extension of Plato's *Euthyphro*
     problem might be thought to undermine the belief that moral truths could be
     "legislated" by anyone. Moreover, Locke speaks of pleasure and pain where we
     have generalized to desire and aversion, so our characterizations of god's role
     will differ from Locke's with regard to those who fail to apportion their desires
     and aversions to the balance of pleasure over pain.

4   Compare with Gregory Kavka's (1985) interpretation of Glaucon's vulnerability
     in Plato's *Republic*.

5   Mackie takes aim not at the somewhat narrow category of moral obligation,
     but at morality (and aesthetics) more generally. But because the argument is
     strongest when put in terms of a person's obligations and her knowledge of
     such, we can retain our focus on this province of the moral realm.

6   I would say that Mackie thinks that nothing *could be* both objective and
     intrinsically prescriptive, but there is textual evidence against this interpretation.
     The most compelling is Mackie's (1977, 48) admission that the existence of a
     god who created us so that we might live morally would indeed saddle us with
     a set of moral obligations. But exactly how Mackie thinks god's existence would
     impugn his arguments for nihilism remains unclear. Why doesn't the fact that
     my parents created me with the intention that I lead a virtuous life generate the
     same result?

7   Saul Kripke famously argued that, given the mythological origin of our concept
     of a *unicorn*, there is in fact no possible world in which unicorns exist. A world
     with creatures that fit the descriptions of unicorns that feature in our ancient
     myths is not a world in which unicorns exist. Use of "unicorn" in the actual
     world would have to involve interaction with unicorns for unicorns to exist in
     some possible world (Kripke, 1972, 23–4, 156–58). If this is right, Mackie's

thesis implies that there is no possible world in which anyone is morally obligated to do anything.

8   Relevant here is the recent controversy over the semantic properties of "water" (or a word that behaves just like it) on a Dry Earth whose inhabitants supposedly have all of our experiences despite there being no water on their planet. See, e.g., Boghossian (1997).

9   For a comparison between the inaccuracies of folk psychology and the inaccuracies of folk physics, and the consequent argument that there are no beliefs and desires, see Paul Churchland (1981). Few still defend the kind of "eliminative materialism" to which Churchland there subscribes.

10   See Harman (1984, 30) for the first interpretation and Garner (1990) for an argument in favor of the second.

11   This is hard to figure out, as "the closest world" at which Huck both has this obligation and knows that he does is one at which Jim must be forced to return to slavery for some legitimate reason having nothing to do with his purported status as property. For surely, if there is a world at which we have a moral obligation to return escaped slaves (as there might be on some teleological theories) this world is radically different – and so quite some "distance" – from our own.

12   Aquinas discusses the issue in a fruitful way when he explains the different kinds of malfunction that can keep *synderesis* – or intellectual understanding of basic virtue – from generating virtuous actions. See Irwin (1988, 1997) for discussion of Aquinas' view and its predecessors.

13   "Besire" is J. E. Altham's (1986) terminology. For criticism of Smith that focuses on the behaviorist aspects of his analysis of direction of fit see Kieran Setiya (2003, 364–66).

14   There is some evidence that certain neurological procedures and medications can bring on *pain asymbolia* wherein patients occupy a state that possesses the representational properties of a typical pain but lacks pain's typically aversive motivational qualities; see Aydede (2005, 32) for discussion. Must we say that states can have only one direction of fit, and that "pain" must refer to just one of these dissociable states? Or can we follow the besire model on which "pain" denotes the complex, and pain asymbolia is really the absence of pain? Do our pre-theoretic beliefs and ordinary patterns of linguistic usage decide the matter in one way or the other?

15   The first philosopher I know of to draw something like this distinction is Francis Hutcheson (1728/1971), who separates "justifying" and "exciting" reasons.

16   Jimeno's story – along with that of fellow officer John McLaughlin – was dramatized in the Paramount Pictures film *World Trade Center* (2006), written by Andrea Burloff and directed by Oliver Stone.

17   Gilbert Harman (1984, 5–7) thinks that we obviously cannot say that the horrible damage the unrepentant murderer is inflicting on his victims and their families provides him with a reason to stop killing, a reason he simply refuses to acknowledge. But this may be because Harman thinks the supremacy of instrumental reason is itself obvious (9). Indeed, Harman's instrumentalist view of reasons, when married to the naturalness of saying that one should do only what one has reason to do, leads Harman to rather perversely suggest that *common sense* finds something wrong with saying that Hitler should not have

ordered the extermination of the Jews (6). Harman subsequently claims that it would not be "strong enough" to simply say Hitler should not have killed so many Jews. But the claim's being too weak would mean that it is nevertheless true; and then the connection between "should" and "reasons" Harman admits would force him to say, contrary to his instrumentalism, that Hitler had a reason not to kill all those Jews after all. The inconsistency has an obvious source. Though nihilism may have its roots in common sense, it is surely not itself a tenet of ordinary thought.

Chapter 4

1   Whereas radical coherentism claims that every justified belief *is* inferred from some others, the kind of minimal coherentism cited here need claim only that a belief *can* be justified without foundations. Minimal coherentism yields radical coherentism only if we assume that there is only one good response to the regress argument, where a kind of "foundherentism" (Haack, 1999) results if we instead allow both non-inferentially justified beliefs and *local holisms* of good, circularly justified belief (Peacocke, 1992). The foundationalist position described below is called "minimal foundationalism" for analogous reasons; it too is compatible with foundherentism.
2   See too Chisholm (1966) and Zimmerman (2006).
3   See Michael Williams (2001) and Donald Davidson (1989) for attempts along these lines.
4   The reply is only "broadly" foundationalist because it need endorse no more of the traditional foundationalist view than its postulation of some non-inferentially justified beliefs. The truth of this tenet is sufficient to rebut the regress argument on its own – we needn't think of the beliefs in question as infallible or indubitable, as grounding all of our inferentially justified beliefs, or as justifying other beliefs through a priori knowable entailments. See Audi (1998, 1999b) for particularly clear discussions of these points.
5   This is not to take a stand on the extent to which infants understand numbers before mastering numerals. See Dehaene (1997) for the evidence.
6   Adults continue to make errors when calculating sums, and we think that this is compatible with their understanding "addition." Is there, then, a set of sensations, behaviors, or dispositions to such that we can identify with grasping the concept? See Kripke (1982) for discussion.
7   See too Ross (1939, 171). According to Chisholm (1966, 76fn.), the term "intuitive induction" was introduced by W. E. Johnson (1921).
8   Kurt Baier (1958) argues that knowledge of a rule's exceptions is a constituent – or part of – knowledge of the rule. This implies that one doesn't really know that lying is wrong unless one knows that it's okay to fib when throwing a surprise party. (In consequence, sticklers for rules, like Aquinas and Kant, either don't know that lying is wrong or they explicitly disavow knowledge they tacitly possess.) G. E. M. Anscombe (1958) argues that the absence of exceptions to the general prohibition on lying is not a known premise from which one's belief in a particular lie's all-things-considered immorality is drawn. Instead, she claims, one's inference to the lie's immorality is non-deductive and sui generis.

(Chisholm [1966] also contemplates this view.) See chapter 5 for more on hedges to general rules.

9   Like most writers citing Kant's works available in English, I cite Kant's texts using page numbers following "Ak" to denote the definitive German edition of his work: *Immanuel Kants Schriften*, Ausgabe der königlich preussischen Akademie der Wissenschaften, Berlin: de Gruyter (1902–). As is also standard, citations for Kant's *Critique of Pure Reason* use "A" to denote the first edition and "B" the second edition of that work followed by page numbers.

10   Note that many views commonly labeled "empiricist" and "rationalist" allow a priori knowledge of particulars or wholly a posteriori knowledge of generalities. For example, Russell also held (1912/1997, 46–59) that we know an individual thing through an act of "conception" whereby we are acquainted with those "universals" expressed by the predicates involved in a definite description the object uniquely satisfies. On a natural interpretation of this account, it has a kind of experience-based knowledge of generalities (acquaintance with universals) grounding all knowledge of particulars. More obvious exceptions include Kant's (1781/1787/1999, 68–69 [A24–25/B39]) famous argument that our knowledge of geometry is grounded in an a priori intuition of space (qua particular thing) and Descartes' (1641/1993) granting himself synthetic a priori knowledge of his own (particular) existence. Given these examples, Mill is overly dogmatic to dismiss those who posit non-inferential knowledge of particular moral facts as not "entitled to the name of thinkers" (1861/1998, 50–51).

11   For non-inferential, perceptualist views of moral knowledge see DePaul (1988); McNaughton (1988); Dreyfus and Dreyfus (1990); Tolhurst (1990); Varela (1992); Greco (2000, ch. 9); Johnston (2001); Watkins and Jolley (2002); and McGrath (2004). Jonathan Dancy (2004) argues, in partial contrast, that we have *a priori* knowledge of the moral quality of particular actions where this is not inferred from our knowledge of general principles of any kind. See Blum (1994); Jacobson (2005); and Goldie (2007) for alternative accounts of how perception might be thought to influence moral judgment, and for critical discussion McKeever and Ridge (2006) and Väyrynen (2007).

12   See 8.1 for defense of the second of these two claims: that non-evaluative knowledge of other minds is not yet moral knowledge.

13   We will return to these matters in earnest in the chapter to come when examining whether "ought" can be inferred from "is" in the manner envisaged by (4)–(5).

14   Perhaps Shafer-Landau (2003, ch. 11) and McKeever and Ridge (2006) have this model in mind when they argue that hedged moral principles are knowable a priori, though they also try to say something about how the absence of exceptions is verified in arriving at an all-in verdict of immorality.

15   Rationalists often describe themselves as arguing that certain moral propositions are *self-evident* (Audi, 1996, 2004, 9–10, 48–49, 81–82, 150–51; Crisp, 2002, 57–59; Stratton-Lake, 2002a, 18–23, 2002b, 113–19; Shafer-Landau, 2003). But this is just to say, in the now common (non-Lockean) sense of "self-evidence" prevalent among analytic philosophers, that if someone has an adequate understanding of such a proposition, this will provide her with prima facie justification for believing it. Since moral principles that are in this sense self-evident needn't be obvious to those with a basic understanding of them, our knowledge of these principles cannot be fully

assimilated to our knowledge of simple mathematical axioms and arithmetic truths. Still, as we discuss in the text, a comparison of moral knowledge to knowledge of moderately complex mathematical principles might be cogently pursued. See, for example, Scanlon's (1998, 62–64) brief examination of the comparison between normative and set-theoretic knowledge.

16   I cite Hume's texts using the book, part, section, and paragraph number format made possible by the critical editions listed in the bibliography. I have also included references to the traditional editions of the *Treatise* and *Enquiries* prepared by L. A. Selby-Bigge and revised by P. H. Nidditch. These are denoted by "SBN" and followed by the relevant page number or numbers.

Chapter 5

1   See Etchemendy (1990/1999) on the respects in which Tarski's (1936/1956) analysis of our concept of logical consequence differs from both its predecessors and heirs. Note that Etchemendy is skeptical about the value of the classical soundness proofs discussed below; see Dummett (1978b) for an important discussion of this issue.

2   This is not to diminish the controversy that surrounds the semantics of indirect discourse, nor the paradoxes that result from the unrestricted employment of "true" in quantificational contexts like (1).

3   In eschewing the grammatical point of view, Hume is followed by Kant, who clearly had an extra-linguistic category in mind when calling "Charity is good" and "One ought to act benevolently" *imperatives* alongside "Be good!" (cf. Foot, 1972).

4   See von Wright, 1951; Hilpinen, 1957/1971; Kanger, 1957/1971; Anderson, 1958, 1967; Chisholm, 1963; Castañeda, 1981; Åqvist, 1984; Hansson, 1997; Feldman, 2001; McNamara, 2006; and Wedgwood, 2007.

5   According to standard deontic logic, all logical truths are obligatory. But these obligations, if indeed they exist, have nothing to do with morality.

6   For instance, the idea of using someone (or his humanity) as an instrument is not necessarily moral in content; see Audi (2004) for discussion.

7   This is not to deny that Kant was mistaken about several of the more subtle ways in which the concepts in question interact in ordinary thought. But he cannot be justly accused, as the Nazi henchman Adolf Eichmann might be, of gross irrationality and incompetence in the interpretation and application of the fundamental tenet or tenets of the Kantian system. On Eichmann's claim to have lived in accord with Kant's ethical system see Arendt (1963/1994, 135–37).

8   Though it has its detractors, my sense is that this is now the view of most epistemologists; see, e.g., Chisholm (1966); BonJour (1980, 1985); Goldman (1986); Pollock (1986); and Audi (1993, 1998).

9   One might try to respond to this line of argument with Audi's (1997b, ch. 11; 2004, 137–39; 2006, 86–90) understanding of intrinsic value building on Moore's (1903/1929, 263) claim that more general good is produced when we add the badness of punishment to the badness of the criminal's offense: as we might somewhat uncharitably put it, "two bads make a good" (cf. Zimmerman, 1983). For a more promising attempt to account for some of the Hegelian intuitions within a broadly consequentialist framework see Feldman (1995).

10   What, though, of Thomson's deontic example? Even if B promised to pay
     Smith five dollars, B's refusing to pay may be in no way bad, wrong, or immoral
     so long as B knows that Smith will use the money to buy a gun and commit
     a heinous crime (cf. Plato, *Republic*, 331c–d; Aristotle, *Nicomachean Ethics*,
     1164b25–1165a12). At least, this is the traditional view of the matter; and
     it is not obviously mistaken. On the other hand, the epistemic reading of
     Thomson's deontic example might be thought to generate a valid argument.
     It may be necessarily true that knowing that B broke a promise warrants belief
     in the immorality of B's action in the absence of contrary evidence. Again, this
     depends on the strength and obviousness of the connection between promise-
     breaking and immorality.

11   Thomson argues that "E plans to torture a baby to death for fun" entails "E
     ought not do what he plans to do" (1990, 17–18). And she may be right about
     this, though there may be some possible world in which sadistic baby-torture is
     necessary to save the galaxy, and E must sign up for neurosurgery to become a
     baby-torturing sadist (albeit a galaxy-saving one). Dostoyevsky's (1880/1990)
     "Grand Inquisitor" occasions a discussion of the moral permissibility of
     torturing infants in extreme cases, though I will leave the beefing up of
     Thomson's premise – to rule out the worlds where this is permissible – as an
     exercise for the reader.

12   Was Saddam compelled by his paranoia to gas the Kurds? If so, was Saddam
     responsible for the extent of his paranoia? If not, was Saddam really to blame
     for ordering the attacks? Gideon Rosen (2004) argues on general grounds that
     immorality stems from either irrationality or ignorance, and that there are few
     circumstances in which we can be justly held responsible for such (see, contra,
     Fitzpatrick, 2008). Still, even if Rosen is right (and I do not think that he is),
     and Saddam is not morally responsible for the atrocity we have described,
     this form of skepticism does not obviously undermine our judgment that the
     act was immoral. Might there be immoral acts for which no one is properly
     held accountable? But then why not judge the tiger's mauling of his handler
     immoral?

13   This problem is made more rather than less pressing by recent skepticism about
     the utility of the a priori/a posteriori distinction; see, e.g., Hawthorne (2007)
     and Williamson (2007).

14   For further discussion of modal epistemology see the essays collected in
     Gendler and Hawthorne (2002).

15   We include a "ceteris paribus" clause to allow for cases of over-determination.
     If S knows P, knows that P entails Q, and believes Q both because she knows it
     is entailed by something she knows and because her incredibly unreliable guru
     told her that Q, we might want to say that she does not know Q. These and
     other subtleties need not concern us here.

16   There are a number of different theories that fall under the "inferential role"
     (or "conceptual role") umbrella. Influential varieties include the work of Hartry
     Field (1977); Gilbert Harman (1986, 1999a); Robert Brandom (1994, 2000);
     and Paul Horwich (1998). For inferentialist accounts of specifically normative
     concepts see Philippa Foot (1958) and Ralph Wedgwood (2001, 2007).

17   To see the necessity of this proviso we need only consider Arthur Prior's famous
     (1960b) example of "tonk" – an artificial expression stipulated to have the

introduction rules classically assigned to "or" and the elimination rules assigned to "and." There is some doubt as to whether "tonk" really expresses a concept. But given the inconsistencies that quickly result from following the rules that we must follow if we are to use the expression in accordance with Prior's stipulations, a speaker would be properly criticized as mad were she to attempt to think (or speak) with its aid. With this in mind, a radically skeptical theorist might propose that moral terms are "tonky" – i.e. defective in something like the way that "tonk" is defective. Though the inconsistency or absurdity-inducing rules that guide the proper use of natural language expressions like "good," "bad," "moral," and "immoral" could not have been stipulated into effect by a logician, a theorist might try to identify these rules and assign them a more organic origin. And if there were introduction and elimination rules guiding proper use of our moral terms, and these rules really were suitably "tonky," we could be criticized for assenting to or executing the licensed inferences, even though (by hypothesis) we must so engage if we are to be granted competence with the terms in question. Just as an even minimally rational person would not use "tonk" in serious reasoning, the skeptic might suggest that we eschew all serious use of moral terminology. Skepticism of this kind would resemble Mackie's nihilism in some respects and, in others, the kind of strong non-cognitivism discussed in 8.2–4. For helpful discussions of these issues see Ryle (1949/2000, 121); Sellars (1953); Foot (1958); Belnap (1962); Dummett (1973); Brandom (1994, 2000); Boghossian (2003); and Williamson (2003).

18   One might think that the inferential role account is obviously too restrictive, as a good mathematics student can be properly granted knowledge of some result even if she skips steps in its proof. In response, the inferentialist might argue that the student must have *tacitly* gone through the steps or that she must at least have the *ability* to do so if challenged by her teacher. If the student cannot reconstruct the reasoning that she has omitted, she has indeed leaped to judgment, and her conviction stops short of knowledge. (She gets partial credit for coming up with the right answer, but full credit cannot be justly awarded.) So as to not complicate the inferential role account beyond measure, we can here treat the ability to supply the missing steps as tacit knowledge of the inference's validity. The clever student tacitly knows that her premises entail her conclusion, and she evinces this knowledge when filling in the missing steps upon request.

19   This is the kind of account Wedgwood (2007) provides for certain normative concepts. For a critical discussion of dispositional accounts of concept possession see Kripke (1982).

Chapter 6

1   Note that Harman thinks that much of what we call perceptual knowledge is really inferential in origin and justification (1973, ch. 11). Moreover, Harman's "Principle Q" (1973, 151–54) has him adding sensitivity to "defeating" considerations by insisting that at the same time as S infers Q as the best explanation of what she knows directly, she must also infer that there is no evidence that would defeat the justification with which she believes Q. These complications need not detain us here.

2 Harman's argument is actually weaker than described, as he admits that there are facts that play no role in explaining our observations. He gives, as an example, facts about what "the average American" wants. These can be admitted as genuine facts because they are in some sense "reducible" to other facts that do explain our observations. (In the case at hand, these will be facts about the preferences of individual Americans.) The question, then, as far as Harman is concerned, is whether moral facts are "reducible" to explanatory facts, and Harman allows that its answer is not yet clear (1977).

3 We can therefore think of our virtue and vice concepts as parts of *common-sense psychology* – a framework we might try to use in our efforts to construct a more accurate or rigorous "scientific" psychology. A natural comparison here would be to *folk physics* – the common-sense views about motion, matter, and force that provided Aristotle and then Newton with a rough – if in many cases systematically erroneous – basis for their scientific physics. For discussion see chapter 3 above, Churchland (1981) and Dennett (1987).

4 Indeed, Hobbes claims, the only real difference between terms like "cowardice" and "vanity" and their morally neutral counterparts is a psychological or *expressive* one (1650, §6). A single trait of character, *glory*, is called "pride" by those it displeases and "just evaluation of self" (i.e. proper self-respect) by those it pleases, where the character trait that is "the opposite of glory" is called "dejection" by those it displeases and "humility" by those it pleases. See too Stevenson (1944, ch. 3) and Hare (1963, 21–29), and for a more subtle "two-factor" account of thick moral concepts Blackburn (1984).

5 Doris and Harman argue against virtue-theoretic psychology from *situationism*. A set of experiments seems to show that our behavior is not determined by stable features of our characters or personalities, but is instead motivated by such things as mood, external pressure, and other features of the "situations" in which we find ourselves. See Isen and Levin (1972); Darley and Batson (1973); Milgram (1974); and Ross and Nisbett (1991). There is a sense, though, in which the situationist critique of virtue theory is tangential to our present concerns. As the situationists acknowledge, we can retain thick, virtue-theoretic explanations of particular actions, even if we drop the assumption that the motives we posit will persist and determine the agent's behavior in a wide range of subsequent situations. (For the acknowledgment see, e.g., Doris [1998, 514] and Harman [1999b, 327–28].) In other words, Sturgeon could retreat to the claim that DeVoto knows, via an abduction, that Woodworth's inaction was motivated by a – perhaps transient – bout of vanity and cowardice. (Though this would then undermine DeVoto's subsequent conclusion that Woodworth was no damn good.)

6 See Yablo (1992) and (2003) for an influential model of how high-level causal explanation might be reconciled with supervenience; and for a recent application to the normative realm Wedgwood (2007, 192–99).

7 On the distinction between "thick" and "thin" concepts and explanations see Williams (1985); Scheffler (1987); Blackburn (1992); Gibbard (1992a,b, 2003); McDowell (1998); Mulligan (1998); Tappolet (2004); and Goldie (2009). Though I follow Williams in equating thickness with informativeness or specificity, it may be that Blackburn (at least) intends a different distinction, as he regularly uses "thin" to denote purely descriptive predicates and "thick" to denote predicates that also encode the speaker's (positive or negative) feelings regarding the actions

and people to which they are applied. Other theorists seem to build into their definition of "thickness" the marriage of evaluative and descriptive components, or even the theoretical claim that the evaluative and descriptive components of thick concepts cannot be "disentangled" from one another. Because "thickness" is used by Williams in a largely technical sense, facts of usage have relatively little evidential bearing on its interpretation. Still, some conceptions of thickness will surely prove more useful than others, and by multiplying meanings the philosophical community risks miscommunication. (It wouldn't be the first time.)

8   Sturgeon's (2002) endorsement of coherentism suggests as much.

Chapter 7

1   See too Haidt *et al.* (2007) cited and discussed in Haidt and Björklund (2008). Note that while the developmental precedence of evaluative concepts does not indicate their greater importance, nor does it indicate the reverse. Though Lawrence Kohlberg (1971, 1976) used the fact of developmental succession to argue that deontic thought is superior to evaluative thought – and so has greater authority when the two conflict – even the most rabid Kohlbergian would refrain from arguing *directly* from succession to greater authority or importance. Instead, Kohlberg's (1973) argument for deontology also invoked the purported fact that people in later developmental stages prefer their (purportedly deontic) ways of thinking to more utilitarian forms of thought along with the purported fact that "philosophers" find deontic moral theories more defensible than utilitarian alternatives.

2   See here, Brian Leiter (2002), who might accuse this claim of begging the question against Nietzsche's moral theory. Though the point is largely terminological, I think we beg no questions here, as Nietzsche is right to think of himself as abandoning (or, in his words, "moving beyond") distinctively moral terms of evaluation, in favor of an alternative evaluative framework. For arguments in favor of this position see Frankena (1967).

3   There has also been substantial work on the neurological instantiation or realization of these processes (Frith and Frith, 1999), with simulation theorists focusing on the role of "mirror neurons." For a recent philosophical discussion of the issues with some mention of their relevance to morality see Goldman (2006).

4   Can they be attributed virtue or described as just? For the spontaneous helping behavior of non-human primates see Warneken and Tomasello (2006).

5   Some researchers would want to include here meta-ethical beliefs regarding the purported "authority-independence" of distinctively moral rules and principles. It seems that children as young as two years of age believe that hitting and stealing would still be wrong even if parents, teachers, and god said it was okay, but that licking their plates and wearing pajamas to school would be perfectly fine if allowed by these figures. Is belief in the authority-independence of moral norms necessary for truly moral thought? See Turiel (1979, 1983); Turiel, Killen, and Helwig (1987); Smetana (1993); and Nucci (2001); and for skepticism Kelly *et al.* (2007).

6   Hume emphasizes that correction of the sentiments requires reason when he compares an "untaught savage" who "regulates chiefly his love and hatred by

the ideas of private utility and injury" to those of us "accustomed to society" and to "more enlarged reflections" who can by certain "suppositions and views ... correct, in some measure, our ruder and narrower passions" (1751/1998, 9.1.8 fn.1). See also 1751/1998, 5.2.22–27.

7   But why is the fact that you are you whereas I am me not a "morally relevant" consideration? Adopting terminology from E. Gellner (1954–55), R. M. Hare (1952, 1954–55, 1963) distinguishes U-type valuations that contain no "personal references" from E-type valuations that do, and argues that it is a matter of the meaning or definition of "morality" that E-type valuations do not express genuinely moral considerations. Strawson more modestly argues that the "abstract virtue of justice" is a "formally universal feature of morality" and it demands that "a man should not insist on a particular claim while refusing to acknowledge any reciprocal claim" (1961, 13). (See, though, MacIntyre [1967/1970] and Sturgeon [1974] for criticism.) Still, it is a further question, addressed in the text below, how non-solipsistic agents resolve the relevant kind of incoherence when it is drawn to their attention.

8   For doubts over whether perceptual knowledge can be used to establish the reliability of perception see Cohen (2002); cf. Van Cleve (2003); Zalabardo (2005); and Brueckner and Buford (2009). It remains a matter of controversy among epistemologists whether facts detected by a faculty can be legitimately or rationally employed in arguing for the reliability of that faculty.

Chapter 8

1   Given Frege's acceptance of truth-conditionally equivalent sentences that express different thoughts (e.g. "Hesperus is lovely" and "Phosophorus is lovely", or "I was wounded" as said by Dr Gustav Lauben and "Dr Gustav Lauben was wounded" as said by Leo Peter) it is odd to find him here infer from the truth-conditional equivalence of the sentences in question to identity in the thought or proposition they express. But, for whatever reason, Frege made the inference and went on to adduce additional grounds in its support.

2   See John Perry (1979) and Stephen Schiffer (1979) for the view that one can have two different belief states with the same propositional content. The possibility is not one we need take seriously here, as an epistemologist adopting this proposal must assess the justification with which one would move from the one belief state to the other. From the epistemologist's point of view, then, accepting the Perry/Schiffer proposal is equivalent to abandoning the Fregean account of value-laden predicates.

3   Indeed, Dickens has Copperfield concluding that Creakle was "an incapable brute." But general pronouncements on the character of a person are more difficult to justify than evaluations of particular actions. See chapter 6 above for discussion.

4   Mill was Moore's main target in the latter's arguments against moral naturalism, and some of the passages in which Mill treats the principle of utility as a "self-evident" truth or a fact of "synonymy" are quoted in the text below. Kant's attitude toward the categorical imperative is more obscure, and our discussion will therefore be restricted to this endnote. Kant seemingly

claims analyticity for "Only actions done from one's knowledge of the moral law are good without limitation," as he thinks we can discern its truth by analyzing our shared concept of what it is to be *worthy of esteem*. (We bring the concept to salience by considering examples.) And he also seems to treat "The categorical imperative is the moral law" as analytic, as we can discern its truth by analyzing the concept of *acting from duty*. Thus, it seems that on Kant's reckoning a complicated conceptual analysis establishes the truth of the categorical imperative. What is synthetic rather than analytic (but nevertheless a priori knowable) is the genuine possibility of someone's acting from the moral law (1785/2002, 33–37 [Ak 4:419–21]). Though this is not a definitional truth, we cannot know it "a posteriori" through observation of actions actually driven by obligation alone, as self-interested motives might be hidden from observation and introspection. We must therefore "synthesize" the concept of *acting from duty* with the concept of *freedom* or *autonomy* to discern the possibility of acting from duty. See the structure of the *Groundwork* as described at Ak 4:392 (1785/2002, 7–8) and the arguments that follow. See chapter 5 above for further discussion of Kant's moral epistemology.

5   For Mill's views on the relation between motives, intentions, and the morality of actions see 1861/1998, ch. 2, and, in particular, "The morality of the action depends entirely upon the intention – that is, upon what the agent *wills to do*" (ibid., 65n.). See too Urmson (1953).

6   Mill's mentor, Jeremy Bentham, claimed, in a similar vein, that the principle of utility lends moral terminology a substantive meaning (1780/1982, ch. 1, x).

7   Those, like John Rawls (1971) and Thomas Scanlon (1998), who argue that "the right" cannot be defined in terms of "the good" will object at this stage of Moore's discussion.

8   See Locke (1690/1991, §157) and chapter 4 for more on the Lockean notion of self-evidence.

9   A. N. Prior suggests that a utilitarian can answer Moore's open-question argument by simply insisting that, as he uses the term "good," nothing but happiness is good (1949, ch.1). But "good" is not an artificial expression whose meaning can be stipulated in this way. Consequently, the attempt at stipulation has the utilitarian closing a question that differs from the one that Moore rightly insists is still open. For further discussion of Moore's open-question argument see Frankena (1939); Goldman (1988a); Ball (1991); Darwall, Gibbard, and Railton (1992); Scanlon (1998); and McKeever and Ridge (2006).

10   The approach has been applied outside ethics as well, with regard to psychological vocabulary (Wittgenstein, 1953/1958) and even logic (Field, 2000), though there is reason to doubt whether Hartry Field's theory is aptly labeled "strongly non-cognitivist" in the sense given that term here.

11   The moral cognitivist might want to hedge this premise to allow that indicative conditionals that suffer from presupposition failures or vagueness have truth-valueless or indeterminate components; a discussion of these issues would take us too far afield.

12   See Wittgenstein (1921/2001). For brevity's sake, we are treating our moral argument (1)–(3) as an arbitrary instance of modus ponens and informally explaining its validity and the soundness of the inference rule in tandem.

13   The correct semantics for indicative conditionals is a source of great
      controversy. And yet, even those who reject the classical account defended by
      Paul Grice (1989) on which indicative conditionals with false antecedents are
      all true, accept the limited claim that conditionals with true antecedents and
      false consequents are all false. Jonathan Bennett calls this position "Adams*"
      and attributes it to the most influential critics of the classical semantics
      including Ernest Adams (1965, 1975, 1998), Dorothy Edgington (1991),
      and Allan Gibbard (1981). Indeed, though Bennett also rejects the classical
      semantics for indicative conditionals and joins William Lycan in calling his
      the "no truth value" account – or "NTV" for short – Bennett actually "denies a
      truth value" to indicative conditionals "only when [the antecedent] is false and
      does not logically, causally or morally imply [the consequent]" (2003, 118).
      (Though Bennett also accepts moral non-cognitivism on independent grounds
      [2003, 106–8].) Vann McGee (1985) and William Lycan (1993) argue that
      when indicative conditionals feature as the consequents of other indicative
      conditionals, counter-examples to modus ponens can result (see 4.2 above for
      discussion). But the view has not gained wider acceptance; and even if it were
      true, it would not impugn the soundness of a restricted form of modus ponens
      from which we might establish the classical validity of (1)–(3).

14   Logicians are not always careful in this regard. Quine, for example, defines
      what it is for one statement to "logically follow" from another by saying, "If one
      statement is to be held as true, each statement implied by it must also be held
      as true" (1972, 4). This is just a mistake. "Some statement is held as true" is
      not a logical truth, unless, as some theologians believe, the universe began with
      an assertion.

15   The last two columns represent our premises. The shaded rows represent those
      cases in which our conclusion is false. But the last two columns of the shaded
      rows each include a "false" so our premises are not both true there. There is,
      therefore, no way to make our premises true and our conclusion false.

16   See Vranas (2008) for an extensive bibliography on imperatival logic and the
      philosophical issues to which it gives rise. For a list of those who try to reduce
      the meaning of imperatives to the meaning of various declarative sentences
      see ibid., 538, n.33. Vranas argues that supplying a correct semantics for
      conditionals forces imperatival logicians to utilize three values – he favors
      "satisfied," "unsatisfied," and "avoided" – and that the resulting system is
      not isomorphic to the logic of declarative discourse. If Vranas is right, neither
      the classical validity of (1)–(3) nor the imperatival validity of (1')–(3') can be
      reduced to the other.

17   See, e.g., Richard's (2008, 63) account of "commitment-validity."

18   "Those emotive theorists who said that the function of moral utterance was to
      evince emotion would ... have been correct if they had substituted the indefinite
      for the definite article" (MacIntyre, 1957, 329). See too Goldman (1988b, 13–14).

19   It "almost" doesn't matter because the non-cognitivist can evade this objection
      by choosing an obvious truth having nothing to do with lying and immorality:
      e.g. the fact that the speaker has asserted that lying is immoral or the fact that
      $2 + 2 = 4$. It is not rational to assert that lying is immoral while doubting these
      last two propositions, but neither is a plausible candidate for the cognitive
      content of "Lying is immoral."

WORKS CITED

Abu-Lughod, L. (1991), "Writing against Culture," in E. E. Fox (ed.), *Recapturing Anthropology*, Santa Fe, NM: School of American Research Press, pp. 137–62.

Adams, Ernest W. (1965), "A Logic of Conditionals," *Inquiry*, 8, pp. 166–97.

Adams, Ernest W. (1975), *The Logic of Conditionals*, Dordrecht: D. Reidel.

Adams, Ernest W. (1998), *A Primer of Probability Logic*, Stanford: CLSI Publications.

Allison, Henry (1990), *Kant's Theory of Freedom*, Cambridge University Press.

Allison, Henry (1996), *Idealism and Freedom: Essays on Kant's Theoretical and Practical Philosophy*, Cambridge University Press.

Alston, William (1976), "Two Types of Foundationalism," *Journal of Philosophy*, 73, 7, pp. 165–85.

Alston, William (1986), "Epistemic Circularity," *Philosophical Studies*, 47, pp. 1–28.

Alston, William (2005), *Beyond "Justification": Dimensions of Epistemic Evaluation*, Ithaca, NY: Cornell University Press.

Altham, J. E. J. (1986), "The Legacy of Emotivism," in G. Macdonald and C. Wright (eds.), *Fact, Science and Morality: Essays on A. J. Ayer's Language, Truth and Logic*, Oxford: Blackwell, pp. 275–88.

Anderson, Alan Ross (1958), "A Reduction of Deontic Logic to Alethic Modal Logic," *Mind*, 67, pp. 100–03.

Anderson, Alan Ross (1967), "Some Nasty Problems in the Formal Logic of Ethics," *Noûs*, 1, pp. 345–60.

Anscombe, G. E. M. (1958), "On Brute Facts," *Analysis*, 18, pp. 69–72.

Åqvist, Lennart (1984), "Deontic Logic," in D. Gabbay (ed.), *Handbook of Philosophical Logic*, Dordrecht: D. Reidel, pp. 605–714.

Arendt, Hannah (1963/1994), *Eichmann in Jerusalem: A Report on the Banality of Evil*, New York: Penguin.

Aristotle (384–322 BC/1984), *Eudemian Ethics*, J. Solomon (trans.), in *The Complete Works of Aristotle*, vol. II, J. Barnes (ed.), Princeton University Press.

Aristotle (384–322 BC/1984), *Nicomachean Ethics*, W. D. Ross, J.O. Urmson (trans.), in *The Complete Works of Aristotle*, vol. II, J. Barnes (ed.), Princeton University Press.

Arrington, Robert L. (1989), *Rationalism, Realism and Relativism: Perspectives in Contemporary Moral Epistemology*, Ithaca, NY: Cornell University Press.

Athanassoulis, Nafsika (2000), "A Response to Harman: Virtue Ethics and Character Traits," *Proceedings of the Aristotelian Society*, 100, pp. 215–21.

Audi, Robert (1993), *The Structure of Justification*, New York: Cambridge University Press.

Audi, Robert (1996), "Intuitionism, Pluralism, and the Foundation of Ethics," in W. Sinnott-Armstrong and M. Timmons (eds.), *Moral Knowledge? New Readings in Moral Epistemology*, Oxford University Press, pp. 101–36.

Audi, Robert (1997a), "Moral Judgment and Reasons for Action," in G. Cullity and B. Gaut (eds.), *Ethics and Practical Reason*, Oxford: Clarendon Press, pp. 125–59.

Audi, Robert (1997b), *Moral Knowledge and Ethical Character*, Oxford University Press.

Audi, Robert (1998), *Epistemology: A Contemporary Introduction to the Theory of Knowledge*, London: Routledge.

Audi, Robert (1999a), "Moral Knowledge and Ethical Pluralism," in J. Greco and E. Sosa (eds.), *The Blackwell Guide to Epistemology*, Oxford: Blackwell, pp. 271–302.

Audi, Robert (1999b), "Self-Evidence," *Philosophical Perspectives*, 13, pp. 205–26.

Audi, Robert (2004), *The Good in the Right*, Princeton University Press.

Audi, Robert (2006), "Intrinsic Value and Reasons for Action," in Horgan and Timmons (2006b), pp. 79–106.

Aydede, Murat (2005), "Introduction: A Critical and Quasi-Historical Essay on Theories of Pain," in M. Aydede (ed.), *Pain: New Essays on Its Nature and the Methodology of Its Study*, Cambridge, MA: MIT Press, pp. 1–58.

Ayer, Alfred J. (1946/1952), *Language, Truth and Logic*, New York: Dover.

Ayer, Alfred J. (1956/1990), *The Problem of Knowledge*, London: Pelican.

Ayer, Alfred J. (1968), "Privacy," in P. F. Strawson (ed.), *Studies in the Philosophy of Thought and Action*, London: Oxford University Press, pp. 24–47.

Baier, Kurt (1958), *The Moral Point of View*, Ithaca, NY: Cornell University Press.

Ball, Stephen (1991), "Linguistic Intuitions and Varieties of Ethical Naturalism," *Philosophy and Phenomenological Research*, 51, pp. 1–30.

Batson, Daniel (1991), *The Altruism Question: Toward a Social-Psychological Answer*, Hillsdale, NJ: Lawrence Erlbaum Associates.

Beah, Ishmael (2007), *A Long Way Gone: Memoirs of a Boy Soldier*, New York: Farrar, Straus and Giroux.

Bealer, George (1998), "Intuition and the Autonomy of Philosophy," in M. Depaul and W. Ramsey (eds.), *Rethinking Intuition: The Psychology of Intuition and Its Role in Philosophical Inquiry*, Lanham, MD: Rowman and Littlefield, pp. 201–39.

Beany, Michael (ed.) (1997), *The Frege Reader*, Oxford: Blackwell.

Bearak, Barry (2009), "Pope Tells Clergy in Angola to Work against Belief in Witchcraft," *The New York Times* (Sunday, March 22), p. 9.

Belnap, Nuel D. (1962), "Tonk, Plonk and Plink," *Analysis*, 22, pp. 130–34.

Bennett, Jonathan (1974), "The Conscience of Huckleberry Finn," *Philosophy*, 49, pp. 123–34.

Bennett, Jonathan (2003), *A Philosophical Guide to Conditionals*, Oxford University Press.

Bentham, Jeremy (1780/1982), *An Introduction to the Principles of Morals and Legislation*, ed. J. H. Burns and H. L. A. Hart (eds.), London: Methuen.

Berlin, Isaiah (1955–56), "Equality," *Proceedings of the Aristotelian Society*, 56, pp. 301–26.

Blackburn, Simon (1984), *Spreading the Word*, New York: Oxford University Press.

Blackburn, Simon (1988), "Attitudes and Contents," *Ethics*, 98, pp. 501–17.

Blackburn, Simon (1992), "Through Thick and Thin," *Aristotelian Society Supplementary Volume*, 66, pp. 285–99.

Blair, James K., Derek Mitchell and Karina Peschardt (1995), *The Psychopath: Emotion and the Brain*, Oxford: Blackwell.

Blair, R. J. R., E. Colledge, L. Murray and D. G. Mitchell (2001), "A Selective Impairment in the Processing of Sad and Fearful Expressions in Children with Psychopathic Tendencies," *Journal of Abnormal Child Psychology*, 29, 6, pp. 491–98.

Blair, R. J. R., L. Jones, F. Clark and M. Smith (1997), "The Psychopathic Individual: A Lack of Response to Distress Cues?" *Psychophysiology*, 34, 2, pp. 192–98.

Bloomfield, Paul (2001), *Moral Reality*, New York: Oxford University Press.

Bloomfield, Paul (2008), "Comment on Doris and Plakias," in Sinnott-Armstrong (2008b), pp. 339–44.

Blum, Lawrence (1994), *Moral Perception and Particularity*, Cambridge University Press.

Boghossian, Paul (1997), "What the Externalist Can Know A Priori," *Proceedings of the Aristotelian Society*, 97, 2, pp. 161–75.

Boghossian, Paul (2000), "Knowledge of Logic," in P. Boghossian and C. Peacocke (eds.), *New Essays on the A Priori*, Oxford: Clarendon Press, pp. 229–54.

Boghossian, Paul (2001), "How Are Objective Epistemic Reasons Possible?" *Philosophical Studies*, 106, pp. 1–40.

Boghossian, Paul (2003), "Blind Reasoning," *Aristotelian Society Supplementary Volume*, 77, pp. 225–48.

Bohannan, Paul (1968), *Justice and Judgment among the Tiv*, Oxford University Press.

BonJour, Laurence (1980), "Externalist Theories of Epistemic Justification," *Midwest Studies in Philosophy*, 5, pp. 53–73.

BonJour, Laurence (1985), *The Structure of Empirical Knowledge*, Cambridge University Press.

BonJour, Laurence, and Ernest Sosa (eds.) (2003), *Epistemic Justification: Internalism vs. Externalism, Foundations vs. Virtues*, Malden, MA: Blackwell.

Boyd, Richard (1988), "How to Be a Moral Realist," in G. Sayre-McCord (ed.), *Essays on Moral Realism*, Ithaca, NY: Cornell, pp. 181–228.

Brandom, Robert (1994), *Making It Explicit: Reasoning, Representing and Discursive Commitment*, Cambridge, MA: Harvard University Press.

Brandom, Robert (2000), *Articulating Reasons: An Introduction to Inferentialism*, Cambridge, MA: Harvard University Press.

Brandt, Richard (1979), *A Theory of the Good and the Right*, Oxford University Press.

Brandt, Richard (1996), *Facts, Values and Morality*, Cambridge University Press.

Brill, Robert H. (1962), "A Note on the Scientist's Definition of Glass," *Journal of Glass Studies*, 4, pp. 127–38.

Brink, David (1984), "Moral Realism and the Skeptical Arguments from Disagreement and Queerness," *Australasian Journal of Philosophy*, 62, pp. 111–25.

Brink, David (1986), "Externalist Moral Realism," *Southern Journal of Philosophy*, Supplement, 24, pp. 23–41.

Brink, David (1989), *Moral Realism and the Foundation of Ethics*, Cambridge University Press.

Broad, C. D. (1930), *Five Types of Moral Theory*, London: Routledge and Kegan Paul.

Brueckner, Anthony and Christopher Buford (2009), "Bootstrapping and Knowledge of Reliability," *Philosophical Studies*, 145, pp. 407–12.

Cappelen, Herman and Ernie Lepore (2005), *Insensitive Semantics*, Oxford: Blackwell.

Carnap, Rudolph (1937), *Philosophy and Logical Syntax*, London: Kegan Paul.

Caro, Mark (2009), *The Foie Gras Wars*, New York: Simon & Schuster.

Carruthers, Peter, Stephen Laurence and Stephen Stich (eds.) (2007), *The Innate Mind*, vol. III, *Foundations and the Future*, Oxford University Press.

Carruthers, Peter and Peter K. Smith (eds.) (1996), *Theories of Theories of Mind*, Cambridge University Press.

Castañeda, Hector-Neri (1981), "The Paradoxes of Deontic Logic," in R. Hilpinen (ed.), *New Studies in Deontic Logic*, Dordrecht: D. Reidel, pp. 37–85.

Chagnon, Napoleon (1974), *Studying the Yanomamo*, New York: Holt, Rinehart, and Winston.

Chagnon, Napoleon (1977), *Yanomamo: The Fierce People*, New York: Holt, Rinehart, and Winston.

Chisholm, Roderick (1957), *Perceiving: A Philosophical Study*, Ithaca, NY: Cornell University Press.

Chisholm, Roderick (1963), "Contrary-to-Duty Imperatives and Deontic Logic," *Analysis*, 24, pp. 33–36.

Chisholm, Roderick (1964), *Philosophy*, Englewood Cliffs, NJ: Prentice Hall.

Chisholm, Roderick (1966), *Theory of Knowledge*, Englewood Cliffs, NJ: Prentice Hall.

Chomsky, Noam (1957), *Syntactic Structures*, The Hague: Mouton.

Chomsky, Noam (1986), *Knowledge of Language: Its Nature, Origin and Use*, New York: Praeger.

Chomsky, Noam (1988), *Language and Problems of Knowledge: The Managua Lectures*, Cambridge, MA: MIT Press.

Chomsky, Noam (1995), *The Minimalist Program*, Cambridge, MA: MIT Press.

Christensen, David (2007), "Epistemology of Disagreement: The Good News," *Philosophical Review*, 116, pp. 187–217.

Churchland, Paul (1981), "Eliminative Materialism and the Propositional Attitudes," *Journal of Philosophy*, 78, pp. 67–90.

Cling, Andrew (2008), "The Epistemic Regress Problem," *Philosophical Studies*, 140, pp. 401–21.

Cohen, Stewart (1986), "Knowledge and Context," *Journal of Philosophy*, 83, pp. 574–83.

Cohen, Stewart (2002), "Basic Knowledge and the Problem of Easy Knowledge," *Philosophy and Phenomenological Research*, 65, 2, pp. 309–29.

Cook, John W. (1999), *Morality and Cultural Differences*, Oxford University Press.

Cooper, Neil (1981), *The Diversity of Moral Thinking*, Oxford: Clarendon Press.

Copp, David (2001), "Realist-Expressivism: A Neglected Option for Moral Realism," *Social Philosophy and Policy*, 18, pp. 1–43.

Copp, David (2007), *Morality in a Natural World: Selected Essays in Metaethics*, Cambridge University Press.

Crisp, Roger (1992), "Utilitarianism and the Life of Virtue," *Philosophical Quarterly*, 42, pp. 139–60.

Crisp, Roger (2002), "Sidgwick and the Boundaries of Intuitionism," in Stratton-Lake (2002c), pp. 56–75.

Cullity, Garrett (2002), "Particularism and Presumptive Reasons," *Aristotelian Society Supplementary Volume*, 76, pp. 169–90.

Dancy, Jonathan (1993), *Moral Reasons*, Oxford: Blackwell.

Dancy, Jonathan (2004), *Ethics without Principles*, Oxford University Press.

Dancy, Jonathan (2006), "What Do Reasons Do?" in Horgan and Timmons (2006b), pp. 39–60.

Daniels, Norman (1996), *Justice and Justification: Reflective Equilibrium in Theory and Practice*, Cambridge University Press.

Darley, John M. and C. Daniel Batson (1973), "From Jerusalem to Jericho: A Study of Situational and Dispositional Variables in Helping Behavior," *Journal of Personality and Social Psychology*, 27, 1, pp. 100–8.

Darwall, Stephen (1983), *Impartial Reason*, Ithaca, NY: Cornell University Press.

Darwall, Stephen (1995), *The British Moralists and the Internal "Ought"*, Cambridge University Press.

Darwall, Stephen (1997), "Reasons, Motives, and the Demands of Morality: An Introduction," in S. Darwall, A. Gibbard, and P. Railton (eds.), *Moral Discourse and Practice: Some Philosophical Approaches*, New York: Oxford University Press, pp. 305–12.

Darwall, Stephen (2006), *The Second-Person Standpoint: Morality, Respect and Accountability*, Cambridge, MA: Harvard University Press.

Darwall, Stephen, A. Gibbard and P. Railton (1992), "Toward Fin de Siècle Ethics: Some Trends," *Philosophical Review*, 101, pp. 115–89.

Davidson, Donald (1984), *Essays on Actions and Events*, Oxford: Clarendon Press.

Davidson, Donald (1989), "A Coherence Theory of Truth and Knowledge," in E. Lepore (ed.), *Truth and Interpretation: Perspectives on the Philosophy of Donald Davidson*, New York: Blackwell, pp. 307–19.

Davidson, P., E. Turiel and A. Black (1983), "The Effect of Stimulus Familiarity on the Use of Criteria and Justification in Children's Social Reasoning," *British Journal of Developmental Psychology*, 1, pp. 46–65.

Davies, Martin and Tony Stone (eds.) (1995), *Mental Simulation: Evaluation and Applications*, Oxford: Blackwell.

Dehaene, Stanislas (1997), *The Number Sense: How the Mind Creates Mathematics*, Oxford University Press.

Deigh, John (1995), "Empathy and Universalizability," *Ethics*, 105, pp. 743–63.

Denis, Lara (2006), "Kant's Conception of Virtue," in P. Guyer (ed.), *The Cambridge Companion to Kant and Modern Philosophy*, Cambridge University Press, pp. 503–37.

Dennett, Daniel (1987), *The Intentional Stance*, Cambridge, MA: MIT Press.

DePaul, Michael (1988), "Argument and Perception: The Role of Literature in Moral Inquiry," *Journal of Philosophy*, 85, pp. 552–65.

DeRose, Keith (2002), "Assertion, Knowledge and Context," *Philosophical Review*, 111, 2, pp. 167–203.

Descartes, René (1641/1993), *Meditations*, J. Cottingham, R. Stoothoff, and D. Murdoch (trans.), in *The Philosophical Writings of Descartes*, vol. II, Cambridge University Press.

DeVoto, Bernard (1942/2000), *The Year of Decision: 1846*, New York: Macmillan.

De Waal, Frans (2006), "Morality Evolved: Primate Social Instincts, Human Morality, and the Rise and Fall of 'Veneer Theory'," in J. Ober and S. Macedo (eds.), *Primates and Philosophers*, Princeton University Press, pp. 1–82.

Dickens, Charles (1849–50/1997), *David Copperfield*, N. Burgis (ed.), Oxford University Press.

Dillon, Sam (2009), "Disabled Students Are Spanked More: Study Looks at Corporal Punishment in Schools in 21 States," *The New York Times* (August 11), p. 10.

Doris, John (1998), "Persons, Situations and Virtue Ethics," *Noûs*, 32, 4, pp. 504–30.

Doris, John (2002), *Lack of Character: Personality and Moral Behavior*, Cambridge University Press.

Doris, John and Alexandra Plakias (2008), "How to Argue about Disagreement," in Sinnott-Armstrong (2008b), pp. 303–31.

Dostoevsky, Fyodor (1880/1990), *The Brothers Karamazov*, trans. R. Pevear and L. Volokhonsky, New York: Farrar, Straus, and Giroux.

Dreier, James (1990), "Internalism and Speaker Relativism," *Ethics*, 101, pp. 6–26.

Dreier, James (1997), "Humean Doubts about the Practical Justification of Morality," in G. Cullity and B. Gaut (eds.), *Ethics and Practical Reason*, Oxford University Press, pp. 81–100.

Dreyfus, Hubert and Stuart Dreyfus (1990), "What is Morality? A Phenomenological Account of the Development of Ethical Expertise," in D. Rasmussen (ed.), *Universalism vs. Communitarianism*, Cambridge, MA: MIT Press, pp. 237–64.

Dummett, Michael (1973), *Frege: Philosophy of Language*, Cambridge, MA: Harvard University Press.

Dummett, Michael (1978a), "Is Logic Empirical?" in *Truth and Other Enigmas*, Cambridge, MA: Harvard University Press, pp. 269–89.

Dummett, Michael (1978b), "The Justification of Deduction," in *Truth and Other Enigmas*, Cambridge, MA: Harvard University Press, pp. 290–318.

Dwyer, Susan (1999), "Moral Competence," in K. Murasugi and R. Stainton (eds.), *Philosophy and Linguistics*, Boulder, CO: Westview Press, pp. 169–90.

Edgington, Dorothy (1991), "The Mystery of the Missing Matter of Fact," *Aristotelian Society Supplementary Volume*, 65, pp. 185–209.

Edwards, Carolyn (1975), "Societal Complexity and Moral Development: A Kenyan Study," *Ethos*, 3, pp. 505–27.

Elga, Adam (2007), "Reflection and Disagreement," *Noûs*, 61, 3, pp. 478–502.

Etchemendy, John (1990), *The Concept of Logical Consequence*, Cambridge, MA: Harvard University Press.

Etchemendy, John (1999), *The Concept of Logical Consequence*, Stanford: CSLI Publications.

Evans, Gareth (1982), *Varieties of Reference*, John McDowell (ed.), Oxford: Clarendon Press.

Feinberg, Joel (1986), *The Moral Limits of the Criminal Law*, vol. III, *Harm to Self*, Oxford University Press.

Feldman, Fred (1995), "Adjusting Utility for Justice: A Consequentialist Reply to the Objection from Justice," *Philosophy and Phenomenological Research*, 55, pp. 567–85.

Feldman, Fred (2001), "Logic and Ethics," in L. C. Becker and C. B. Becker (eds.), *Encyclopedia of Ethics*, 2nd edn., New York: Routledge, vol. II, pp. 1011–17.

Feldman, Richard and Earl Conee (1985), "Evidentialism," *Philosophical Studies*, 48, pp. 15–34.

Field, Hartry (1977), "Logic, Meaning and Conceptual Role," *Journal of Philosophy*, 74, pp. 379–409.

Field, Hartry (2000), "A Priority as an Evaluative Notion," in P. Boghossian and C. Peacocke (eds.), *New Essays on the A Priori*, Oxford: Clarendon Press, pp. 117–49.

Filonowicz, Joseph (2008), *Fellow-Feeling and the Moral Life*, Cambridge University Press.

Fischer, John Martin (1999), "Recent Work on Moral Responsibility," *Ethics*, 110, pp. 93–139.

Fischer, John Martin and Mark Ravizza (1998), *Responsibility and Control: A Theory of Moral Responsibility*, Cambridge University Press.

Fitzpatrick, William (2008), "Moral Responsibility and Normative Ignorance: Answering a New Skeptical Challenge," *Ethics*, 118 (July), pp. 589–613.

Flanagan, Owen (1993), *Varieties of Moral Personality: Ethics and Psychological Realism*, Cambridge, MA: Harvard University Press.

Fogelin, Robert (1994), *Pyrrhonian Reflections on Knowledge and Justification*, New York: Oxford University Press.

Foot, Philippa (1958), "Moral Arguments," *Mind*, 67, pp. 502–13.

Foot, Philippa (1972), "Morality as a System of Hypothetical Imperatives," *Philosophical Review*, 81, 3, pp. 305–16.

Foot, Philippa (1981), *Virtues and Vices*, Berkeley: University of California Press.

Frankena, W. K. (1939), "The Naturalistic Fallacy," *Mind*, 48, pp. 464–77.

Frankena, W. K. (1967), "The Concept of Morality," *University of Colorado Studies: Series in Philosophy*, 3, pp. 1–22; reprinted in G. Wallace and D. M. Walker (eds.) (1970), *The Definition of Morality*, London: Methuen, pp. 146–73.

Frankfurt, Harry (1971), "Freedom of the Will and the Concept of a Person," *Journal of Philosophy*, 68, pp. 5–20.

Frege, Gottlob (1897/1997), "Logic," reprinted in part in Beaney (1997), pp. 227–50.

Frith, Chris D. and Uta Frith (1999), "Interacting Minds: A Biological Basis," *Science*, 286 (November 26), p. 1692.

Garner, R. T. (1990), "On the Genuine Queerness of Moral Properties and Facts," *Australasian Journal of Philosophy*, 68, pp. 137–46.

Garrett, Don (1997), *Cognition and Commitment in Hume's Philosophy*, New York: Oxford University Press.

Garrow, David J. (1986), *Bearing the Cross: Martin Luther King Jr. and the Southern Christian Leadership Conference*, New York: HarperCollins.

Geach, Peter T. (1957–58), "Imperative and Deontic Logic," *Analysis*, 18, pp. 49–56.

Geach, Peter T. (1960), "Ascriptivism," *Philosophical Review*, 69, pp. 221–25.

Geach, Peter T. (1965), "Assertion," *Philosophical Review*, 74, pp. 449–65.

Gellner, E. (1954–55), "Logic and Ethics," *Proceedings of the Aristotelian Society*, 10, pp. 157–78.

Gendler, Tamar Szabó and John Hawthorne (eds.) (2002), *Conceivability and Possibility*, Oxford: Clarendon Press.

Gettier, Edmund (1963), "Is Justified True Belief Knowledge?" *Analysis*, 23, pp. 121–23.

Gibbard, Allan (1981), "Two Recent Theories of Conditionals," in W. L. Harper, R. Stalnaker, and C. T. Pearce (eds.), *Ifs*, Dordrecht: D. Reidel, pp. 211–47.

Gibbard, Allan (1990), *Wise Choices, Apt Feelings: A Theory of Normative Judgment*, Cambridge, MA: Harvard University Press.

Gibbard, Allan (1992a), "Morality and Thick Concepts – I, Thick Concepts and Warrant for Feelings," *Aristotelian Society Supplementary Volume*, 66, pp. 267–83.

Gibbard, Allan (1992b), "Reply to Blackburn, Carson, Hill and Railton," *Philosophy and Phenomenological Research*, 72, pp. 969–80.

Gibbard, Allan (2003), "Reasons Thick and Thin," *Journal of Philosophy*, 100, pp. 288–304.

Gilligan, Carol (1982), *In a Different Voice*, Cambridge, MA: Harvard University Press.

Ginet, Carl (1975), *Knowledge, Perception and Memory*, Dordrecht: D. Reidel.

Goldie, Peter (2007), "Seeing What Is the Kind Thing to Do: Perception and Emotion in Morality," *Dialectica*, 61, pp. 347–61.

Goldie, Peter (2009), "Thick Concepts and Emotion," in D. Callcut (ed.), *Reading Bernard Williams*, London: Routledge, pp. 94–109.

Goldman, Alan (1988a), *Moral Knowledge*, London: Routledge.

Goldman, Alan (1988b), *Empirical Knowledge*, Berkeley: University of California Press.

Goldman, Alvin (1967), "A Causal Theory of Knowing," *Journal of Philosophy*, 64, pp. 357–72.

Goldman, Alvin (1976), "Discrimination and Perceptual Knowledge," *Journal of Philosophy*, 73, pp. 771–91.

Goldman, Alvin (1986), *Epistemology and Cognition*, Cambridge, MA: Harvard University Press.

Goldman, Alvin (2006), *Simulating Minds: The Philosophy, Psychology and Neuroscience of Mindreading*, Oxford University Press.

Goodman, Nelson (1955), *Fact, Fiction, and Forecast*, Cambridge, MA: Harvard University Press.

Gopnik, Alison and Andrew Meltzoff (1997), *Words, Thoughts, and Theories*, Cambridge, MA: MIT Press.

Gopnik, Alison and Henry Wellman (1992), "Why the Child's Theory of Mind Really is a Theory," *Mind and Language*, 7, pp. 145–71.

Gordon, Robert M. (1986), "Folk Psychology as Simulation," *Mind and Language*, 1, pp. 158–71.

Gordon, Robert M. (1995), "Sympathy, Simulation and the Impartial Spectator," *Ethics*, 105, pp. 727–42.

Goswami, Usha (ed.) (2002), *Blackwell Handbook of Childhood Cognitive Development*, Malden, MA: Blackwell.

Gowans, Chris (ed.) (2000), *Moral Disagreements: Classic and Contemporary Readings*, London: Routledge.

Greco, John (1993), "Virtues and Vices of Virtue Epistemology," *Canadian Journal of Philosophy*, 23, pp. 413–32.

Greco, John (2000), *Putting Skeptics in Their Place*, Cambridge University Press.

Grice, Paul (1989), *Studies in the Way of Words*, Cambridge, MA: Harvard University Press.

Grossbard-Shechtman, A. (1984), "A Theory of Allocation of Time in Markets for Labour and Marriage," *Economic Journal*, 94, pp. 863–82.

Guyer, Paul (1993), *Kant and the Experience of Freedom*, Cambridge University Press.

Guyer, Paul (2008), *Knowledge, Reason and Taste: Kant's Responses to Hume*, Princeton University Press.

Haack, Susan (1999), "A Foundherentist Theory of Empirical Knowledge," in Louis Pojman (ed.), *The Theory of Knowledge: Classical and Contemporary Readings*, 2nd edn., Belmont, CA: Wadsworth, pp. 283–93.

Haidt, Jonathan (2001), "The Emotional Dog and Its Rational Tail: A Social Intuitionist Approach to Moral Judgment," *Psychological Review*, 108, pp. 814–34.

Haidt, Jonathan and Fredrik Björklund (2008), "Social Intuitionists Answer Six Questions about Moral Psychology," in Sinnott-Armstrong (2008b), pp. 181–218; 241–54.

Haidt, Jonathan, Fredrik Björklund, and Scott Murphy (2000), "Moral Dumbfounding: When Intuition Finds No Reason," unpublished manuscript.

Haidt, Jonathan and Matthew A. Hersh (2001), "Sexual Morality: The Cultures and Reasons of Liberals and Conservatives," *Journal of Applied Social Psychology*, 31, pp. 191–221.

Haidt, Jonathan, and Craig Joseph (2007), "The Moral Mind: How 5 Sets of Innate Moral Intuitions Guide the Development of Many Culture-Specific Virtues, and Perhaps Even Modules," in P. Carruthers, S. Laurence, and S. Stich (eds.), *The Innate Mind*, vol. III, *Foundations and the Future*, Oxford University Press, pp. 367–92.

Haidt, Jonathan, Silvia H. Koller and Maria G. Dias (1993), "Affect, Culture, and Morality, or Is It Wrong to Eat Your Dog?" *Journal of Personality and Social Psychology*, 65, pp. 613–28.

Haidt, Jonathan, V. Lobus, C. Chiong, T. Nishida and J. DeLoache (2007), "When Getting Something Good is Bad: Young Children's Reactions to Inequity," unpublished manuscript.

Haji, Ishtiyaque (1998), *Moral Appraisability*, Oxford University Press.

Hale, Bob (1993), "Can There Be a Logic of Attitudes?" in J. Haldane and C. Wright (eds.), *Reality, Representation and Projection*, New York: Oxford University Press, pp. 337–63.

Hamlin, J. Kiley, Karen Wynn and Paul Bloom (2007), "Social Evaluation by Preverbal Infants," *Nature*, 450, pp. 557–59.

Hampton, Jean (1998), *The Authority of Reason*, Cambridge University Press.

Hansson, Sven Ove (1997), "Situationist Deontic Logic," *Journal of Philosophical Logic*, 26, pp. 423–48.

Hare, R. M. (1952), *The Language of Morals*, Oxford: Clarendon Press.

Hare, R. M. (1954–55), "Universalizability," *Proceedings of the Aristotelian Society*, 10, pp. 295–312.

Hare, R. M. (1963), *Freedom and Reason*, Oxford University Press.

Hare, R. M. (1970), "Meaning and Speech Acts," *Philosophical Review*, 79, pp. 3–24.

Harman, Gilbert (1973), *Thought*, Princeton University Press.

Harman, Gilbert (1977), *The Nature of Morality: An Introduction to Ethics*, New York: Oxford University Press.

Harman, Gilbert (1984), "Is There a Single True Morality?" in D. Copp and D. Zimmerman (eds.), *Morality, Reason, and Truth*, Totowa, NJ: Rowman & Allanheld, pp. 27–48.

Harman, Gilbert (1986), "The Meaning of the Logical Constants," in E. Lepore (ed.), *Truth and Interpretation: Perspectives on the Philosophy of Donald Davidson*, Oxford: Blackwell, pp. 125–34.

Harman, Gilbert (1999a), *Reasoning, Meaning, and Mind*, Oxford University Press.

Harman, Gilbert (1999b), "Moral Philosophy Meets Social Psychology: Virtue Ethics and the Fundamental Attribution Error," *Proceedings of the Aristotelian Society*, 99, pp. 315–31.

Harman, Gilbert (2000a), "Moral Philosophy and Linguistics," in K. Brinkmann (ed.), *Proceedings of the 20th World Conference of Philosophy*, vol. I, *Ethics*, Bowling Green, OH: Philosophy Documentation Center, pp. 107–15; reprinted in Harman (2000b), pp. 217–26.

Harman, Gilbert (2000b), *Explaining Value and Other Essays in Moral Philosophy*, New York: Oxford University Press.

Harman, Gilbert, and Judith J. Thomson (1996), *Moral Relativism and Moral Objectivity*, Oxford: Blackwell.

Hauser, Marc (2006), *Moral Minds*, New York: HarperCollins.

Hawthorne, John (2007), "A Priority and Externalism," in S. Goldberg (ed.), *Internalism and Externalism in Semantics and Epistemology*, Oxford University Press, pp. 201–18.

Herman, Barbara (1981), "On the Value of Acting from the Motive of Duty," *Philosophical Review*, 90, 3, pp. 359–82.

Herman, Barbara (1985), "The Practice of Moral Judgment," *Journal of Philosophy*, 82, 8, pp. 414–36.

Herman, Barbara (2008), "Morality Unbounded," *Philosophy and Public Affairs*, 36, pp. 323–58.

Heumer, Michael (2005), *Ethical Intuitionism*, Houndmills, UK: Palgrave Macmillan.

Hilpinen, Risto (ed.) (1957/1971), *Deontic Logic: Introductory and Systematic Readings*, Dordrecht: D. Reidel.

Hobbes, Thomas (1650), *Human Nature or the Fundamental Elements of Polity*; reprinted in part in D. D. Raphael (ed.) (1969/1991), *The British Moralists*, Indianapolis: Hackett, vol. I, §§1–20.

Hoffman, Martin (2000), *Empathy and Moral Development*, Cambridge University Press.

Holland, John H., Keith J. Holyoak, Richard E. Nisbett and Paul R. Thagard (1986), *Induction: Processes of Inference, Learning and Discovery*, Cambridge, MA: MIT Press.

Holton, Richard (2002), "Principles and Particularisms," *Aristotelian Society Supplementary Volume*, 76, pp. 191–209.

Hooker, Brad (2002), "Intuitions and Moral Theorizing," in Stratton-Lake (2002c), pp. 161–83.

Hooker, Brad and Margaret Little (eds.) (2000), *Moral Particularism*, Oxford University Press.

Horgan, Terry and Mark Timmons (2006a), "Cognitivist Expressivism," in Horgan and Timmons (2006b), pp. 255–98.

Horgan, Terry and Mark Timmons (eds.) (2006b), *Metaethics after Moore*, Oxford University Press.

Horwich, Paul (1998), *Meaning*, Oxford University Press.

Hudson, W. D. (1967), *Ethical Intuitionism*, New York: St. Martin's Press.

Hume, David (1739–40/2000), *A Treatise of Human Nature*, David Fate Norton and Mary J. Norton (eds.), Oxford: Clarendon Press.

Hume, David (1751/1998), *An Enquiry Concerning the Principles of Morals*, Tom L. Beauchamp (ed.), Oxford: Clarendon Press.

Hutcheson, Francis (1728/1971), *Illustrations on the Moral Sense*, Bernard Peach (ed.), Cambridge University Press.

Irwin, Terence H. (1988), "Some Rational Aspects of Incontinence," *Southern Journal of Philosophy*, Supplement, 27, pp. 49–88.

Irwin, Terence H. (1997), "Practical Reason Divided: Aquinas and His Critics," in G. Cullity and B. Gaut (eds.), *Ethics and Practical Reason*, Oxford University Press, pp.189–214.

Isen, Alice M. and Paula F. Levin (1972), "Effect of Feeling Good on Helping: Cookies and Kindness," *Journal of Personality and Social Psychology*, 21, 3, pp. 384–88.

Jackson, Frank (1974), "Defining the Autonomy of Ethics," *Philosophical Review*, 83, pp. 88–96.

Jackson, Frank and Philip Pettit (1995), "Moral Functionalism and Moral Motivation," *Philosophical Quarterly*, 45, pp. 20–40.

Jacobson, Daniel (2005), "Seeing by Feeling: Virtues, Skills and Moral Perception," *Ethical Theory and Moral Practice*, 8, pp. 387–409.

James, William (1897/1956), *The Will to Believe and Other Essays in Popular Philosophy*, New York: Dover.

Johnson, W. E. (1921), *Logic*, London: Cambridge University Press.

Johnston, Mark (2001), "The Authority of Affect," *Philosophy and Phenomenological Research*, 63, pp. 181–214.

Joyce, Richard (2001), *The Myth of Morality*, Cambridge University Press.

Kahneman, Daniel, Paul Slovic and Amos Tversky (eds.) (1982), *Judgment under Uncertainty: Heuristics and Biases*, Cambridge University Press.

Kahneman, Daniel and Amos Tversky (1996), "On the Reality of Cognitive Illusions," *Psychological Review*, 103, pp. 582–91.

Kamm, Frances (1993), *Morality and Mortality*, vol. I, *Death and Whom to Save from It*, New York: Oxford University Press.

Kamtekar, Rachana (2004), "Situationism and Virtue Ethics on the Content of Character," *Ethics*, 114, pp. 458–91.

Kanger, Stig (1957/1971), "New Foundations for Ethical Theory," in Hilpinen (1957/1971), pp. 36–58.

Kant, Immanuel (1781/1787/1999), *Critique of Pure Reason*, P. Guyer and A. Wood (trans.), Cambridge University Press.

Kant, Immanuel (1785/2002), *Groundwork for the Metaphysics of Morals*, Alan Wood (trans. and ed.), New Haven: Yale University Press.

Kant, Immanuel (1797/1996), *Metaphysics of Morals*, Mary Gregor (ed.), Cambridge University Press.

Kaplan, David (1989), "Demonstratives," in J. Almog, J. Perry, and J. Wettstein (eds.), *Themes from Kaplan*, Oxford University Press, pp. 481–564.

Kaufmann, Walter (ed.) (1956/1975), *Existentialism from Dostoevsky to Sartre*, New York: Penguin.

Kavka, Gregory (1985), "The Reconciliation Project," in D. Copp and D. Zimmerman (eds.), *Morality, Reason, and Truth*, Totowa, NJ: Rowman & Allanheld, pp. 297–319.

Kelly, Daniel, Stephen Stich, Kevin Haley, Serena Eng and Daniel Fessler (2007), "Harm: Affect and the Moral/Conventional Distinction," *Mind and Language*, 22, 2, pp. 117–31.

Kelly, Thomas (2005), "The Epistemic Significance of Disagreement," in J. Hawthorne and T. Szabó Gendler (eds.), *Oxford Studies in Epistemology*, Oxford University Press, pp. 167–96.

Killen, Melanie and Judith Smetana (eds.) (2006), *Handbook of Moral Development*, Mahwah, NJ: Lawrence Erlbaum Associates.

Kim, Jaegwon (1984), "Concepts of Supervenience," *Philosophy and Phenomenological Research*, 45, pp. 153–76.

Kim, Jaegwon (1988), "What Is 'Naturalized Epistemology'?" in J. Tomberlin (ed.), *Philosophical Perspectives 2, Epistemology*, Atascadero, CA: Ridgeview, pp. 381–405; reprinted in H. Kornblith (ed.) (1994), *Naturalizing Epistemology*, 2nd edn., Cambridge, MA: MIT Press, pp. 33–56.

Kim, Jaegwon (1992), "Multiple Realizability and the Metaphysics of Reduction," *Philosophy and Phenomenological Research*, 52, pp. 1–26.

Klein, Peter (1999), "Human Knowledge and the Infinite Regress of Reasons," in J. Tomberlin (ed.), *Philosophical Perspectives 13*, Oxford: Blackwell, pp. 297–332.

Klinnert, M. D., R. N. Emde, P. Butterfield and J. J. Campos (1987), "Social Referencing: The Infant's Use of Emotional Signals from a Friendly Adult with Mother Present," *Annual Progress in Child Psychiatry and Child Development*, 22, pp. 427–32.

Kohlberg, Lawrence (1971), "From Is to Ought: How to Commit the Naturalistic Fallacy and Get Away with It in the Study of Moral Development," in T. Mischel (ed.), *Cognitive Development and Epistemology*, New York: Academic Press, pp. 151–235.

Kohlberg, Lawrence (1973), "The Claim to Moral Adequacy of the Highest Stage of Moral Judgment," *Journal of Philosophy*, 70, pp. 630–45.

Kohlberg, Lawrence (1976), "Moral Stages and Moralization: The Cognitive Developmental Approach," in T. Lickona (ed.), *Moral Development and Behavior: Research and Social Issues*, New York: Holt, Rinehart, and Winston, pp. 31–53.

Koops, Willem, Daniel Burgman, Tamare J. Ferguson and Andries F. Sanders (eds.) (2009), *The Development and Structure of Conscience*, New York: Psychology Press.

Kornblith, Hilary (ed.) (2001), *Epistemology: Internalism and Externalism*, Cambridge, MA: MIT Press.

Korsgaard, Christine (1986), "Skepticism about Practical Reason," *Journal of Philosophy* 83, 1, pp. 5–25.

Korsgaard, Christine (1996a), *Creating the Kingdom of Ends*, Cambridge University Press.

Korsgaard, Christine (1996b), *The Sources of Normativity*, Cambridge University Press.

Kripke, Saul (1972), *Naming and Necessity*, Cambridge, MA: Harvard University Press.

Kripke, Saul (1982), *Wittgenstein on Rules and Private Language*, Cambridge, MA: Harvard University Press.

Layman, Stephen (1991), *The Shape of the Good: Christian Reflections on the Foundations of Ethics*, Notre Dame University Press.

Leiter, Brian (2002), *Nietzsche on Morality*, London: Routledge.

Lewis, David (1972), "Psychophysical and Theoretical Identifications," *Australasian Journal of Philosophy*, 50, pp. 249–58.

Lewis, David (1989), "Dispositional Theories of Value," *Aristotelian Society Supplementary Volume*, 63, pp. 113–37.

Lewis, David (1996), "Elusive Knowledge," *Australasian Journal of Philosophy*, 74, 4, pp. 549–67.

Locke, John (1690/1991), *Essay Concerning Human Understanding*, reprinted in part in D. D. Raphael (ed.) (1969/1991), *The British Moralists*, Indianapolis: Hackett, vol. I, §§154–223.

Lycan, William (2003), *Real Conditionals*, Oxford University Press.

Lyons, David (1965), *The Forms and Limits of Utilitarianism*, Oxford University Press.

McCloskey, Michael (1983), "Intuitive Physics," *Scientific American*, 248, pp. 122–30.

McClosky, H. J. (1963), "A Note on Utilitarian Punishment," *Mind*, 72, p. 599.

McDowell, John (1979), "Virtue and Reason," *The Monist*, 62, pp. 331–50.

McDowell, John (1985), "Values and Secondary Qualities," in T. Honderich (ed.) *Morality and Objectivity*, London: Routledge and Kegan Paul, pp. 110–29; reprinted in Geoffrey Sayre-McCord (ed.) (1988), *Essays on Moral Realism*, Ithaca, NY: Cornell University Press, pp. 166–80.

McDowell, John (1995), "Might There Be External Reasons?" in J. E. J. Altham and R. Harrison (eds.), *World, Mind and Ethics: Essays on the Ethical Philosophy of Bernard Williams*, Cambridge University Press, pp. 68–85.

McDowell, John (1998), *Mind, Value, and Reality*, Cambridge, MA: Harvard University Press.

McGee, Vann (1985), "A Counterexample to Modus Ponens," *Journal of Philosophy*, 10, 349–51.

McGrath, Sarah (2004), "Moral Knowledge by Perception," *Philosophical Perspectives*, 18, pp. 209–28.

McGrath, Sarah (2007), "Moral Disagreement and Moral Expertise," in R. Shafer-Landau (ed.), *Oxford Studies in Metaethics*, vol. IV, Oxford University Press, pp. 87–107.

MacIntyre, Alasdair C. (1957), "What Morality is Not," *Philosophy*, 10, pp. 325–35; reprinted in G. Wallace and D. M. Walker (eds.) (1970), *The Definition of Morality*, London: Methuen, pp. 26–39.

MacIntyre, Alasdair C. (1959), "Hume on 'Is' and 'Ought'," *Philosophical Review*, 68, 4, pp. 451–68.

MacIntyre, Alasdair C. (1981/2007), *After Virtue*, 3rd edn., University of Notre Dame Press.

McKeever, Sean, and Michael Ridge (2006), *Principled Ethics: Generalism as a Regulative Ideal*, Oxford: Clarendon Press.

Mackie, John L. (1977), *Ethics: Inventing Right and Wrong*, London: Penguin.

McNamara, Paul (2006), "Deontic Logic," in E. Zalta (ed.), *Stanford Encyclopedia of Philosophy*, available online at http://plato.stanford.edu/entries/logic-deontic/.

McNaughton, David (1988), *Moral Vision*, Oxford: Blackwell.

Malle, Bertram F., Louis J. Moses and Dare A. Baldwin (eds.) (2001), *Intentions and Intentionality: Foundations of Social Cognition*. Cambridge, MA: MIT Press.

Meltzoff, Andrew N. and Alison Gopnik (1993), "The Role of Imitation in Understanding Persons and Developing a Theory of Mind," in S. Baron-Cohen, H. Tager-Flusberg, and D. J. Cohen (eds.), *Understanding Other Minds: Perspectives from Autism*, New York: Oxford, pp. 335–66.

Mikhail, John (2008), "The Poverty of Moral Stimulus," in Sinnott-Armstrong (2008a), pp. 353–60.

Milgram, Stanley (1974), *Obedience to Authority*, New York: Harper and Row.

Mill, John Stuart (1861/1998), *Utilitarianism*, Roger Crisp (ed.), Oxford University Press.

Miller, Richard W. (1985), "Ways of Moral Learning," *Philosophical Review*, 94, 4, pp. 507–56.

Moody-Adams, Michelle (1997), *Fieldwork in Familiar Places*, Cambridge, MA: Harvard University Press.

Moore, G. E. (1903/1929), *Principia Ethica*, Cambridge University Press.

Moore, G. E. (1912), *Ethics*, London: Oxford University Press.

Moser, Paul and Thomas Carson (eds.) (2001), *Moral Relativism: A Reader*, New York: Oxford University Press.

Mulligan, Kevin (1998), "From Appropriate Emotions to Values," *The Monist*, 81, pp. 161–88.

Murphy, Jeffrie G. (1973), "Marxism and Retribution," *Philosophy and Public Affairs*, 9, pp. 217–43.

Murphy, S., J. Haidt and F. Björklund (2000), "Moral Dumbfounding: When Intuition Finds No Reason," *Lund Psychological Reports*, 1, Lund University, pp. 1–15.

Nagel, Thomas (1970), *The Possibility of Altruism*, Oxford University Press.

Nagel, Thomas (1979), *Mortal Questions*, Cambridge University Press.

Nagel, Thomas (1986), *The View from Nowhere*, Oxford University Press.

Nelson, Mark (1995), "Is It Always Fallacious to Derive Values from Facts?" *Argumentation*, 9, pp. 553–62.

Nichols, Shaun (2002), "How Psychopaths Threaten Moral Rationalism: Is It Irrational to Be Immoral?" *The Monist*, 85, pp. 285–304.

Nichols, Shaun (2004), *Sentimental Rules*, Oxford University Press.

Nielsen, Kai (1972), "Against Moral Conservatism," *Ethics*, 82, pp. 113–24.

Nietzsche, Friedrich (1886/1966), *Beyond Good and Evil*, Walter Kaufmann (trans.), New York: Random House.

Nisbett, R. E. and D. Cohen (1996), *Culture of Honor: The Psychology of Violence in the South*, Boulder, CO: Westview Press.

Nozick, Robert (1974), *Anarchy, State and Utopia*, New York: HarperCollins.

Nozick, Robert (1981), *Philosophical Explanations*, Cambridge, MA: Belknap Press.

Nucci, Larry P. (2001), *Education in the Moral Domain*, Cambridge University Press.

Nussbaum, Martha C. (1990), *Love's Knowledge*, Oxford University Press.

O'Neill, Onora (1975), *Acting on Principle*, New York: Columbia University Press.

Parfit, Derek (1984), *Reasons and Persons*, Oxford University Press.

Parfit, Derek (2001), "Rationality and Reasons," in D. Egonsson, J. Josefsson, B. Petersson, and T. Ronnow-Rasmussen (eds.), *Exploring Practical Philosophy: From Action to Values*, Aldershot: Ashgate, pp. 17–39.

Peacocke, Christopher (1992), *A Study of Concepts*, Cambridge, MA: MIT Press.

Peacocke, Christopher (1998), "Implicit Conceptions, Understanding and Rationality," *Philosophical Issues: Concepts*, 9, pp. 43–88.

Peacocke, Christopher (2000), "Explaining the A Priori: The Programme of Moderate Rationalism," in P. Boghossian and C. Peacocke (eds.), *New Essays on the A Priori*, Oxford: Clarendon Press, pp. 255–85.

Peacocke, Christopher (2004), *The Realm of Reason*, Oxford University Press.

Perry, John (1979), "The Problem of the Essential Indexical," *Noûs*, 12, pp. 3–21.

Persily, Nathaniel, Jack Citrin and Patrick Egan (2008), *Public Opinion and Constitutional Controversy*, Oxford University Press.

Peterson, Christopher and Martin P. Seligman (2004), *Character Strengths and Virtues: A Handbook and Classification*, Washington, D.C.: American Psychological Association; New York: Oxford University Press.

Pitcher, George (1970), "Pain Perception," *Philosophical Review*, 79, 3, pp. 368–93.

Plato (1987), *The Complete Works*, J. M. Copper (ed.), Indianapolis: Hackett.

Pollock, John (1974), *Knowledge and Justification*, Princeton University Press.

Pollock, John (1986), *Contemporary Theories of Knowledge*, Totowa, NJ: Rowman and Littlefield.

Portmann, John (2000), *When Bad Things Happen to Other People*, London: Routledge.

Price, Huw (1994), "Semantic Deflationism and the Frege Point," in S. L. Tsohatzidis (ed.), *Foundations of Speech Act Theory: Philosophical and Linguistic Perspectives*, London: Routledge, pp. 132–55.

Prinz, Jesse (2007), *The Emotional Construction of Morals*, Oxford University Press.

Prinz, Jesse (2008a), "Is Morality Innate?" in Sinnott-Armstrong (2008a), pp. 367–406.

Prinz, Jesse (2008b), "Reply to Dwyer and Tiberius," in Sinnott-Armstrong (2008a), pp. 427–37.

Prior, Arthur N. (1949), *Logic and the Basis of Ethics*, Oxford: Clarendon Press.

Prior, Arthur N. (1960a), "The Autonomy of Ethics," *Australasian Journal of Philosophy*, 38, pp. 199–206.

Prior, Arthur N. (1960b), "The Runabout Inference-Ticket," *Analysis*, 21, pp. 38–39.

Pryor, Jim (2000), "The Sceptic and the Dogmatist," *Noûs*, 34, pp. 517–49.

Quine, W.V.O. (1970/1983), *Philosophy of Logic*, Cambridge, MA: Harvard University Press.

Quine, W.V.O. (1972), *Methods of Logic*, New York: Holt, Rinehart, and Winston.

Quine, W.V.O. (1969), "Epistemology Naturalized," in *Ontological Relativity and Other Essays*, New York: Columbia University Press, pp. 69–90.

Railton, Peter (1986), "Moral Realism," *Philosophical Review*, 95, pp. 163–207.

Railton, Peter (1992), "Pluralism, Determinacy and Dilemma," *Ethics*, 102, pp. 720–42.

Railton, Peter (1996), "Moral Realism: Prospects and Problems," in Sinnott-Armstrong and Timmons (1996), pp. 49–81.

Railton, Peter (2003), *Facts, Values and Norms*, Cambridge University Press.

Rawls, John (1955), "Two Concepts of Rules," *Philosophical Review*, 64, pp. 3–32.

Rawls, John (1971), *A Theory of Justice*, Cambridge, MA: Harvard University Press.

Rawls, John (2000), *Lectures on the History of Moral Philosophy*, B. Herman (ed.), Cambridge, MA: Harvard University Press.

Reynolds, David S. (2006), *John Brown, Abolitionist: The Man Who Killed Slavery, Sparked the Civil War, and Seeded Civil Rights*, New York: Vintage.

Richard, Mark (2008), *When Truth Gives Out*, Oxford University Press.

Ridge, Michael (2006), "Ecumenical Expressivism: Finessing Frege," *Ethics*, 116, pp. 302–36.

Rosen, Gideon (2004), "Skepticism about Moral Responsibility," *Philosophical Perspectives, Ethics*, 18, pp. 295–313.

Ross, Lee D. and Richard Nisbett (1991), *The Person and the Situation: Perspectives of Social Psychology*, New York: McGraw Hill.

Ross, W.D. (1930), *The Right and the Good*, Oxford: Clarendon Press.

Ross, W. D. (1939), *The Foundations of Ethics*, Oxford: Clarendon Press.

Russell, Bertrand (1912/1997), *The Problems of Philosophy*, John Perry (ed.), Oxford University Press.

Ryle, Gilbert (1949/2000), *The Concept of Mind*, London: Penguin.

Salmon, Nathan (1989), "The Logic of What Might Have Been," *Philosophical Review*, 98, pp. 3–34.

Scanlon, Thomas (1998), *What We Owe to Each Other*, Cambridge, MA: Harvard University Press.

Scheffler, Samuel (1987), "Morality through Thick and Thin: A Critical Notice of *Ethics and the Limits of Philosophy*," *Philosophical Review*, 46, pp. 411–34.

Schiffer, Stephen (1979), "Naming and Knowing," in P. French, T. Uehling, and H. Wettstein (eds.), *Contemporary Perspectives in the Philosophy of Language*, Minneapolis: University of Minnesota Press, pp. 28–41.

Schroeder, Mark (2008), *Being For*, Oxford University Press.

Schueler, G. F. (1988), "Modus Ponens and Moral Realism," *Ethics*, 98, pp. 492–500.

Searle, J. (1962), "Meaning and Speech Acts," *Philosophical Review*, 71, 4, pp. 423–32.

Sellars, Wilfrid (1953), "Inference and Meaning," *Mind*, 62, pp. 318–38.

Sellars, Wilfrid (1963), *Science, Perception and Reality*, London: Routledge and Kegan Paul.

Setiya, Kieran (2003), "Explaining Action," *Philosophical Review*, 112, 3 (July), pp. 339–93.

Sextus Empiricus (1562/1949), *Writings*, 4 vols. (Loeb Classical Library), Cambridge, MA: Harvard University Press.

Shafer-Landau, Russ (1994), "Ethical Disagreement, Ethical Objectivism, and Moral Indeterminacy," *Philosophy and Phenomenological Research*, 54, pp. 331–44.

Shafer-Landau, Russ (2003), *Moral Realism: A Defense*, Oxford: Clarendon Press.

Shope, Robert K. (1983), *The Analysis of Knowing: A Decade of Research*, Princeton University Press.

Sidgwick, Henry (1874/1981), *The Methods of Ethics*, 7th edn., Indianapolis: Hackett.

Siegel, Susanna (2005), "Which Properties Are Represented in Perception?" in T. Szabo Gendler and J. Hawthorne (eds.), *Perceptual Experience*, Oxford University Press, pp. 481–503.

Simner, Marvin L. (1971), "Newborn's Response to the Cry of Another Infant," *Developmental Psychology*, 5, pp. 136–50.

Singer, Peter (1972), "Famine, Affluence, and Morality," *Philosophy and Public Affairs*, 1, pp. 229–43.

Sinnott-Armstrong, Walter (ed.) (2004), *Pyrrhonian Skepticism*, Oxford University Press.

Sinnott-Armstrong, Walter (2006), *Moral Skepticisms*, Oxford University Press.

Sinnott-Armstrong, Walter (ed.) (2008a), *Moral Psychology*, vol. I, *The Evolution of Morality: Adaptation and Innateness*, Cambridge, MA: MIT Press.

Sinnott-Armstrong, Walter (ed.) (2008b), *Moral Psychology*, vol. II, *The Cognitive Science of Morality: Intuition and Diversity*, Cambridge, MA: MIT Press.

Sinnott-Armstrong, Walter (ed.) (2008c), *Moral Psychology*, vol. III, *The Neuroscience of Morality: Emotion, Brain Disorders, and Development*, Cambridge, MA: MIT Press.

Sinnott-Armstrong, Walter and Mark Timmons (eds.) (1996), *Moral Knowledge? New Readings in Moral Epistemology*, New York: Oxford University Press.

Skorupski, John (1997), "Reasons and Reason," in G. Cullity and B. Gaut (eds.) *Ethics and Practical Reason*, Oxford University Press, pp. 345–68.

Smart, J. J. C. (1984), *Ethics, Persuasion and Truth*, London: Routledge and Kegan Paul.

Smart, J. J. C. and B. Williams (1973), *Utilitarianism: For and Against*, Cambridge University Press.

Smetana, Judith (1993), "Understanding of Social Rules," in M. Bennett (ed.), *The Development of Social Cognition: The Child as Psychologist*, New York: Guilford Press, pp. 111–41.

Smith, Michael (1994), *The Moral Problem*, Oxford: Basil Blackwell.

Smith, Michael (2004), *Ethics and the A Priori*, Cambridge University Press.

Snare, Francis (1980), "The Diversity of Morals," *Mind*, 89, pp. 353–69.

Sosa, Ernest (1980), "The Raft and the Pyramid," in P. French, T. Uehling, Jr., and H. Wettstein (eds.), *Studies in Epistemology* (Midwest Studies in Philosophy, vol. V), Minneapolis: University of Minnesota Press, pp. 3–25.

Sosa, Ernest (1994), "Philosophical Skepticism and Epistemic Circularity," *Aristotelian Society Supplementary Volume*, 68, pp. 268–90.

Sosa, Ernest (1997), "How to Resolve the Pyrrhonian Problematic: A Lesson from Descartes," *Philosophical Studies*, 85, 2/3, pp. 229–49.

Sosa, Ernest (2007), *A Virtue Epistemology: Apt Belief and Reflective Knowledge*, vol. I, Oxford: Clarendon Press.

Sosa, Ernest and Jaegwon Kim (eds.) (2000), *Epistemology: An Anthology*, Malden, MA: Blackwell.

Sreenivasan, Gopal (2002), "Errors about Errors: Virtue Theory and Trait Attribution," *Mind*, 111, pp. 47–68.

Sripada, Chandra S. (2008a), "Nativism and Moral Psychology: Three Models of the Innate Structure That Shapes the Contents of Moral Norms," in Sinnott-Armstrong (2008a), pp. 319–43.

Sripada, Chandra S. (2008b), "Reply to Harman and Mikhail," in Sinnott-Armstrong (2008a), pp. 361–65.

Stanley, Jason (2005), *Knowledge and Practical Interests*, New York: Oxford University Press.

Steup, Matthias and Ernest Sosa (eds.) (2005), *Contemporary Debates in Epistemology*, Oxford: Blackwell.

Stevenson, C. L. (1944), *Ethics and Language*, New Haven: Yale University Press.

Stevenson, C. L. (1963), *Facts and Values*, New Haven: Yale University Press.

Stich, Stephen (1988), "Reflective Equilibrium, Analytic Epistemology, and the Problem of Diversity," *Synthese*, 74, pp. 391–413.

Stich, Stephen (1990), *The Fragmentation of Reason*, Cambridge, MA: MIT Press.

Stocker, Michael (1979), "Desiring the Bad: An Essay in Moral Psychology," *Journal of Philosophy*, 76, pp. 738–53.

Stoljar, Daniel (1993), "Emotivism and Truth Conditions," *Philosophical Studies*, 70, pp. 81–101.

Stratton-Lake, Philip (2000), *Kant, Duty and Moral Worth*, London: Routledge.

Stratton-Lake, Philip (2002a), "Introduction," in Stratton-Lake (2002c), pp. 1–28.

Stratton-Lake, Philip (2002b), "Pleasure and Reflection in Ross's Intuitionism," in Stratton-Lake (2002c), pp. 113–36.

Stratton-Lake, Philip (ed.) (2002c), *Ethical Intuitionism: Re-evaluations*, Oxford: Clarendon Press.

Strawson, Peter F. (1961), "Social Morality and Individual Ideal," *Philosophy*, 36, pp. 1–17.

Strawson, Peter F. (1962), "Freedom and Resentment," *Proceedings of the British Academy*, 48, pp. 1–25.

Stueber, Karsten (2006), *Rediscovering Empathy: Agency, Folk Psychology, and the Human Sciences*, Cambridge, MA: MIT Press.

Sturgeon, Nicholas (1974), "Altruism, Solipsism, and the Objectivity of Reasons," *Philosophical Review*, 83, pp. 374–402.

Sturgeon, Nicholas (1984), "Moral Explanations," in D. Copp and D. Zimmerman (eds.), *Morality, Reason and Truth*, Totowa, NJ: Rowman and Littlefield, pp. 49–78.

Sturgeon, Nicholas (1986), "Harman on Moral Explanations of Natural Facts," *Southern Journal of Philosophy*, Supplement, 24, pp. 69–78.

Sturgeon, Nicholas (1995), "Evil and Explanation," *Canadian Journal of Philosophy*, Supplement, 21, pp. 155–85.

Sturgeon, Nicholas (2001), "Moral Skepticism and Moral Naturalism in Hume's Treatise," *Hume Studies*, 27, 1, pp. 3–83.

Sturgeon, Nicholas (2002), "Ethical Intuitionism and Ethical Naturalism," in Stratton-Lake (2002c), pp. 184–211.

Tappolet, Christine (2004), "Through Thick and Thin: *Good* and Its Determinables," *Dialectica*, 58, pp. 207–21.

Tarski, Alfred (1936/1956), "On the Concept of Logical Consequence," in *Logic, Semantics, Metamathematics*, Oxford: Clarendon Press, pp. 409–20.

Tersman, Folke (2006), *Moral Disagreement*, Cambridge University Press.

Thomson, Judith J. (1971), "A Defense of Abortion," *Philosophy and Public Affairs*, 1, pp. 47–66.

Thomson, Judith J. (1976), "Killing, Letting Die, and the Trolley Problem," *The Monist*, 59, pp. 204–17.

Thomson, Judith J. (1990), *The Realm of Rights*, Cambridge, MA: Harvard University Press.

Thomson, Judith J. (2008), "Turning the Trolley," *Philosophy and Public Affairs*, 36, pp. 359–74.

Timmons, Mark (ed.) (2002), *Kant's Metaphysics of Morals: Interpretive Essays*, New York: Oxford University Press.

Tolhurst, William (1990), "On the Epistemic Value of Moral Experience," *Southern Journal of Philosophy*, Supplement, 29, pp. 67–87.

Turiel, Elliot (1979), "Distinct Conceptual and Developmental Domains: Social Convention and Morality," in H. Howe and C. Keasey (eds.), *Nebraska Symposium on Motivation, 1977: Social Cognitive Development*, Lincoln, NE: University of Nebraska Press, pp. 77–116.

Turiel, Elliot (1983), *The Development of Social Knowledge*, Cambridge University Press.

Turiel, Elliot, Melanie Killen and Charles Helwig (1987), "Morality: Its Structure, Functions and Vagaries," in J. Kagan and S. Lamb (eds.), *The Emergence of Morality in Young Children*, Chicago University Press, pp. 155–244.

Unger, Peter (1975), *Ignorance: A Case for Skepticism*, Oxford University Press.

Unger, Peter (1995), "Contextual Analysis in Ethics," *Philosophy and Phenomenological Research*, 55, pp. 1–26.

Unger, Peter (1996), *Living High and Letting Die*, New York: Oxford University Press.

Unwin, Nicholas (1999), "*Quasi*-Realism, Negation and the Frege-Geach Problem," *Philosophical Quarterly*, 49, pp. 337–52.

Unwin, Nicholas (2001), "Norms and Negation: A Problem for Gibbard's Logic," *Philosophical Quarterly*, 51, pp. 60–75.

Urmson, J. O. (1953), "The Interpretation of the Moral Philosophy of J. S. Mill," *Philosophical Quarterly*, 3, pp. 33–9.

Van Cleve, James (1979), "Foundationalism, Epistemic Principles and the Cartesian Circle," *Philosophical Review*, 88, 1, pp. 55–91.

Van Cleve, James (2003), "Is Knowledge Easy – or Impossible? Externalism as the Only Alternative to Skepticism," in S. Luper (ed.), *The Skeptics: Contemporary Essays*, Aldershot: Ashgate, pp. 45–59.

van Roojen, Mark (1996), "Expressivism and Irrationality," *Philosophical Review*, 105, pp. 311–55.

Varela, Francisco (1992), *Ethical Know-How*, Stanford University Press.

Väyrynen, Pekka (2007), "Some Good and Bad News for Ethical Intuitionism," *Philosophical Quarterly*, 58, pp. 489–511.

Väyrynen, Pekka (2009), "A Theory of Hedged Moral Principles," in Russ Shafer-Landau (ed.), *Oxford Studies in Metaethics*, vol. IV, Oxford University Press, pp. 91–132.

Vogel, Jonathan (1990), "Cartesian Skepticism and Inference to the Best Explanation," *Journal of Philosophy*, 87, 11, pp. 658–66.

Vogel, Jonathan (2000), "Reliabilism Leveled," *Journal of Philosophy*, 97, pp. 602–23.

von Wright, G. H. (1951), "Deontic Logic," *Mind*, 60, pp. 1–15.

Vranas, Peter (2008), "New Foundations for Imperative Logic I: Logical Connectives," *Noûs*, 42, 4, pp. 529–72.

Wainryb, C. and E. Turiel (1994), "Dominance, Subordination, and Concepts of Personal Entitlements in Cultural Contexts," *Child Development*, 65, pp. 1701–22.

Walker-Andrews, A. S. (1998), "Emotions and Social Development: Infants' Recognition of Emotions in Others," *Pediatrics*, 102, pp. 1268–71.

Wallace, G. and D. M. Walker (1970), "Introduction," in G. Wallace and D. M. Walker (eds.), *The Definition of Morality*, London: Methuen, pp. 1–20.

Walton, Kendall L. (1973), "Pictures and Make-Believe," *Philosophical Review*, 82, pp. 283–319.

Walton, Kendall L. (1978), "Fearing Fictions," *Journal of Philosophy*, 75, pp. 5–27.

Warneken, Felix and Michael Tomasello (2006), "Altruistic Helping in Human Infants and Young Chimpanzees," *Science*, 311, pp. 1301–3.

Watkins, Michael and Kelly Dean Jolley (2002), "Pollyanna Realism: Moral Perception and Moral Properties," *Australasian Journal of Philosophy*, 80, pp. 75–85.

Watson, Gary (1975), "Free Agency," *Journal of Philosophy*, 72, pp. 205–20.

Wedgwood, Ralph (2001), "Conceptual Role Semantics for Moral Terms," *Philosophical Review*, 110, pp. 1–30.

Wedgwood, Ralph (2007), *The Nature of Normativity*, Oxford: Clarendon Press.

Weinberg, Jonathan, Shaun Nichols and Stephen Stich (2001), "Normativity and Epistemic Intuitions," *Philosophical Topics*, 29, pp. 429–60.

Wheatley, Thalia and Jonathan Haidt (2005), "Hypnotic Disgust Makes Moral Judgments More Severe," *Psychological Science*, 16, pp. 780–84.

White, Douglas R. and Michael L. Burton (1988), "Causes of Polygyny: Ecology, Economy, Kinship and Warfare," *American Anthropologist*, 90, pp. 871–87.

Wiggins, David (1991), "Moral Cognitivism, Moral Relativism, and Motivating Moral Beliefs," *Proceedings of the Aristotelian Society*, 91, pp. 61–85.

Wiggins, David (1995), "Categorical Requirements: Kant and Hume on the Idea of Duty," in R. Hursthouse, G. Lawrence, and W. Quinn (eds.), *Virtues and Reasons*, Oxford: Clarendon Press, pp. 279–330; originally published in *The Monist*, 74 (1991), pp. 297–330.

Wikan, Unni (1996), *Tomorrow, God Willing: Self-Made Destinies in Cairo*, Chicago University Press.

Williams, Bernard (1979), "Internal and External Reasons," in R. Harrison (ed.), *Rational Action: Studies in Philosophy and Social Science*, Cambridge University Press, pp. 17–28; reprinted in Williams (1981), pp. 101–13.

Williams, Bernard (1981), *Moral Luck*, Cambridge University Press.

Williams, Bernard (1985), *Ethics and the Limits of Philosophy*, Cambridge, MA: Harvard University Press.

Williams, Michael (2001), *Problems of Knowledge*, Oxford University Press.

Williams, Michael (2004), "The Agrippan Argument and Two Forms of Skepticism," in Sinnott-Armstrong (2004), pp. 121–45.

Williamson, Timothy (1992), "Vagueness and Ignorance," *Aristotelian Society Supplementary Volume*, 66, pp. 145–62.

Williamson, Timothy (2000), *Knowledge and Its Limits*, Oxford University Press.

Williamson, Timothy (2003), "Understanding and Inference," *Proceedings of the Aristotelian Society*, 73, pp. 249–93.

Williamson, Timothy (2007), "Philosophical Knowledge and Knowledge of Counterfactuals," *Grazer Philosophische Studien*, 74, pp. 89–123.

Wilson, James Q. (1993), *The Moral Sense*, New York: Free Press.

Wittgenstein, Ludwig (1921/2001), *Tractatus Logico-Philosophicus*, D. Pears and B. McGuiness (trans.), London: Routledge Classics.

Wittgenstein, Ludwig (1953/1958), *Philosophical Investigations*, 3rd edn., G. E. M. Anscombe (trans.), Englewood Cliffs, NJ: Prentice Hall.

Wolf, Arthur P. and W. Durham (2005), *Inbreeding, Incest and the Incest Taboo*, Palo Alto, CA: Stanford University Press.

Wolf, Susan (1990), *Freedom within Reason*, Oxford University Press.

Wong, David (2006), *Natural Moralities*, Oxford University Press.

Wright, Crispin (2001), "On Basic Logical Knowledge," *Philosophical Studies*, 106, pp. 41–85.

Yablo, Stephen (1992), "Mental Causation," *Philosophical Review*, 101, pp. 245–80.

Yablo, Stephen (2003), "Causal Relevance," *Philosophical Issues*, 13, pp. 316–27.

Yaffe, Gideon (1999), *Liberty Worth the Name: Locke on Free Agency*, Princeton University Press.

Zagzebski, Linda (1996), *Virtues of the Mind*, Cambridge University Press.

Zahn-Waxler, Carolyn and Marion Radke-Yarrow (1982), "The Development of Altruism: Alternative Research Strategies," in N. Eisenberg (ed.), *The Development of Prosocial Behavior*, New York: Academic Press, pp. 109–37.

Zalabardo, José L. (2005), "Externalism, Skepticism, and the Problem of Easy Knowledge," *Philosophical Review*, 144, pp. 33–61.

Zimmerman, Aaron (2006), "Basic Self-Knowledge: Answering Peacocke's Criticisms of Constitutivism," *Philosophical Studies*, 128, pp. 337–79.

Zimmerman, Aaron (2007), "Hume's Reasons," *Hume Studies*, 33, 2, pp. 211–56.

Zimmerman, Aaron (2009), "A Conflict in Common-Sense Moral Psychology," *Utilitas*, 21, 4, pp. 401–23.

Zimmerman, Michael (1983), "Evaluatively Incomplete States of Affairs," *Philosophical Studies*, 43, pp. 211–24.

Zimmerman, Michael (1988), *An Essay on Moral Responsibility*, Totowa, NJ: Rowman and Littlefield.

INDEX